SELECTED PROSE

PROSE

of

BOBBIE
LOUISE
HAWKINS

Also by Bobbie Louise Hawkins

Fifteen Poems (Belladonna Collaborative, 2012)

Absolutely Eden (United Artists Books, 2008)

Bijoux (Farfalla Press, 2006)

Sensible Plainness (Bijou Books, 1995)

Bitter Sweet (Bijou Books, 1995)

Fragrant Trappings (Bijou Books, 1995)

The Sanguine Breast of Margaret (North and South Press, London, 1992)

My Own Alphabet (Coffee House Press, 1989)

One Small Saga (Coffee House Press, 1985)

A Sense of Humor (Toothpaste Press, 1983)

Almost Everything (Coach House Press, 1982)

En Route (Little Dinosaur, 1982)

Trammel: Thought, Question, Treasure (Island, Canada, 1982)

Talk, radio play (PBS, 1980)

Live at The Great American Music Hall, LP (Flying Fish, 1982)

Frenchy And Cuban Pete (Tombouctou, 1977)

Back To Texas (Bear Hug Books, 1977)

Fifteen Poems (Arif Press, 1974)

Own Your Body (Black Sparrow Press, 1973)

SELECTED PROSE

of

BOBBIE LOUISE HAWKINS

Edited by

BARBARA HENNING

BLAZEVOX [BOOKS]
Buffalo, New York

ISBN: 978-1-60964-100-9
First Edition
Cataloging-in-publication data is available from the Library of Congress.
Printed in the United States of America

Almost Everything was originally published by Coach House Press/Long River Books, USA, 1982 (collecting *Back to Texas, Frenchy and Cuban Pete,* and *Other Stories*). *The Sanguine Breast of Margaret* was originally published by North and South Press, Middlesex, England, 1992. *Back to Texas* was originally published by Bear Hug Books, 1977, USA. *Frenchy & Cuban Pete and Other Stories* was originally published by Tombouctou, 1977, USA; and Verlag Gunter Ohnemus, 1980, Germany.

Thanks to Chuck Miller for his illustrations for *Back to Texas.*

Thanks to Krystal Languell, Mia Bruner and Kylee Weiss for help with proofreading and editing. Special thanks to Maureen Owen for meeting with Bobbie, and HR Hegnauer for helping to facilitate this book in all of its stages.

Cover collages by Bobbie Louise Hawkins.
Cover, interior design, and typesetting by HR Hegnauer.

BlazeVOX [books]
76 Inwood Place
Buffalo, NY 14209
blazevox.org

21 20 19 18 17 16 15 14 13 12   01 02 03 04 05 06 07 08 09 10

3 PREFACE

7 BACK TO TEXAS

9 When you're stoned on grass ...
12 I've always been impressed ...
13 Last October ...
15 Used car salesmen ...
18 One of the best times ...
21 The Irish came to Texas ...
23 I get to talking ...
25 What were we talking about ...
27 My Uncle Horace had ...
28 You knew ...
37 I knew yawl ...
39 Are you my aunt ...
40 We were living ...
41 Mama, show Billie-Jean how ...
45 ... providing for their own family ...
48 When Mama had pelligrisy ...
50 When my father died ...
51 A letter to My Grandaughter
56 The houses where my grandmother ...
58 So what I knew ...
59 She was small and sweet and tough ...
61 Running Set of Lies
66 Mae, are you feeling good?
68 It was a big old house ...
69 ... this was up north ...
70 Them two little girls ...
71 The first book ...
72 ... what we did to the old man ...
73 The old man used to wake up ...
74 Mae, not to change ...
76 You know how ...
77 Let's see ...

78 You know, Crystal
80 When we were living ...
82 ... five hundred dollars ...
85 Beezer was small ...
88 When my cousin Velma ...
91 From Abilene to Lubbock ...
92 I just don't hardly ...
95 Marvin answered the door ...
97 I've been a practising lawyer ...
100 Frank bought ...
103 Everything begins as a dot ...
104 When I was little ...
107 When Billy-Bob married ...
109 Didn't Billy have ...
110 By the time I was fifteen ...
112 Aunt Ada came ...
114 Pearl said ...
115 I used to love ...
117 Curtis stuck his foot ...
118 Thirty-thirty's what they ...
119 For their wedding trip ...
121 You heard anybody ...
122 We was setting there ...
124 Well, I'll tell yawl ...
128 You feel like ...

131 FRENCHY AND CUBAN PETE

133 Frenchy and Cuban Pete
137 The Boyfriend
141 A Special Condition
143 I Dreamed Last Night
146 I Owe You One
147 Free State of Winston
149 Old Security
153 Twice

154   Little Ernie

157   Bathroom / Animal / Castration Story

159   Dolores

163   Bellagio

164   Pitches and Catches

168   Curry

170   Old Vivvy

172   Piece of Trash

176   Why Does Anyone ...

177   How Has ...

178   There's An Old ...

179   It's A Phony

180   Got From Yeats' 'Celtic Twilight'

181   The Dismay of:

182   Take Love, For Instance ...

183   Plan

184   Some Bits

185   N E W   S T O R I E S

187   The Elevation of Terre Haute is 50 Feet

189   Salamander

191   A Sense of Humour

192   Rosario

193   Doing Psychology

195   Roots

197   Her Name

199   The Child

204   A Moral Tale

209   T H E   S A N G U I N E   B R E A S T   O F   M A R G A R E T

349   P H O T O G R A P H S

363   I N T E R V I E W

SELECTED PROSE

PROSE

of

BOBBIE LOUISE HAWKINS

PREFACE

When I was at Naropa University for the Summer Program in June 2011, Bobbie came to my prose chat and we planned to get together later in the week. Meanwhile, in the poetics library, I picked up a copy of her novel, *One Small Saga,* and read it that same night. It is beautifully written prose with poetic disjunction and rhythm, the story of a young artist on a journey to Belize with her new husband. I wanted to interview Bobbie about the book; unfortunately she was ill, and I wasn't able to see her that week. So we conducted our interview over the telephone. One phone call can lead to another, one book to another. When I started reading little editions of her poetry and stories, I came across *15 Poems,* published by Arif Press in 1974 with only 426 copies in the world, a series of poems about love and loss that could rival HD's poetry; in the introduction Robert Duncan writes, "A magic then comes into it, a would-be witchcraft in spirit. . . her art in the poem . . . to liberate in self and in the world the workings of a womanly imperative." This was a perfect book for the Belladonna Collaborative, and they republished it in 2012.

I didn't start this project with the goal of editing Bobbie's *Selected Prose* or getting *15 Poems* back into print. I had intended a short interview, maybe a couple of hours. While we were talking one day, Bobbie mentioned that one of her books was out of print, *Almost Everything,* and that *The Sanguine Breast of Margaret* was only available in the UK. She wanted to find someone to republish these books, especially as e-books. I said I'd talk to Geoffrey Gatza at BlazeVOX and see if he would be interested. He said he would definitely like to make her books available as e-books, and also in print, as a *Selected Prose.* It was clear to me that Bobbie wasn't well enough to see this book through the stages of publication, so I volunteered to help. The stories needed to be typed, reformatted and proofread. Krystal Languell helped with proofreading and revising, and interns from Belladonna, Mia Bruner and Kylee Weiss gave many hours to typing and scanning. Then Bobbie and I decided to expand the interview and include a section in the book. HR Hegnauer designed the layout and the cover using Bobbie's collages. Both HR and Maureen Owen also helped Bobbie with proofreading and going through photographs. Putting this book together has definitely been a group project. Almost all of us working on the book are members of the Belladonna Collaborative. When I was talking to Bobbie about some captions to the photographs, she said, "You've done so much work Barbara. Please make yourself the editor."

I don't want to say a lot about this book but there are a few things that might be interesting to know before reading the stories. At first, I was reading Bobbie's novels as autobiographical fiction and so I'd talk about them in terms of "the narrator" and the "main character." I remember Bobbie saying something like, "What do you mean fiction? This is about my life." She went on, "Robert Duncan once said there is no such thing as fiction. And that makes more sense than almost anything. And when at one point I started looking back through my stories, I thought, I have almost never written a fictional line in my life. Your mind gets on something and you just meander along with it. I don't think that's fiction. It's all autobiography." The stories in *Back to Texas* are about her mother and their relatives and about growing up in Texas. In *The Sanguine Breast of Margaret,* she retells in a fictional framework the story of she and Bob Creeley traveling to Guatamala with their four children in 1959.

In the 1950's American women were portrayed in the news and television as in love with their refrigerators and pink dishwashers. *The Sanguine Breast of Margaret* is the story of a 1950's bohemian artistic family involved in quite a different way of living, poverty as simply a bothersome side effect. But wow, what a lot of work when you are on the road in a broken-down van with four small children and not enough money to get to where you're going, washing diapers in roadside bathrooms. And yet a moment of danger becomes a moment of beauty. Exhausted, the main character, Margaret is driving through Mexico while Patrick sleeps. "Driving in the darkest small hours of the morning oncoming headlights would splay out across the wet windshield like exploding stars" (23).

Once Bobbie said to me: "I mean my relatives, dear, were incredible, and it was all because of that habit of sitting around a big kitchen table with a coal oil lamp and telling stories, just passing around the table from one person to the next. That was a major entertainment. Everyone would laugh even if it was the fiftieth time they'd heard this story because it was like a performance. So as a child I had that background." While interviewing Bobbie and transcribing, it sometimes seemed as if I were orchestrating a series of new narratives. Walter Benjamin writes, "Every morning brings us the news of the globe, and yet we are poor in noteworthy stories." We don't have to be so poor with a storyteller like Bobbie around. By including this interview with these already acclaimed stories, we are bringing into print new noteworthy stories, stories she has entertained her friends and students with over and again. It is my pleasure to have been part of this process.

—Barbara Henning
New York City, 2012

BACK
TO
TEXAS

When you're stoned on grass and drinking wine and it's really festive ... a lot of people, eight or ten, and everybody feeling privileged and pleased to be there and to be so happy ... I'm talking about yesterday afternoon and evening. It was a birthday party. We were five of us waiting there for the birthday boy and the others and the cake and they all turned out to be about three hours late because of the traffic ... so we sat talking and enjoying it ... a fire in the fireplace ... and they did finally arrive; coming through the door. It felt like old-time family Christmases, waiting for the ones who lived farther away. And at some time during the evening ... the dilemma on grass if there's a lot of jazzy talking is to remember any of it later ... so this Sunday morning I started remembering it with pleasure and thinking I probably talked too much but not really feeling worried about it and there was a moment in it that suddenly I remember I said ... feeling really high and delighted to get it out at last ... I don't even know if it was true but it felt so accurate ... we had been talking about school's being narrower in some inverse ratio—like—the longer you're there the less it's got to tell you, and I remember saying the dues are worth it; all that's worth it ... and what suddenly came out that I'm remembering lying here in bed is—I said with all the certainty and pleasure of revelation, "Nothing in my life ever happened that was as important to me as learning to read."

And this morning I'm hung on remembering I said that as if the statement itself has turned to metal and I can hold it and gauge it; as if it were negotiable. A riffle like flip-cards in my mind of—wouldn't I pay it like a coin to have had this different or that different, as if that feeling, and being so definite saying it, really has to prove out.

My daddy was a good-looking woman chaser. He looked like Clark Gable and darkened his moustache with my mother's Maybelline mascara in private so he was angry when he saw the kid, me, standing in the bathroom door watching him.

Pictures of me then show me as a skinny, spooky kid. I was really quiet. If I broke a dish I hid it under the most complicated mess of crumpled paper I could make, filling the trash to hide my dangerous broken dish. He had a lousy temper and I never ... I guess I never will get rid of that secret self-protection I learned then.

They both were fighters, my mother and father. I remember him pulling the tablecloth off the table when his breakfast didn't suit him ... what a mess. And the time she threw a meat cleaver after him and it stuck in the door jamb inches from his head. He stopped and she says he turned pale. But he left. Time and again he left and when he came back (it's called coming-back-home) after a few months or whatever time, they'd get along until they didn't.

We moved all over Texas, never more than six months in a place (usually it was closer to three or four) and they fought wherever they were together. So I never made any friends that lasted and everything was various depending on whether it was just my mother and me or whether my father was there; and whether they were trying to run a restaurant together or whether my mother was working as a waitress ... do you know that breakfast-shift, dinner-shift, swing-shift vocabulary? ... or there was once when she worked in a candy factory coating chocolates and putting the identifying little swirl on top. What I remember most often is that we were just the two of us living in a bedroom in somebody's house and my mother's salary would run ten dollars a week and the room plus board for me, and the landlady's looking after me, would run seven.

I don't mean to make this sound pathetic.

At some time during that, when I was five, I started school and I was a whiz. I went through the first and second grade the first year and I went through the third and fourth grade my second year and the third year when I was seven I was in the fifth grade and broke my arm twice so I got slowed down.

That would have been when we were in Mineral Wells. My father was with us then and we were living in a three-room house with a yard and honeysuckle on the porch at the bottom of a hill that was notable for a line of twenty-foot-high block letters filled with regular light bulbs that in the night glared out WELCOME toward the highway.

I loved that sign. It felt like being in church to stand at the base of those letters.

Just to finish that part of the story the next year we went to New Mexico and I went from being a whiz to passing the sixth grade "conditionally." I was a kind of half-dummy thereafter. I don't remember whether I had any notion of what went wrong.

It feels like years of chaos.

My father finally truly left around then. We sat in my Aunt Hannah's house south of Albuquerque and he roamed in the night around the house yelling Mae and my Uncle Horace would yell back Mae doesn't want you anymore, and I've got a .22 here, and my father finally left for good.

But, while I feel like that has to be told somehow, these few pages going the way they've gone, what I really want to mention and it took me until yesterday to get it into the air, is that all that time, and right from the first, reading was my darling pleasure.

I'VE ALWAYS BEEN IMPRESSED ...

I've always been impressed by the ability some people have to remember everything, things from a long time back, the name of a first grade teacher, whatever.

What I have instead is page after page of random notes to remind me.

Miz VanArt with the gun under her pillow and bullet holes in her door eating squabs in Mineral Wells

horny toads

the old man throwing his shoe through the window and putting shoe polish in his nose

the lady with the crazy daughter

In a book like this, the "plot" is whether it can come together at all. It might help to think of it as having *gathered* more than having been written. It's got about as much plan to it as tumbleweeds blown against a fence and stuck there.

Last October for the first time in more than twenty years I went back to Texas.

I went from San Francisco to my mother's house in Albuquerque and the next day about mid-morning the two of us left there driving her three-year-old air-conditioned Buick, headed east.

"We're going to have the sun beating on our backs all the way to Cline's Corners," she said. And, "Honey, get Mama a cigarette. They're in my purse. Do you want to drive?"

"Sure, if you want me to. You sure it won't make you nervous?"

"I'll just get us through the city limits. I know how all these freeways go."

"Are you supposed to smoke cigarettes?" I handed her the one I had lighted.

"Oh, I'm not supposed to but it won't hurt anything. Just, I'm not supposed to smoke so much that I get to coughing. Any kind of a cough plays hell with my throat."

When we were into the Sandias east of the city where the freeway turns into a more old-fashioned highway she pulled over and stopped to let us switch places.

"This car handles *really well* at fifty-five," she told me.

"O.K. Mama."

She began an instantaneous nesting in the midst of Kleenex, brought out chewing gum, put her purse where she could get it.

I put the seat back a couple of inches, checked the rear view mirror, pulled out onto the tartop.

"You're just used to those *little* cars that don't have much power," she said. "This car'll creep right up on you if you don't pay attention. You'll think you're just poking along and if you look at the speedometer it'll be on eighty or ninety."

She pulled a plastic package of slippers out of the glove

compartment and exchanged her high heeled shoes for them. She clicked the radio on.

The radio has a way of acting like a messenger. They play so many songs that if you're in any kind of a particular "catch" there's bound to be one that starts rising up above the rest like it's got your name on it.

If the song is at all popular it seems like that's the only thing they're playing after awhile.

Merle Haggard came in on us singing that song that has the line in it *Sing me back home, turn back the years* ... That song was number one all the time we spent driving around. We kept car company for just under three weeks, me, Mama, and Merle. It was like old times.

Used car salesmen, itinerant preachers and fry cooks have a hard time getting credit: bad risks, too mobile.

Amarillo, Lubbock, Abilene, San Angelo, Sweetwater, Houston, Galveston; my daddy was a six foot three Irish frycook. We followed the general rule. On short notice or no notice at all he'd have Mama and me in the car and gone. When he ran out of towns he'd just start over.

It wasn't until many years later, I mean quite recently, that it occurred to me to wonder how many of those abrupt departures had to do with jealous husbands; or to a woman whose demands were finally strong enough to override his charm.

"Are you feeling carsick, Jessie? Jack, Jessie's feeling carsick! Here honey, trade places with me. Hang your head out the window. The wind on your face'll do you good. Pull over, Jack! She's going to vomit! You better stop the car!"

There I'd be, shoved out the window of the car as it veered to the side of the road ... my mother pushing me farther out at the same time she clutched my skirt. My father, resentful and swearing, would slam the car to a stop and I'd stand beside the road in the settling dust, retching green bile.

"She's bilious! I told you in Brownfield that we should stop and eat something!"

Jack looks, disgusted, at the side of his car, pulls up a young cotton plant to wipe at the side of his car. His name was Walter but he called himself Jack. It was the current hero name. Jack Armstrong, the All-American Boy was a radio favourite. A current song was Cowboy Jack:

> Your sweetheart waits for you, Jack
> Your sweetheart waits for you
> Out on the lonely prairie
> Where skies are always blue

And she always did. In every town.

Breaded veal cutlets, flour and milk gravy, shrunken peas, a wilted lettuce leaf with a slice of tomato and a big dab of mayonnaise going a darker yellow at the edges ... all over Texas.

(You know, nobody wanted that place. Time and again the U.S. turned it down. Aaron Burr wanted it for awhile but Jefferson ruined him. James Monroe let Texas go by to get Florida. Daniel Webster resigned as secretary of state when President John Tyler started considering it. That great patriot-author Edward Everett Hale wrote a sixteen-page pamphlet against "the introduction into the Union of an un-principled population of adventurers, with all the privileges of a state of naturalized citizens." The title of that pamphlet was How To Conquer Texas, Before Texas Conquers Us.)

Mineral Wells: Jack takes the tablecloth (one of many times) and with a pull crashes breakfast onto the floor; dishes, eggs, bacon, gravy, biscuits, and a full pot of coffee.

Galveston: Handsome Jack springs to the aid of the blonde young woman who stands ... ("I know that type," Mae snorted to a friend of hers en route to the lake, "she's going to move two inches into the water and say I wish somebody would teach *me* to swim.") ... ankle deep in the water, looking at him archly, her arms wrapped around herself, pretending to shiver. "I wish somebody...."

Abilene and Austin: Handsome Jack breaks his wife's nose two separate times in different towns.

Lubbock: Jack looks back to see the meat cleaver thrown by his wife quiver in the door frame inches from his head.

And in which of those towns did Jack go down on one knee and hold his arms open toward me, saying, "Are you going to leave your daddy, honey?" And I came flying back while Mae stood at the door with her suitcases packed.

"Alright then," she said into my tears, "but someday *you're* going to want to leave him and when you do we'll go."

Children are so easy to get around.

Once he held two coins out to me, a nickel and a dime.

"Which one do you want," he asked, "the big one or the little one?"

Of course I knew the difference and I took the dime and saw the disappointment on his face.

"Why do you want that one? This one is bigger."

So, seeing that he really wanted me to take the nickel I put the dime back and took the nickel and he got on with his joke.

"Look here," he yelled to my mother, "she took the nickel instead of the dime because it's bigger!"

"We should be at Cline's Corners in about ten minutes."

"I believe it's right over that hill yonder, babe. You go straight ahead on the ridge and then circle back."

Mama went on with her story. "One of the best times that I remember when we were kids was when we lived out there south of Abilene on a farm. We had a big old two-story farmhouse with a great big earth tank down at the back. There was a spring above that fed into it. This big old tank had a gravel bottom and fresh water run into it all the time out of this spring. Then on the far side there was a place that it run out. That earth tank was us kids' joy and pleasure. We'd swim in it all summer then we'd skate on it all winter. We'd go down there and build us a big fire on the bank. We'd go out on that ice and skate and slide until we was tired and cold. Then we'd go get warm at the fire. We used to take eggs down there to boil in a bucket or some kind of meat to cook on a stick over the fire.

"In the fall after the feed had been gathered and brought in our stepdaddy would take these great big field rakes— it's like a plough—you pull it with horses ... and he'd start at one end of that field and he'd rake all the stalks to the centre of the field. There'd be a pile of stalks four or five feet high and real wide, five or six feet, and it would go all the length of the field which was ... heavenly days ... a *good* mile long!

"We'd wait until some night when the wind was in the right direction and we'd get the neighbours' kids that was our ages to come over ... it was when the wind would be blowing from one end of that pile to the other end ... that direction. We'd start burning that pile at one end and we'd stay down there until it had burned across the whole length of the field which normally took until the wee small hours of the morning. We'd play games around the fire and take food down there to cook.

"We really had a fine time when we were little ones and had a chance to have it," her voice was wistful.

"What made all that change?"

"They had an influx of grasshoppers. It was four or five years in a row that the grasshoppers ate *everything.* They ate the feed. They ate the cotton. They'd just ... you know ... as the little cotton came out of the ground they'd just bite it off right down at the ground. This happened for three or four years.

"It wasn't just us. It was *everybody* in this whole area.

"At the time it started we had fourteen nice milk cows plus all the calves that we had for beef, and young bulls. And we had chickens and pigs, the things you keep to kill off.

"The first two or three years, well, the *first* year we did alright on the proceeds of former crops. Then the next year my stepdaddy had to borrow some money from the bank to make a crop. Alright, they got wiped out by the grasshoppers again *that* year. Everybody did. Then the next year *everybody* borrowed toward a crop. Everybody was in the same position that third year because the bankers in self-defense had to lend the money for crops because it was their only hope of getting their money back.

"Then when it happened again the next year, well, the farmers either had to turn over everything they had to the bank, their farming tools and cattle and all, or they had to sell it all for next to nothing. Whatever they had the banks took. It was bad all the way around.

"So at that time everybody moved to towns to try and get work because there wasn't any work on the farms."

"Would that have been around the time that Peter was nine? Was that why he had to go off and saw wood?"

"No, he didn't have to. He did that because my step-daddy was so mean to him that he just couldn't stand it any longer. He just got up and left. But my stepdaddy did have a nice son that was our stepbrother. That's where Peter went. What *he* was doing ... yes, come to think of it that was during the same time … what the stepbrother was doing, he went way back into wooded country and he cut wood for people that had wood stoves, which was most people. Then they would haul it to whoever wanted it or they'd take it to the wood yard in the town."

"Look. There's snow on the mountains over Santa Fe."

"First snow of the season. If I remember it right we got it even earlier last year."

"So then you moved to town?"

"My stepdaddy got some kind of job. I don't remember what. Oh, one thing, he was one of these what they used to call faith doctors."

"He was?"

"Yeah he … uh, cool it a little, babe. You'll be right there in a minute. Top of the bridge. Now it's the next one.

"Yeah, he did a lot of people a lot of good. For instance there was this one man that come to him that had his toes curled under just like this."

She held her hand out with the fingers under to show me.

"Oh, honey, you can just go straight ahead and then take a left," she interrupted herself.

"I should go right shouldn't I?"

"You *can* go either one but if you go left we'll come out at Cline's Corners and get us a Coke."

"O.K."

"It's easier than making that big swirl.

"This man's toes had been that way for *years*. My step-daddy worked with those some way and talked to that man and when he got through … this man had told him he'd give him *any* amount of money if he got those toes straightened out. He got those toes straightened out and the man give him ten or fifteen dollars."

THE IRISH CAME TO TEXAS ...

The Irish came to Texas building the railroads as they came, the cheapest labour available. There were some Chinese and some Negroes but mostly that company of men was filled out of the latest wave of Irish to hit the country. Hardly arrived, eyes still full of ... think of it ... the pictures you've seen of Ireland if you've never been there. All that soft green and blue hazed over by mists ... deep valleys with fog ... lakes ... all that growing green stuff.

And think of the Great Plains; land flat as a table and immense, far as the horizon; the sky an inverted bowl to hold the tiny work gang in, like ants; the sky huge and pale blue with chicken hawks gliding in slow circles, held up by the rising heat.

For another instance: St. Patrick drove the snakes from Ireland, but Texas has all four of the poisonous snakes to be found in the U.S. (rattlesnake, coral snake, water moccasin and copperhead.)

This is, as it's clear, a fantasy of that time and place and those persons but few things are probable. They lived in a mess of shacks and material, in the simple fact of back-breaking work. And every morning a huge sun rose to blast them; the rails too hot to touch; the muscles and haul of getting them into place. And when a man straightened to ease his back he must have had that perspective line of the rail that had already been laid stretching back in a perfect pointer, himself on the balance end of it; lips cracked, dry skin turning to leather in a sirocco sandstorm; still heat with twisters on the horizon in season. ("The old man was so scared of tornadoes that he'd have us kids and mama all crammed together in the storm cellar most of the night all through the season. We wouldn't no more than get to sleep before he'd be dragging at the covers and swearing at us.")

Many of them took Cherokee women. That nation, the Cherokee nation, got dispersed so early and the women weren't secured.

What I really have on my mind just at this minute is how that Irish-Cherokee got seeded out across that vast distance by the time they had stopped. There's a high percentage of residents across the Texas plains who've got that mix in them.

There must have been a lot of interplay ... I mean that both those lots of people believed in visionary realities at least part of the time. And it hangs on. The Hardshell Baptists, the Holy Rollers, the snake handlers. My grandmother has second-sight and my Aunt Ethel has the gift-of-tongues.

But there are other aspects to it. My Aunt Ethel waited to claim her own son in a dime store in a one-street Texas town some forty years ago because two women, as they passed by him said, Look at that cute little Indian boy. She waited until they were at the far end of the store and couldn't see her hurry him out and home. One of her younger sisters was there and saw it all, got hustled out as well, and there was at least the looseness to let it turn into a family joke.

"I get to talking and let the car get down to fifty-five," Mama said.

"Well, we got through town," I answered.

"We'll be in Texas pretty quick. Did I tell you about the time I brought Maggie and Rachel over here? They were just little bitty things, you know, and I brought them over here. I had told them that all my people lived in Texas. We got up there to that sign ... you know that stone map shaped like Texas? I said to them, You see that? That means we're in Texas! Of course there wasn't a thing there except wide open country. Maggie raised up and looked all around and she said, Well! Where is everybody?

"But if Rachel didn't show her ass over there! You know how she can when she gets on one of them tears.

"I had a real nice setup. I bought 'em funny books. They got in the back seat and I turned on the air conditioner. In the car we just had a ball.

"The minute we got over there ... I thought they would *play* with the kids ... the big kids ... which *they* wanted to. But nossir! Rachel would *not* do it. She wanted my attention every minute.

"I was trying to visit with Hannah, trying to visit with Ethel, trying to visit with Peter and Maxine and here she come ... for the fiftieth time in the hour ... I said, Well honey, it'll be alright! I said, Don't get so fussed up over it. Just go ahead and play. She *jumped* up and down, and went to *screaming* at the top of her voice. She said, You don't *like* me! and I *hate* you! You're not my grandmother *anymore!* You'll *never* be my grandmother again because *I hate you!* You're not even my *friend!!*

"Brother! I went outside ... I didn't get a *big* one ... I got a little bitty keen elm switch and I come back in there and I went to *work* on her with it! I said, I *am* your grandmother and I *do* love you and you *do* love me!! *Right?* And she said, Yes, grandmother, yes.

"Then she went home and told you that I whipped her with a whip! It was just a little old keen switch because I didn't want to do her too much damage. I had to get her about three times! I never saw her act like that in my life!"

"She's got to learn to control it or she'll never have anything but hell on earth. That's Ethel exactly! That's Ethel the way she was when she was a kid!"

"Oh yeah?"

"No ... (musing) I don't remember Ethel throwing temper fits like that till after she was grown and married. (laughing) But boy, she goes off on them now!

"She told me about her and Hannah getting into a squabble and she said, "I got so mad at her that I just couldn't think what to say to her" ... and she was just dying laughing ... "And I told her she was a *liar* and a *thief!*"

"I said, Ethel, you and I have never got mixed up that bad yet but if we ever do you better be smart and not call me either of those names! I said, Because the day you do you and I are going to tangle!"

"I think that sounds pretty mild."

"A *liar* and a *thief?*"

"Yeah, when you get as angry as you can get and the best you can come out with is something like a liar and a thief...."

"Oh, she wouldn't think of saying bitch or son-of-a-bitch or something like that."

"I bet it relieved her to say it. She enjoyed it later."

"Yeah. I told her I said, Ethel, you know what I'd of done if I'd've been Hannah? Ethel said, No. I said, I would've never spoke to you again as long as I lived! You'd of been right off the board as far as I was concerned if you'd of called me a liar and a thief."

"That's a good song, that Merle Haggard song."

"Oh. What song is that, honey?"

"What were we talking about?"

"You were telling me about when you and Horace and Hannah spent the winter in east Texas," I answered.

"I can't get too *interested* in telling about that.

"Well, Hannah and Horace they was going down there because the doctor had told Horace that the paint was starting to affect his lungs and cause him problems with his breathing. So they come by and got you and me from Peter's and Maxine's, I guess, when they lived at Hawley. Then we went down into southeast Texas.

"And Horace was ... oh ... we found this great big old farmhouse, you know, just on a lovely ... a big old house ... It belonged to his family. Lots of land around it and lots of dead trees, mesquite trees, and a *huge* fireplace, almost a walk-in thing, really big, natural stone. They took a trailer with beds and bedsteads and cooking pots and pans and a gasoline stove. We set up our kitchen and living room in this big room with the fireplace.

"And the ... oh ... we'd have the best meals! This was a big ranch and his people ... well you know at that time if anybody needed beef they just killed a calf and dressed it out and divided it around among the family. Then when they needed another one they'd do the same thing. So they furnished us with all kinds of fresh meat, lots of Rhode Island Red eggs ... you know those brown eggs ... and milk and butter and cream. You never saw the like. Just running over.

"Horace cleared one room there by the fireplace ... by the *room* with the fireplace ... and he took the car and the trailer ... little two-wheeled trailer ... and he went out ... He just brought in great loads of those dead logs and filled that room up with them.

"It would come big snows and we'd just build big roaring fires in the fireplace. It was more fun. The people around there would give dances. Somebody would clear out a couple of great big rooms and the local musicians would play for the dance and we'd go and we'd dance all night. Stop at midnight for a barbecue dinner or something like that and after we all got through eating we'd dance until morning, then we'd all go home.

"It come big snows! It'd just come *big* snows and everything'd be covered, all those pretty trees. We really enjoyed it. We'd put on rubber boots and heavy coats and get out, Hannah and me, and take walks through the snow.

"Horace set him out a trapline, just an old-fashioned trapline and he'd go out and walk his trapline every day. He'd catch coyotes, skunks ... they have beautiful fur, of course, in the wintertime ... coyotes have beautiful fur too. There was two or three other kind of animals. I don't know whether there was any foxes but it seems like he got a few fox furs. He did that for a pastime and that paid for all our expenses!"

"How old were you all then?"

"Well ... you was six months old ... wait a minute ... you was eighteen months old so that made me about nineteen. Hannah was about twenty-one or twenty-two and Horace was ten years older ... eleven ... He was eleven years older'n Hannah. He'd have been about thirty-two or three.

"They had these huge fieldstone storage rooms there, like a big barn.

Horace kept his furs and things out there, the pelts, stretched out over boards, and he cured them out there. Seems like we stayed there ... we stayed down there about six weeks."

"Did it help his lungs?"

"Oh yes, he got alright. He hadn't been down or anything. The doctor just told him it was best for him to get away from that paint for awhile."

MY UNCLE HORACE HAD ...

My Uncle Horace had eyes as pale as water and the greatest private playhouse in the world. Of course he called it a *store house* ... the old barn. And the reasons he gave me and Sonny as to why we should stay out were reasonable. Dryrot: the barn was bound to have dryrot and we could fall through the loft floor and injure ourselves drastically. Tetanus: since all the doors were padlocked shut our entry was gained by climbing the accumulation of cast-off machine parts, old bedsprings and junk in general that was stacked against the back of the barn and piled high enough to let us reach a square loft door. Uncle Horace projected the results of a scratch from that metal as if it had all been soaked in whatever the poison is that pygmies or whoever it is tip their arrows with. He had other reasons but they're less sensational and harder to remember.

What never got stated was what everybody knew. Horace was one of those people who can't stand to throw anything away but he couldn't live in the midst of it all. So he "stored" it. The barn was a symbol for a kind of peace of mind. He was keeping the residue of his life secure there. Old books of wallpaper samples, mail order catalogues with fabric swatches glued to the pages, fencing foils; it drove him wild to learn that we had been there. Once when we were high up a tree and keeping quiet to avoid doing dishes we saw him come from the house, realize we weren't in sight and head for the barn ... almost on tiptoe. He put his ear to the wall to hear us, but there wasn't any sound. Up the tree we kept quiet. He took his keys out and unlocked one of the doors. We could hear him inside moving around the piles of boxes and trunks, looking to see whether we were hidden. For him I guess it was desperate.

For our part, we were fans of the Katzenjammer Kids, Pirates, Robin Hood; and we were cronies. Such a sight as Uncle Horace scouring out the hiding places in the barn was a kind of triumph for us.

He was a decent man but he was easy to bypass.

YOU KNEW ...

"You knew he shot himself?"

"I knew he shot himself," I answered.

"But honey, poor thing, he's better off."

"I never understood, when he went into the hospital what exactly was the matter with him?"

"Well, the thing of it was he had started to Idaho to see Florence and the kids and spend Thanksgiving with them. He got to ... not Cortez, Colorado ... but up in that area and he had a stroke. He *knew* something had happened to him so instead of stopping *there* and going to a Vets hospital ... or *any* hospital and giving the Veterans the bill he turned around and drove his car back to Albuquerque and went into the Vets hospital there.

"Bert what's-his-name, that electrician that was a friend of his called me up one day and said, Mae, have you seen or heard anything from old Horace? And I said, No, I sure haven't. And he said, Well, he started for Florence's and that's the last I heard, said, He hadn't been home and I tried to call him at Florence's and he hadn't been there ... hadn't heard from him in months.

"So Florence called me or I called her, I don't remember which and anyway her daddy never got there. So none of us couldn't figure it out. I called Hannah and Bud. Bud didn't know anything. So Bert one day said he just happened to think maybe he's up at the Veterans hospital. So he went and checked. Horace was there and he'd been there a month."

"Why didn't Horace get in touch with somebody and tell them he was there?"

"He was just too sick or he didn't have the mind for it. You see a car on this side?"

"Naw ... well ... yeah, but it's way up there."

"It's not far enough that I'd have time to go around this truck.

"He had a blood clot lodged between his heart and his kidney and it was running his blood pressure up so high that it was real dangerous. So, anyway, they had to go in there and get it and that was when his brother Wendell come up to be there.

"They went in there to get it and they'd give him so much blood thinner stuff trying to dissolve it that after the operation the blood would just run out around those stitches. It'd collect in here ... just a *ball* of it ... a *pile* of it in his stomach ... and they'd have to go in there to get it out. They operated on him three times in three days. The third time I told Wendell I said, For god's sake tell that stupid doctor to put a drain tube in there to drain off the excess blood. They can always give him more blood but he *cannot* stand them going in and out and in and out, you know. So the doctor come in to talk to us and Wendell asked him about that and he said, Why, I hadn't *thought* about *that*. So they put in a drain tube.

"By that time they were giving him a blood coagulant but they'd already give him so much of the other stuff that they just cancelled out.

"Then his kidneys failed. They had to put a bunch of stuff in him to try to purify his kidneys, his urine or something.

"The last time they brought him out of there they told me, they said, There's something wrong with one of his legs. He acts like one of his legs is paralyzed. I said, Well, it couldn't be nothing except another blood clot. It was behind his knee and they left it go. They waited until he had gangrene in his foot before they ever done anything. It was moving right up his leg. Honey, it was as purple as if you'd painted it with purple ink.

"By that time Wendell had gone home and he'd left a written thing up there that if there was anything anybody in the family had to sign they were to let me sign it. They called me at 7:30 one morning ... no ... they called me one night to tell me to be up there at 7:30 the next morning and I'd have to sign a thing for them to take his leg off. Boy, what a hardship. That like to have *killed* me. I went up there and I told them ... see, he was in the intensive care unit ... and I said, I'm not signing *anything* until I see that leg *myself!* They took me right in there and, Jessie ... his foot and his leg was purple just on a slant to his knee. They was going to take his leg off below his knee and it just so happened that they had a real good specialist in this line of stuff that had flown in that morning from Chicago or somewhere and he said, Oh no! He said, You take that leg off below the knee and you'll have to go in again and take it off way up here. So he went in and he took it off right here. So he got it.

"Poor Horace. He'd had so much pentathol. That stuff'll drive you crazy. You get a certain amount of brain damage from that the way it cuts your respiration. It cuts your blood pressure and slows you heart down. You don't get enough blood and oxygen to your brain. That's the reason I get these hallucinations after I've had too much of it.

"After my last operation when Alice come to visit me she was sitting in a chair near the bed and I started chuckling and she said, What are you laughing about? And I said, I'm going to tell you I know it isn't true so you won't think I'm crazy but I just saw the most beautiful white cat in the world come through the window and jump onto the floor and go under your chair. And she *jumped* up and started looking all around for that cat. I said, Alice, it's *bound* to be a hallucination. We're three floors up!

"Anyway, I'd go up there to see Horace, poor thing, and he'd talk plumb crazy more often than not. I'd take him stacks and stacks of magazines. You remember how he loved to read magazines? Everybody I knew give me magazines to take him.

"I went up there one day and he says, Boy! he said, You know I got up this morning about two or three clock and I was tired of this bed and I just walked downtown. See he still didn't know his leg was off. And he said, You know they had to come down there and *get* me! He said, They went down there and hunted me up and brought me back here and *tied* me to this bed. He'd talk real crazy.

"He kept reaching around and feeling his *spine,* you know how knotty it is, and he'd say, You just feel back there where they cut me open up and down my back. I said, Horace, they didn't operate on your back! That's your *backbone!* I'd say something like that to him and he'd just say, Oh.

"Wendell was there and he'd talk to him every day. He never did know Wendell had been there. H.N., his cousin, an older man, come up there to see him. He never did know that H.N. had been there. His sister and her husband come, he didn't remember it."

"When did he know his leg was off?"

"Well, they told him. They just went in there one day and told him about his leg being off but the next day he didn't remember it. He wasn't himself to know.

"Well, he stayed in there quite a long time. You see, one thing was, he had to learn to walk. They had two kinds of artificial legs. One was lightweight, made out of aluminum, you know. It was a newer model and much easier to manage, but no, he wouldn't have it. He had to have one of those old-fashioned kind that's carved to look like a leg. Weighed thirty or forty pounds.

"So of course he couldn't get around with it.

"One day the woman at the hospital called me and she said, I want to know why you haven't come after Mr. Lambert! Said, He's sitting out on the front walk in a wheelchair with all of his things packed and out there waiting for you to come and pick him up! To *me!* That was after he'd got that artificial leg and he could walk a little bit. But he was a real case. I didn't dare take him. I said, Well that's just too damned bad! You better go out there and get him and put him back to bed! *Because,* I said, You come right down to it he's not anything to me. He's got family of his own and

I don't have anything but a one-bedroom apartment and I don't have *no* way of taking care of him or looking after him and I'm not able to lift him. One thing, it was *blowing a blizzard.* I said, He don't have any business coming out of there!

"So Florence come over. Bert called Florence and she got on a plane and flew over.

"Horace wanted to go back out to that little trailer house of his. But it wasn't self-contained. It didn't have a toilet, no running water."

"He probably wanted to be independent."

"Yes, but Jessie there was just no way. So Florence come over. I said, Now Florence, I want to tell you something! Before you take Horace out of that hospital. I do *not* want you to bring him *here*. I said, You fix a place for him and you take him to it. Well, you know what she did? She got me to take her over so she could get his pickup ... that was Sunday ... and she went over there and got Horace and she brought him to me *bag* and *baggage!* She just didn't want to clean that trailer! It didn't have as much room in it as one room. She could have gone out there and cleaned it herself but she wanted to get somebody else to clean it.

"Well, that was on Sunday and he set around there and he ranted and cussed and ranted and raved and he run Bert down...."

"Why was he running Bert down?"

"Well, he turned against Bert and me. We was the people that really stuck by him all the time he was in hospital."

"Why did he turn against you?"

"Well ... he just ... because I didn't come to get him that day for one thing and because Bert didn't come to get him for another one. And I didn't think in his weakened condition that he had any business changing beds as cold as it was. It was in the middle of winter.

"Besides, I wasn't able. I had already fooled with him and all the kinfolks that come to visit him until I was just down. I drawed over six hundred dollars out of the bank while he was in the hospital just to feed the extra company I had. Of course there wasn't a one of them that didn't offer to help with the groceries.

"Anyway, she brought him over to me and I had to make the couch down every night. And he had to pull that heavy old wooden leg off every night to go to bed. Florence got him a two pound coffee can to pee in and the first thing he did was knock it over when he got up in the morning and it spilled all over the rug and the floor. And her and Bud didn't even offer to help clean it up. I had to get down on the floor and scrub it up right in their face.

"So this went on till Thursday and still she wasn't saying nothing about taking him to a place. Thursday morning I got up and I called her into the kitchen … I hadn't slept all night for dreading it … and I said, Florence I don't care what you do with your daddy but I want him out of this apartment today. I said, I have done my share for your daddy. And I said, You took his money and spent it … you see, he had almost three thousand dollars in the safe at the hospital. We all thought he was going to die. So Bert and Florence went in there and talked to him … told him he ought to sign a paper to let Florence get that money out of there … so he did. He signed the paper. The next day he didn't even remember it. Florence went in and got that money and she told me, Well, I'm going to go home and pay up all my bills. I said, Florence, for god's sake don't spend that money. I said, Put it in a savings account and hold it! I said, I don't think Horace's going to die, and he's going to need that money. She went home and spent every damned bit of it! When poor old Horace got out … well, he hadn't got out of the hospital when they let him take a plane up there to spend Christmas with Florence. When he come back he said, I told her if she could just give me a thousand dollars of that money she could keep the rest … and said, You know, she couldn't even do *that!*"

"That's a shocker."

"Oh, that just turned me against Florence!

"So I said, You taken your daddy's money and spent it and if he don't have the money for a place to stay well you get him on a plane and you take him home with you. I said, He's not my responsibility. I want him out of here and I want it done today. So she got up and went over and got somebody to clean up that little trailer and she put him in it and went and got him some groceries and a few other things and went off and left him there."

"When did Bud get him?"

"Bud got him ... oh, it wasn't long after that. It was just a little while later."

"Bud really tried to do well by him didn't he?"

"He sure did, honey. He had a *world* of patience with him. But see, Horace had the leg off on this side. I think it was this one. Yes, I'm sure it was. And *then* he had another stroke on *this* side that partially paralyzed him."

"Good Lord."

"He was just getting to be ... he was a real mental case and *awfully* handicapped physically. Bud was as good to him as he could be. Hannah even cooked extra stuff ... her and Douglas lived just down the street in that same house they live in now ... she'd cook things that she *knew* he liked, like corn bread and things like that that he'd always liked. She'd take that stuff over there and sweet milk to have with it ... that's what he always ate at home...."

"I remember he used to crumble cold corn bread in a glass of cold milk and eat it with a spoon."

"He loved that. So she'd bake and she'd cook things and take them up there and the minute she'd walk in through that door he'd just start cussin her and calling her an old bitch and everything else."

"Why did he do that?"

"Because he just ... honey, he was crazy. He just had it in for everybody."

"He didn't have much of a life by then. I guess he just hated anybody that still had a life."

"I said, *Never* again would I pray for anybody to live except if it's the Lord's will and if it's for the best. Because I got the elders to come up there and pray for him and give him a blessing. The doctors would say, I don't know *what* on *earth* is holding that man here! He should have been dead *days* ago! He don't have a thing going for him and he's got *everything* against him. And he suffered the agonies of the damned."

"He was always such a quiet man. I tended to feel sorry for him."

"Honey, I tell you Horace was sort of mean down underneath. He used to accuse Hannah of messing around with men. He hit her one time in the face and busted her nose all to pieces. That was when you was a little girl. She had to go to the doctor and get her nose fixed. Then she'd have to go back to him. She got a little hat with a veil across here to hide her black eyes and her broke nose. Well, that's what caused her to finally leave him. She stopped loving him then."

"How long did he stay with Bud?"

"Oh, a year or more. And Bud was just so good to him ... you know, and sweet and kind ... he'd come home from work every afternoon to take his daddy for a walk. Get him by the arm and help him. And he'd talk to him in just the gentlest voice.

"Well, they had all these guns around. You remember him and Bud was always fooling around with guns. And he started keeping one of them guns alongside him all the time. He wouldn't lie down on the couch without that gun alongside him. Scared Hannah to death.

"One day the girl was over there cleaning up the house and Horace was fooling with that gun. He got up and come into the kitchen and he dropped that gun on the floor.

"He asked her to hand it to him so she picked it up and

handed it to him. Then he asked her to help him get down the steps into the back yard. And she did.

"And he just walked out there and set down in a chair that was there and just put that gun to his head and blow-ed his brains out."

"*I knew* yawl'd like peas and corn bread for supper! Douglas said if you're going to do a lot of cooking why don'tcha make a roast or a chicken or something like that. But I said I'll bet you that Mae and Jessie can't get fresh black-eyed peas. I said I'm going to cook peas and corn bread and have fresh butter."

"Well, it's really good."

"I love it."

"Would anybody like a slice of raw onion?"

"Yeah. Me."

"I can't eat raw onion. I'd love to but it'd tear me up. I'd be sick for the next two days."

"Well, Mae, how's your throat?"

"The first operation it was better. The doctor said it was blocking up my breathing, all that growth. He said, You're going to feel like a new woman when you start getting your fair share of oxygen. And it was true. I just felt half-drunk. You know how you feel when they give you pure oxygen? Well, after the first operation it was like the air I breathed was pure oxygen. But the second operation has really set me back. I feel worse now than I did before I had the first one."

"Are you supposed to talk?"

"Listen, you know how *they* are! Let a doctor boss you and you're as good as buried. They want you to stop anything and *everything!* Dr Macauley heard him tell me not to talk and not to smoke and I guess he saw the look on my face. He just went to laughing. He said to Dr Dillon, that was the other doctor, he said, Don't you have anything better to do with your time than stand there and pound your head on the wall?"

"Well, isn't this trip hard on you?"

"Jessie's doing most of the driving. If I get sick we'll just head home."

"Where yawl going from here?"

"I thought we'd just go straight over to Abilene. I want to be sure to see mama and that way if I get sick I'll have done that much."

"Jessie, Bud's really anxious to see you. And wait'll you see those little old kids. How long's it been since you saw Danny and Darlene?"

"They were real little."

"Are you my *aunt* or my *cousin* or what?"

"I guess we're cousins. I'm your daddy's cousin."

"Jessie's the one that knows all about poems, Darlene. Why don't you get your poem and read it for her. Darlene wrote a poem at school today."

"Well, it's just a little one. The teacher said it was really nice." The slim child thumbed through an assortment of papers, then stood straight, holding one. She had short dark hair cut close to her head and enormous eyes.

"May you be happy," she read in a clear high voice, "And live a good life Find a good husband And be a good wife."

WE WERE LIVING ...

We were living in New Mexico when Bud and I were kids together. When I went back there a couple of months ago I saw an article in the newspaper deploring the state of the poor deprived children who couldn't afford to get into the municipal swimming pool and were reduced to swimming in the irrigation ditches. The sense of it was that charitable organizations should provide free tickets. Another instance of bureaucratic nose-poking. Anybody who'd swap a deep ditch with the water moving in it for a cement pool with chlorine is some kind of a fool. Well, a *usual* kind of a fool.

The ditch Bud and I swam in was a five-minute walk down the dirt road and a turn right for about another five minutes, along the ridged dirt that made the bank. The moisture rose up into the air, softening it, and there was a constant warm smell of mud and weeds gone rampant, the smell of chlorophyll.

The "flume" was a wooden chute, about three feet wide with sides about two feet high that carried water from a higher ditch and dumped it into ours. Where the water fell a deeper hole had been dug and the ditch widened into a larger pool. The chute was angled about twenty degrees and had slick green moss growing along the bottom. We could go to the top and climb in, sit down, turn loose of the sides and get rushed along, as good as a roller coaster, propelled by footdeep water, to the end where we dropped about six feet into the ditch and were rolled and tumbled back up to the surface usually about ten or fifteen feet farther down.

"I was sorry to hear about your daddy," I told Bud. Grown up now with a small moustache.

He looked at me intently for an instant, then ducked his head in a way he always had to keep his feelings in.

"Yeah. I guess it couldn't be helped."

"Mama, show Billie-Jean how you can sit on your hair."

"Mama, let me brush your hair."

Until my grandmother was an old woman she pulled her hair into a bun at the back of her neck. At night when she let it down it fell to her knees. Her daughters were always after her to let them brush it. They took it as a personal treasure. And one of the things she hated most in the world was to have her hair messed with. She was tender-headed but she was also tender-hearted and she'd sit with her teeth gritted after the tangles were out and let one or another of her girls brush the hair that at first was raven black, then salt and pepper, then gray; and by the time it was gray it was me ... "Grandmama let me brush your hair." And when she couldn't stand it a moment longer she'd snap, "That's enough now!" and take the hairbrush ... and as quickly she'd smile and be her own gentle self, the snap being a reflex and not anger. It was always a gift to brush her hair.

She was a scant five feet tall and worked as hard as a full-sized man.

Especially after she married her second husband who lost everything that came to his hand. He had red hair and a mean disposition.

In Texas when you say of somebody "He married a red-headed woman," or, "She married a red-headed man," you're saying Lookout! Maybe nobody says it when the red-head's a gentle one and that's the discrimination. Maybe that phrase itself is a kind of word for redheads who are bad tempered. Whatever. The fact is: the second time around my grandmama married a red-headed man who was as sour as she was sweet. It must have been a surprise to her. Her first husband, Mr. Chapman, had been a good husband, a good father and a frugal man.

"The first thing us kids learned about the old man was not to walk in kicking distance," my mother said.

There were thirteen kids in all lumping together the ones my grandmother had by Mr. Chapman, the ones the old man had by his first wife and the ones they had together. At least the old man didn't show any preference for his own. He was as bad as he could be to all of them.

My mother stood up to him when she was twelve. She was a substantial twelve-year-old. The old man had Ada in the kitchen and was mad at her about something. Ada was the first child he had with my grandmother ... a sad scrawny thing all her life ... she ended up married to a squint-eyed mechanic named Steve who took up where the old man left off. Anyway, "He was hitting her with his fists just like she was a man." She must have been about eight; and my mother picked up a piece of stove wood and said, "You old son-of-a-bitch if you hit her again I'll kill you!" And he laid off.

I meant to talk about my grandmother but it's hard to avoid the old man. By the time I really remember him he had taken to his bed to die.

He was about twenty years older than my grandmother. She was in her twenties when they married. I must have been born when he was around sixty and he went to bed when he was sixty-three. He didn't pass away until he was in his nineties so there was some small margin of error there, which nonplussed him not at all. He had a running, full-scale deathbed scene for more than thirty years.

My mother and her sisters would go to Abilene for a visit and would invite Grandmama to come home with them for awhile. There were always other people in the house who could tend to the old man.

She'd say, "Well ... Papa *has* been feeling a little better lately. I'll go ask him."

There'd be a roar from the next room.

"You're doing what no woman has ever done!" he'd yell. "You're leaving your husband on his deathbed. You go right ahead but know that I won't be here when you get back!"

That was his constant theme ... for thirty years. And Grandmother would come back to say, "Papa isn't really feeling well enough for me to go, honey."

My memory of him is mostly that if he wanted anything he'd start swearing at the top of his lungs and my Grandmother would rush to him saying, "Yes, Papa?"

He wore long-handled underwear for pajamas and at times he would undertake a minor trip away from his bed. I remember there would be big pooches like air bubbles in the long-handles at his knees and elbows and seat. He'd stomp to the bathroom or the kitchen glaring and swearing at anyone he met. There was always a sense of scurrying when the old man moved around. Everybody getting out from under foot.

Apart from the scene in the kitchen he only got his come uppance three times that I know of:

The Ku Klux Klan got after him one year when he had made a crop and had money in the bank and was sending my Uncle Peter to school barefoot after the snows had started. One morning there was a note on the kitchen screen door: "Get your boy some shoes. KKK." He paid no attention and three days later a note on the door said, "We're coming for you tonight. KKK." And he took Peter into town and bought him some new shoes.

The second time was: In Texas in the summertime when it's really hot the practice on farms is to pull the metal bedsteads out of the house and set them up under trees or on the side of the house opposite to where the sun rises; and everybody sleeps out. Well, the old man always woke up before anybody and he always took it personally that the others were still lying there after he slung his legs over the side of the bed. So he woke them by swearing at them. There was a time when he was making Ada his particular scapegoat and he'd jump her every morning. My mother had taken Ada on as her special charge and one night she told her, "Tomorrow morning when the old man starts swearing at you tell him to go to hell and take out across the sticker patch. I'll bring you something to eat in the orchard."

I want to describe a sticker patch for anybody who's never seen one. In some parts of the Texas plains the stickers are the only green things in sight. They flourish no matter what. They layout huge and uneven and absolute. It's possible for kids who go barefoot to memorize their local sticker patches like a geographer memorizes maps. It saves time to be able to traverse a sticker patch's bald spots instead of having to go around it.

The next morning in grey dawn the old man started raking the air with his daily message and Ada swung her own skinny kid legs over the bed, mumbled, "Go to hell," and set out running with the old man hard on her heels. She hit the sticker patch and immediately shifted into an intricate series of little hops and jumps like Little Liza across the ice. The old man hit the sticker patch right after her. His momentum overrode his tender feet and carried him five or six or ten feet into it before he was stopped. Like a cripple, a different man, he turned to start the long hobbling way back, picking his step by step, walking on the sides of his feet.

My mother took Ada some cold biscuits and preserves to the orchard, and Ada came home for supper, coming in quietly to take her place. The old man didn't say a word.

The third time was, he did finally die. Most of his "mourners" had tight pursed lips while the preacher talked about his virtues.

But my grandmother really cried. She really had loved that mean old fool.

"...providing for their own family, you know. They didn't have to think of much money because there wasn't a lot of stuff to do and a family's main concern was raising enough foodstuff during the growing season to support them until the next growing season.

"Everybody knew how to cure their own hams and bacon and put up their own sausages and can their vegetables and kill and dress out their own beef. Had their own eggs and chickens and milk, butter, and about the only thing they'd have to bother with would be sugar and coffee and flour.

"We always grew a big corn crop. After the ears dried we'd take the husks off and stack it in the corn crib ... take it easy, babe. You're letting the speedometer creep up. I don't know *why* Buick stopped putting those beepers on the speedometer! You could set them, you know, at the speed you didn't want to go over and they'd make a real racket:

"I don't need a beeper, Mama. I've got you."

"Well ... anyway, when we wanted cornmeal we'd get out and work the corn off those ears, rubbing them against an old rub board, and put it in baskets. Then my stepdaddy would take it to the corn mill. They'd stone-grind it. Then they'd bring it back. Mama would sift it. The fine stuff that would go through the sifter she kept to make bread with and the coarse stuff that wouldn't go through the sifter, well, that went to the chickens and pigs.

"That was the best cornmeal you ever ate! It just made the *best* corn bread!

"Another thing we used to do, we had a rub board that the boys had put nails through from the back side so it made a real rough surface, a kind of grater, and before the corn got too hard and dry we'd rub ears over that grater. Then you'd have to sift it. When you did it that way you saved the price of the mill but you got a lot more big rough pieces in it. But none of it was ever wasted because it went to the pigs and chickens. People didn't waste anything! Everything was put to good use.

"There was lots of neighbours. Of course, they lived quite a way apart from one farm to the next. Everybody had cattle and calves growing up. The neighbours would all take turns butchering a beef. The men would divide it up equally between so-many families because there was no way of keeping it. In the wintertime you could keep it. But in the summertime if you'd get hungry for fresh beef ... they'd kill one at our place and butcher it out. Then the next week they'd kill one at the next place. It was so much better than the meat you get now! It was so good.

"Then every winter we'd put up two or three hogs."

"I thought that after grandmama and the old man got married that he wasted that farm of hers. I thought you never had that place long after they got married."

"No, I think that Mama ... my mother wasn't a good manager, honey. As Mama said, she was raised up to sit on a silk pillow and sew a fine seam. The phrase had a ritual cadence."

"How was that? You mean her family was better off or something?"

"Well, you see ... she was raised by an old aunt ... whatever she called her. I can't remember her name. And they had plenty.

"She taught Mama how to do fine sewing. Hand-sewing because they didn't have any sewing machines. Everything was made by hand.

"In fact they even took the cotton and carded it. Have you ever seen a cotton carder? They would card this cotton and then they'd get it to rolling in long strings and they'd keep spinning it out some way until it made a thread.

"Then they'd weave their own material and they'd cut those materials to make whatever by hand. Even the men's suits and their own petticoats and dresses and all that.

"Mama knew how to do all that. My mother said that when she got married she had ten quilts that she had pieced and quilted as well as all her own linens and things."

"When Mama had pelligrisy we put hoops on over the wagon bed and stretched cloth over them and set out to go to east Texas where there was supposed to be an old black man could cure it.

"He had all these little cabins in the woods and the people that come to be cured lived in the cabins. Every morning and every evening he boiled up a mess of what looked like weeds that he gathered in a big old cast-iron pot and everybody that was there had to drink a glass of it. Even the ones that wasn't sick had to drink a glass of it. Us kids really hated it.

"We stayed there about a month and then we started home when Mama got better.

"Well, one evening just at dark we come to an old house beside the road. There wasn't nobody lived there and we thought to spend the night there under a roof for a treat.

"We brought the broom in and swept out a couple of the rooms and we made down pallets and we all went to bed.

"Well, the room Mama and the old man were in had an old wood stove against one of the walls. Mama woke out of a sound sleep hearing that stove rattle. Then she heard footsteps going across the floor and out of the room. She called out to Ernie, he used to sleepwalk when he was a boy, but there wasn't no answer. The footsteps just went on back into the other room and then they stopped so she figured he was back on his pallet and she started to go back to sleep.

"Then the footsteps come back into the room and she heard them cross the floor again back to the old wood stove, and she could hear like he was climbing onto that old wood stove. She was worried that he was going to get hurt so she struck a match and lit a candle but there wasn't anybody there. Nobody on the stove, nobody in the room at all, just the old man asleep. So she got up and went to look at the kids and they were all asleep too.

"She went back to her own place and laid down and as soon as she blew the candle out somebody jumped down off the stove in the dark and went walking across the floor and out of the room.

"Well, there wasn't nobody else heard it but Mama didn't get to sleep all night for those footsteps crossing the room and climbing onto that old stove and jumping down and walking back across the room.

"She knew she wasn't dreaming and that it had to be her second-sight so she just resigned herself to it and laid there listening.

"The next day we learned down the road that a man had killed his wife in that house nearly twenty years before and he stood on that stove to hoist her body into the space over the ceiling boards to hide it."

WHEN MY FATHER DIED ...

"When my father died ... see, he broke with his family before he ever met my mother ... and he never went back except for his parents' funeral. And when he died there was a write-up in the paper said he was from one of the most prominent families in this big county that he come from. So you know they were bound ... they wouldn't say that if they didn't have a lot of property and stuff. Well, us kids should get our daddy's part of that stuff and over all these years it would be increasing, you know.

"I think they tend to have a statute of limitations on that, Mama."

"Well, they may do it but under the circumstances that they wasn't any notification of *any* kind or no provision of *any* kind that we know of we still might be able to do something about it.

"And Emmett went back there one time and he come back and said, You ought to go back east and visit some of your relatives, he said, They're *all* wealthy and they're all lawyers and doctors and writers and artists and ... all of that, you know."

"How long was he there? How did he meet them? I mean ... you don't even know who your relatives are in the east do you?"

"Well no ... I mean it's back in east Texas somewhere ... or back in the east ... he said *east.* I just wish Mama would write to him before she dies and get the name of the county at least where my daddy was born and raised ... And if I could get the name of that county I could get old John Henry Fisher to get on it and tell him I'd give him a certain percent of whatever came out of it ..."

(a long pause for the contemplation of advantage)

"Yeah, we've got too much air in the tires. Are you getting tired?"

A LETTER TO MY GRANDAUGHTER

Dear Jessie I am thinking to day of you when you were the very sweetest of little girls. Your Mama was working and you were staying with me. And I thought of how much we loved you. So much your Aunt Louella who was just a little bit older than you prayed for your Mother to die so we could keep you Thank the good Lord he knew and had a better answer to that prayer.

You wanted to know a few things about my life. I can assure you dear it has been quite different to yours. My Mother died when I was 2 years old. My father remarried when I was 5 years old and lived just 1 year after his marriage. 2 months after his death my Step Mother gave birth to a little baby boy and she died with Pneumonia. When the baby was 1 month old the baby's Uncle my Step Mother's brother got homes for the baby and me. My little half brother was killed in the 1st World War in France 3 days before the War ended.

I can remember a few little interesting events that happened during my Step Mother's life time. We lived close to a big creek. My Step Mother decided one day she would take my little Step Brother and me and go visiting. We had to go through this creek bottom. On the way back home we were attacked by a bunch of wild hogs. Some one had cut down a tree. It was bent over. My Step Mother threw us children up in the tree and climbed up into it herself. I can imagine how worried my Father must have been about us. I had a wonderful Father dear. I know that by what people has told me about him. Everybody that knew him loved him and I loved him dearly. I remember he bought my Step Mother a big yellow turkey gobbler. She was real proud of it because of the colour. There were lots of wild turkeys them days and Father wanted to go out and kill one and he wanted to take her gobbler and stake him and he would gobble and the turkeys would come to him. Well she didn't want him to but he promised her he would be careful but he killed the wild turkey and Mothers yellow gobbler too and she cried about it.

In my new house I don't think I was ever really happy or unhappy. I went to school for 4 years just long enough to learn to read and write and arithmatic as the old tune goes played to the tune of a Hickory stick. Which was used very often. Not in school but at home. The people I lived with sure believed in using the rod but love they knew nothing about. If they loved or cared for me they never let me know. Once I started to the well for a bucket of water. Mr. Womack had a big dog. He was standing on the steps in front of me. I just kinda kicked him out of my way. He threatened to give me a whipping for that. 2 boys he had hired called the dog off to the field and shot him. He never did know what happened to the dog. I didn't either until I married one of the boys and he told me.

That was my first husband. I was 14 years old the 25th of December. We were married the 25th of July 1896. Eunice our first baby was born 16 June 1897. Our second baby was born August 27th 1900 just 2 weeks before the great Galveston Flood. My 3rd baby a little boy was born the 3rd day of August in 1902. On December 3rd 1902 my baby died. On the day my baby died his Father was seriously ill with Pneumonia and died on Sunday which was 3 days later.

I went then with my 2 little girls and lived with their Grandmother and Grandfather until I married your Grandfather Peter Joseph Chapman in 1904. We had 5 children. Lost one little baby girl when she was 12 days old. We had 1 boy and 3 little girls your Uncle Peter and Aunt Ethel and Aunt Hannah and your Mother who was 7 months old when her Father died in April 1913 with cancer of the stomach in Willis Montgomery County Texas.

I left there and taken the children and went back to Mitchell County and lived with them. Most of the time with your Aunt Bertha and her husband Will Gatliff who was real kind to me and the children.

I stayed there until I married Mr. Ingram in Oct. 1st 1914 in Colorado City Texas. We had 5 children 2 boys and 3 girls. Lost both our boys. That left me 7 children out of the 13.

So you see darling there hasn't been too much happiness mixed up in my life but I am not complaining. I have been blessed in so many ways.

As you know, Mr. Ingram died in 1953.

My children and grandchildren have been such a comfort and blessing to me. If I make no mistake I have 7 children 21 grandchildren 31 Great Grandchildren 2 Great Great Grandbabys, expecting another one in December. That will be Jimmy's baby. I may never see them but I am proud of them. I have 2 new Great grandsons. One will be 2 weeks old next Monday and one will be 2 weeks old next Saturday. Of course dear this isn't old stuff but I thought maybe you would like a little of the new along with the old.

Talking about old stuff I wonder if you can imagine pretty print material selling for 1 ct a yard. I can remember when we sold butter for 5 cts a lb and thought we were getting a good price for it. We had an old fashioned wooden churn and a churn Dasher. The lid that fit on the churn had a hole in the centre. You put the handle of the dasher through that. Sometimes we would have to churn for hours before the cream would turn to butter but Oh what good butter and buttermilk we had. But you would really get tired churning.

Your Grandfather fixed me a milkbox. We had a windmill and a wonderful well of water. He bored a hole in each end of this box and put a pipe in each hole. We let the windmill run all the time and that cold water was running through this box all the time ... I kept the milk jars and butter bowls wrapped in cloth and the milk and butter was just as cold as the water. And we really enjoyed it. We also irrigated a garden from the well. We had a beautiful garden out by the well and most all kinds of vegetables. I went to the garden the day your Uncle Peter was 2 weeks old to gather vegetables for dinner, had on a loose dress with just a yoke in it and it just hung loose from this yoke. Had a pan of vegetables gathered and when I stooped down to pick it up there was a big tarantula half out and half in the yoke of this dress. That is half of it was in between my dress and slip and the other half outside. So I didn't pick up the pan. I just left it and caught my dress and slip up on each side of the thing and held it out away from me until I got back to the house and the dining table. My oldest daughter was in the kitchen. I just eased the whole mess on the table. She picked up a stick of wood and put it on it and mashed it. I unfastened my dress and it fell out on the table. I know the Lord was certainly with me in that deal to keep me from being scared so bad and to be composed enough not to start fighting at it. If I had it would have run back in my clothes and would have bitten me. As it was it never moved or changed position. I really think dear I do have a Guardian Angel that watches over me. Once when I was little it was coming up a cloud fixing to rain. Mr. Womack had bundled a lot of fodder in the field and if it rained on it it would ruin it so he wanted Aunt Nannie and me to go and help him put it in the wagon so he could haul it in before it got wet. We were gathering it up in our arms. I felt something wriggling next to my body and I held the bundle out from me and a grown rattlesnake fell to the ground. I had picked it up with the bundle of fodder.

A few funny little things happened. Once I had gone across the field to visit a little neighbour girl. On the way back home I had to pass some cows. There was one in the bunch that would fight but I thought maybe she wouldn't notice me but I was mistaken. I had passed her just a little way when she spied me and here she come. There was a little creek between me and the corral fence. When I got to that creek I was sure she was going to catch me. I let out a pretty loud scream and it scared the cow and she dug the ground up a good little ways trying to stop. I had a real hearty laugh about it all when I got over my scare.

Well dear, I guess that is about all. Of course there were a lot of things that happened I guess that I don't remember but I guess this is about all you care to read. Hope it isn't too boring.

Your grandmother who loves you very much.

THE HOUSES WHERE MY GRANDMOTHER ...

The houses where my grandmother and the old man lived when I was little were various but the same, one story high, weathered and tired, used up. What paint still clung was only a further complication of the rotting wood.

There was usually a sagging wooden porch for taking the evening air after supper and a rocking chair for grandmama and the babies.

She would start with the youngest and rock it to sleep, then she'd carry it to bed. She'd rock and sing, cradling the children against her, moving up the line through the older ones until there would be a rebel who could stop it all by declaring fiercely, "I'm too *old* to be rocked to sleep!"

Inside those houses there would be a smell throughout of too many lives, as if animals lived in the walls. A memory smell that stayed into present time as a woman's hair will take the smell of frying onions while her hands still smell of the fresh onions she sliced to be fried.

Oilcloth covered the table, flowers or checks, cracked and worn through to the fabric, the pattern spoiled by the overwhelming pattern of wear. On the floor the linoleum had been used into islands of patternless brown at the sink, the stove, around the table.

The kitchen chairs were wired together, some became stools with a row of broken bits along one edge like teeth to show where the back had been. Straw chairs burst through underneath to remain a static explosion, fixed, under the board that was laid across to be sat on.

The corrosion of time is accelerated by poverty. Things grow old faster. Cheap dresses hung unevenly from their first washing. Plastic buttons melt against the iron. Cheap bright colours fade and run. Cheap shoes begin to curl up at the toes the first wearing, reaching for that foetal position old shoes take when they die. The shoestrings break, are taken out, knotted, returned to the shoe a blot marring the clear x's.

All the rooms except the kitchen held beds, iron and brass bedsteads that moved from house to house with mattresses made of feathers or of stuffed cotton turned hard as rock.

All the appurtenances, called by name, often travesties of the original intention, were there. The *rug* worn to rags, trails walked through to the floorboards, was there to be swept. A lumpy shape, humps and hollows of displaced batting, springs a threat, was the *couch,* or the *sofa* or even the *davenport.*

And boxes of old clothes, old toys, old objects no one could throw away because there was still some good left in them, the *belongings* were stacked under the beds and along the walls.

The pride and blindness of the poor, their persons as their houses, *worn,* worn down to the thread. Lined hands, lined faces, none of that ease of muscles a little money gives.

In all that grubbiness and unspoken despair the children were the joy. They were fresh however. Their necks were nuzzled, their sides and feet were tickled to make them scream. They slept and waked in poverty's matriarchy. All those daughters, my grandmother's daughters, with husbands who came and went, had babies who came and stayed.

If my grandmother passed her childhood without feeling loved, the children and grandchildren who grew up near her had no such problem.

It was so intimate, ripe with reality.

SO WHAT I KNEW ...

So what I knew of those houses where the old man lay always dying was the middle time when they sat between farm country and the town, usually in some old farmhouse that went with nearby land that somebody else was farming. If you haven't seen the place you've seen the pictures.

And by the time my eyes were in my head they were in the houses that they would be in forever, in succession.

The yards for those houses were hard-packed dry dirt where whatever grass that grew was accidental and doomed, a few tall sprigs of dusty green that must finally join the rest; dead roots in hard clay. The only green with any hope, a jagged mixture of rough grass and wild mint, would signal a leaky faucet.

What else was common?

Wrecked cars out back, a woodpile and a raised iron cauldron for making soap out of accumulated fat drippings and lye water from wood ash, a playhouse, its walls outlined by lines of small rocks under a shade tree, a profusion of bent pots and broken crockery and misshapen dolls, their eyes staring.

And Franklin Delano Roosevelt, as absolute as the sun and the moon. It doesn't seem at all political to me that I can't stand to hear a word against him.

His WPA and CCC made the first jobs to be counted on by one whole generation of Texas young men from poor homes.

One of the boys grandmama talks about losing went over a cliff in the back of a CCC truck and was killed.

"Mama knew it the minute it happened. She stopped in the middle of the kitchen floor and started crying and said Joey is laying on the ground. His head's broke open on a rock. And sure enough we got the telegram the next day."

SHE WAS SMALL AND SWEET AND TOUGH ...

She was small and sweet and tough, moving among the various armed camps of that household. The kids chose up sides daily and stopped just short of killing each other.

As when Peter one day had sharpened his axe and was chopping at whatever caught his eye. Hannah was always a tease and she angled off what she was doing to put her finger down on a good-sized wood chip that Peter was aiming for.

"You better move your finger. I'm getting set to chop that piece of wood."

"You better not chop this piece of wood because I ain't planning to move my finger off of it."

They both were truthful.

Hannah didn't move her finger and Peter did chop the wood. Wills of iron.

Hannah ran to the house screaming with her finger pouring blood and dangling, caught only by a piece of skin.

Grandmama boiled a needle and some thread and sewed the finger on and it took. It had a lump where it had been cut through and Hannah couldn't move it much. Then a couple of years later she got into the bad habit of finger-twisting. She grabbed Mae's hand once to give her a twist and Mae twisted first. Hannah's finger gave a loud crack and swelled up for a week or two and when the swelling went down the lump was only half the size it had been and she could move it a lot more.

Mae took a milk pail once: "I didn't think of it as *stealing*. It was more like it just didn't seem fair to me that they had all those new pails stacked up and we just had one old bucket. So when I went home I just took a pail along with me. I picked out a good one. But when Mama saw it she went dead quiet and asked me where I got it. Well, I couldn't sit down for a week. And I had to take the pail back. I couldn't even just take it back and sneak it onto the pile. I had to take it back to Mr. Holliday and tell him I took it. It was the only time in my life that Mama ever whipped me."

I remember the two times in my life grandmama ever whipped me.

The first was when my Aunt Louella had climbed onto my mother's bed to play and I got territorial about it. I got a broom and went to work on her. She got tangled in the covers trying to get away and my grandmother found me there pounding on the lump under the covers and screaming, "This is my Mama's bed!"

The second time was when I was alone in the house and locked grandmama out. She circled the outside of the house as I circled the inside to be standing there solemnly looking out at every door and window as she came to it.

RUNNING SET OF LIES

There was a running set of lies that got handed to me all the time I was growing up. Whenever Issue-Number-One came up all the women's faces changed and all the girls were lied to.

I realize it was a *conservative* ... as in *protective* ... device, but at my end of it it added up to a lot of confusion.

For instance, on my fourteenth birthday a boy who was maybe sixteen was going to come to the apartment and formally ask my parents if he could take me on my first official date. They had agreed that he could ask so it seemed likely the answer was yes.

I went to the corner drugstore to hang out with my friends and my mother showed my father some presents I had got that morning one of which was the classic Five Year Diary which, when she laid it down, fell open to what I had immediately written in on receiving it, so as not to forget. The week before in a movie house with my friends I had kissed the boy who was due to arrive around four this afternoon. It was there in black and white with exclamation marks for ecstasy.

That entry proved to be the first and last of that "diary." One thousand eight hundred and twenty-four days down the drain, precluded by stupidity.

I had taken the abstraction of *My Diary* as an allowance, proof against getting hoisted on the hook because you wrote it down. The power of a defined occasion. And I learned the way it really was when I got home and faced those two faces. There was no doubt that I had made a mistake.

My mother took me into the kitchen to talk to me.

Kissing in the movies is vulgar.

But worse than that ... and she rang the shift on me ... no girl should kiss a boy until they're engaged.

I couldn't believe it ... that she was saying it. I looked

at her and she looked as solemnly back as if she meant to stand by that statement against come what may. I couldn't believe it. I mean ... she came off a *farm.*

And when Aunt Ethel's baby came seven months after she was married it was because she had got tired of carrying it and swallowed a bottle of castor oil.

I mean to say the girls and women were falling left and right and if there wasn't a good cover-up story to preserve the myth ... a bottle of castor oil to produce a fully developed eight pound premature baby ... of course there was acceptable leeway because she *was* married ... then you became an example of life's other side. And the sin was to be that example.

Given some proposal of *winning* you looked around and just saw the losers. I don't doubt it had to do with ... I came from a rockbottom *poor* family that *aspired* to the lower middle class, and most of them made it. Some of them did better. But the time I'm talking about was when they were still talking it up and learning the gestures at the movies and learning what their desires were by window shopping.

It was hopeless. It was truly intellectual. The *ideal* occurred in conversation as the *real,* and what was really happening was shameful, not to be mentioned. The fear of going lower was the real motive power. And the only *lower* was to be in the same place but disgraced as well. Just a step away. But it loomed downward like something you could avoid and the imagination of it was a misstep would do it.

Or you could jump. You could be finally desperate and jump. Louella was my mother's youngest half-sister, Grandmama's last baby. "This is my baby," she'd say introducing her, even when she was grown. She was about four years older than me so when I was fourteen she was eighteen. We made a summer visit to Abilene that year and I felt awkward and pleased to walk on the street with her, the soldiers whistling and she being so cool, paying no attention.

She was a soft full-bodied beauty with blonde hair pulled up in a '40s Betty Grable pompadour and platform ankle-strap shoes. She was proud of her hands and I thought she was right to be. She had curvaceous fingers with exact long nails. She changed her nail polish every time she changed her lipstick so they would match.

Abilene was packed full of soldiers. There was a rumour for awhile that a black regiment was going to be stationed there and the old man, Louella's father, swore that he was going to buy an acre of land and a shotgun and he meant to shoot any of em that set foot on his property. He had no notion of patriotism.

It was his usual kind of bad-mouthing. He was on relief and didn't have the hard cash to buy a shotgun shell, much less a shotgun, much less an acre of land.

Louella fell in love with a handsome and sweet-natured Italian from Detroit. They married. Ten months later Louella had twins, a boy and a girl. The boy was dark and larger with black straight hair and (after they changed colour) black eyes. The girl was tiny and blue-eyed with blonde curls. All by the book.

But there was a curve. A month before the babies were born Louella applied for the army's family allotment and learned that it was already being paid out to a wife and two children back in Detroit.

The Italian really loved her, too. He begged her to stay with him and cried. He kept crying and swearing that he'd get a divorce and that all he wanted was Louella.

But her heart was broken.

She had the babies and went on the town. That open. Within two months she was pregnant again and married to a man who turned out to be a forger and went to prison.

It seemed to me then and it seems to me now that I had about as much chance in that economy as a snowball in hell. I had a glamoured mind and I sure did want to be close to somebody.

When I was just turned seventeen I was knocked up by Blacky James in a small town near Lubbock while I was on a visit to my Aunt Hannah. He was a prize-winning diver, a cheer-leader at Texas Tech, and he wanted to be an FBI agent. He wore fancy hand-tooled boots and rode in local rodeos. He was really flashy.

It was like the sky fell in. It was a dimensional change. It was my turn. And I fought it with the slimmest, most ignorant resources. I became a living breathing salvage project. I walked around in a daze with my ears ringing from quinine and my skin parboiled from hot baths. I jumped off every table in sight.

I'd gone back to Albuquerque and it was a coincidence that my mother decided just then to go to Texas for a visit.

I called Blacky's house as soon as I could, but he was back at school.

And the self-preservation scheme went on. On a blazing hot day I went out with a pick-axe to dig a trench in the hard clay back of the garage. It seemed more to the point somehow to make a useless trench than to just dig at random. It gave me a chance to see where I'd been.

As a trench it was pathetic; a foot wide, a foot deep, and as long as it had to be. The clay was as hard as stone. Every inch counted.

At one moment my mother and aunt stood watching me, their eyes like tabulators.

"I'm getting some exercise," I gasped.

"You better get in the house," Aunt Hannah said drily, "you look green."

Mrs. James was an invalid. She spent her time in bed. When she got up it was to clamber creep into a nearby wheelchair. She had dyed red hair and was fat. Her skin was gray white. The small bedroom stank with her smell.

"She knows a good thing when she sees it," she spat at us, meaning me. "She had to mess around and now she's got what's coming to her and she thinks she's going to get herself a college boy for its daddy."

Mr. James stood near the head of the bed watching us. He was quiet. It was clear that his wife was the master of the moment.

We had been quiet too. Shamed. We were shamed. But my mother has never passed up an opponent in her life.

"You filthy mouthed old woman. You turn your talk around or I'll haul you out of that bed and climb all over you! I don't care if you are a cripple!"

The upshot was that Blacky was telegraphed to come home.

But of course it amounted to nothing. There was nothing in it to begin with ... not like a place to be.

The three of us drove around in a car to "talk about it."

Blacky explained how this would all be a large problem to him. And it was true.

"If you don't want him honey you don't have to have him," my mother said. "You know I'd love any baby of yours no matter where it came from."

To make a long story short I had an abortion. One way out. One way to get on with it.

Almost home free.

I can't think why it's so much like people walking along the highway with their backs to the traffic and high odds against them. And it's the only highway.

MAE, ARE YOU FEELING GOOD?

"Mae, are you feeling good? I mean ... I know you're not feeling *good* but you think you're recovering and getting over ... ?"

"It's real slow."

"I don't see where they cutcha."

"They didn't. They went down through my mouth and got it."

"Thank goodness! I was expecting Mae to have a scar there and one there of some sort."

"No. They put a ... You know they go down in your throat and work just like the time they had to go up into my kidney. They went up thru my bladder. They've got these little mirrors and these teeny-weensy little lines that they can run down into there. The first one wasn't a bit bad. I mean it took a long time to get over ... but...."

(Crystal brings in iced tea)

"Why didn'tcha just have the *maid* bring those in?"

"She's taking her rest." (laughing)

"Didja get the house clean enough before she got here this morning to keep from embarrassing her?"

"Naw, I'm not *about* to embarrass *the maid*."

"Well, Crystal, thank you kindly."

"Are you going to stand up or are you going to sit down?"

"I'll be back in a minute."

"Where I'm nursing that old woman she just can't stand it if the house is a mess when the maid comes!"

"You mean you have to straighten up?"

"I keep the part I live in straight."

"Well, this is the maid's day off so I get to relax today."

"I told Crystal when we got here this morning I said If I ever look at another man it'll be because he's got money enough to hire me a maid and a cook and a yardman. Because nothing else much interests me...." (laughing)

"I'm telling you the truth ... I've been that way a long time."

"If I'da been doing the kind of work Ada has been doing I'd of latched onto me a rich man a long time ago."

"I bet you would've. I've had some chances too, Mae. I've even been told 'take that old man' and he died in no time!"

"If you get one with enough money then you could *hire* somebody to come in and look after him!"

"This old man was in a wheelchair and I was nursing his sister. They lived together...."

"Let me tell you one thing before I forget it...."

"He would've married me. He died about thirty days...."

"Fred said something about he was coming home the end of this month. I said, Call me before you do because I'm thinking about running off with the yardman. I have this big fat old guy comes and mows the lawn once a week. Fred just went to laughing. He said, If that's what my baby wants that's what I want her to have. I said, You know how much trouble I give the men. I said, Boy, I don't have no time for 'em. And he said, I realize that, but Boy, I sure did enjoy the little dab of trouble you give me."

I sat on Grandmama's bed and held her hand. Everybody else was doing the doing. It sounded like they had finally got her where they could take care of her despite herself.

"When Floyd come to visit last week with his twin babies I thought Mama was just going to wear herself out! All she wanted to do was hold those babies. We finally had to just take them away from her. Floyd put them in their little baskets and we put them all the way across the room against the wall. And she still just wouldn't take her eyes off those baskets. The least little sound from one of those babies and she'd raise up and look over to try to see it."

"It was a big old house and a pretty one but hadn't anybody lived in it as long as we could remember. Us kids wouldn't go anywhere near it. We had to pass it every day when we walked to school but we kept well down into the road when we passed by.

"Well, this day I'm talking about it had been raining and the only way I could keep my shoes out of the mud was to walk high on the slope that ran up toward the old house. I don't know why I was walking by myself. I guess I got kept in after school or something.

"Anyway, there wasn't nobody with me and it was getting near sundown. Well, the closer I come to that old house the slower I walked. I just knew there was going to be something jump out and grab me.

"By the time I got in front of the door I wasn't moving more than an inch in a minute and sure enough that front door that hadn't ever been open was open. Just the screen door was there and I could see right through it.

"Well, at first what I saw I thought it was a little girl. Then I saw it was a woman. Not all of her. It was just a head. It was floating there about three feet off of the floor and it had long yellow hair that fell straight down all the way to the floor and it was looking right back at me through the screen door. I just went on walking like nothing was the matter, looking at it and it looking back until I got past where I could see it. Then I cut and run until I couldn't run no more. I remember everybody was just setting down to supper when I come bolting through the back door shaking all over and white as a sheet."

" ... this was up north where the ghost stories really are something ... We were all told to steer clear of this place. It was a big old mansion with stained glass windows. You really could see lights in there at night in some of the rooms. But it was just somebody circulating stories and then using the place for drinks and gambling. That's how most ghost stories go.

"At the same time I'm firmly convinced that there's millions of restless spirits walking this earth."

"Oh my! I am too. I mean, I have some understanding of it now."

"I'll say...."

"Jessie, reach up there and turn that light on. Turn it so it comes on this side. Or somewhere where it won't be in her face. That'll be alright."

"Them two little girls was named Cora and Dora. They was twins. They had an older sister ... I don't remember what her name was. That Cablet girl, Mama, that had the baby....

"Miz Cablet would come down and she'd *talk* to Mama. She'd act so mournful and so sad, and I finally caught on that it was this oldest girl she was talking about. Finally this girl had a baby.

"Well, all this Miz Cablet would do would be to treat that girl like she was dirt. She turned Mama against her. She turned us kids against her. "I told Mama, I said, Mama, I think that's real mean of Miz Cablet to talk that way about her daughter. I said, I want to go down there and see that baby!

"Mama said it was alright. So Hannah and me went down there and here Cora and Dora was flitting around, you know. And the mother was acting like she had a leper in her house. She was setting, the daughter, was setting over in the corner in an old-fashioned rocker with that tiny little baby. She just had her head bowed over it like this, you know. She didn't even raise up her head when we come in.

"I went over and I told her, I said, We've come down here to see your little baby. And she looked like she was so happy.

"It was the cutest little baby. I never could stand that woman after that."

"The first book he wrote was 'Chasing the Wild Asparagus.'"

"Who wrote?"

"Euell Gibbons."

"That's what made him famous."

"He didn't have any education. He just got out and went to scouting and snooping about these wild foods. He's wrote about four books now."

"You know that joke that ends up 'you ever *shit* a pine tree?'"

" ... what we did to the old man, he was real skittish and he'd hooked up a thing out at the henhouse so if anybody went in there...."

"It'd rattle a can in the house."

"Yeah. So he rigged it up and two or three days went by without nothing rattling out there and us kids was getting restless about it. So we hooked up to his hookup. He'd just doze off to sleep and we'd pull our string. It'd sound like the damn roof was falling in! We had him jumping and running for three or four nights in a row. Finally I got started laughing and couldn't stop and give it all away. He come in mad as hell after his latest trip out the the henhouse and as soon as he saw me laughing he guessed it. He yelled, What are you damned kids up to now!"

"The old man used to wake up in the middle of the night and think he couldn't breathe. He used to have the idea that at night all the oxygen in the room would get used up and he was going to die in his sleep. Anyway, he used to wake up and just run snorting for the window and throw it up and stick his head out and take big breaths, like he'd just come up out from under the water.

"Well, this one night he woke up almost too late, that is, he didn't think he could make it to the window. So he reached down and grabbed up one of his shoes and heaved it toward the window. There was all the crash of the glass breaking and he figured he'd saved his life. But the next morning he saw that he'd broke the mirror over the chest of drawers.

"Another thing, you know how he used to shove Vix up his nose? When he had a cold he'd rub Vix all over his chest and on his temples, and then for good measure he'd stuff it up his nose and swallow some as well.

"Well, one night he woke up with a cold and he headed for the drawer where the Vix was kept and he went through that whole routine. But the next morning he found out that he'd used a jar of white shoe polish."

"Mae, not to change the subject but you look good."

"She looked awful tired last night."

"How'd you like me to prepare the liver?"

"Do you pound liver?"

"I'll tell you how I prepare it and you can do it any way you want to. I turn it in flour ..."

"Yeah, Mama likes it that way and cooked brown."

"Turn it in flour that has salt and pepper in it."

"Then put gravy on it and let it simmer."

"If you turn it in flour and fry it brown and pour the grease off. Then put just a little water in the pan and put a lid on...."

"I don't put *any* water it at all. I just fry it *really* slow for a long time and it comes out fried real crisp. Then if you want gravy you can make it in the pan afterwards."

"I start the grease and fry the onions until they're absolutely brown. So the whole pan has that taste of brown onions. Then I take the onions out to the side. Then I turn the liver in flour and lay it in the pan and put it on a low fire and just cook it for a long time."

"On a low fire?"

"So it comes out really brown."

"Hannah cooked some at the house one time. It really amazed me. She put the liver in there and she braised it very lightly. It wasn't even tan. Just enough to set the flour. Then she put the onions she cut up into the pan on the range. And she added *milk.*"

"Well, then you're going to end up with stewed onions."

"That's exactly what happened."

"That's the way I fix it *except* I take the liver and salt and pepper it and turn it in flour. Then I put it in hot grease and I brown it real good. Then I pour off every drop of that grease and I put some water in the bottom of the pan. I slice my onions thick and lay them all over the top and I put a lid on it and I turn it low."

"I can't get onions to come out right unless I cook them first."

" ... so when I get through I have my onions *and* gravy *and* liver ..."

"I cook 'em in separate pans a lot of times you know."

"I've tried making liver and onions like that, you know, like Papa used to eat. He'd have the gravy and all just gooey. You could actually take the onions off the top and have the liver and gravy on the bottom."

"You know how Louella's husband is about Sally."

"I don't appreciate that type."

"Who is that?"

"Louella's husband. He *acts* like a prude."

"He says, I have to keep an eye on Sally. She's the sexiest little bitch I ever saw in my life. Not that *I'd* touch her, mind you! I told Louella, I said, You better *watch* him!"

"Yes, she had."

"Damned well better."

"He looks at her just like she was a *bowl* of something *good* to eat!"

"She is beautiful and I'm not kidding you. She's got that long dark hair."

"I guess I never saw her."

"She's Louella's youngest."

"Peter's got the worst crush on her you ever heard of!"

"Well, any man would. Just to look at her."

"She was a lovely little girl. I saw her a couple of years ago and she was a little doll then."

And my grandmother says from the bed, "Well, she's a grown girl now."

LET'S SEE ...

"Let's see ... She's in Root isn't she?"

"I should have called her back yesterday."

"Why dontcha just set down here ..."

"Is that light too bright for you, grandmama?"

"In Root for the Ethel Leary residence ..."

"Root. Ethel Leary. You don't have it? Alright, let's have that. Slow down. What was it? 2472 ... ? Operator? Well, she's gone. We'll just try this and if it ain't the number we'll just call the operator and say that Information gave us the wrong number. She was in just too damned big of a hurry!" (dialing).

"Are yawl ready for your lunch now?"

"Lord, no!"

"I should've called Ethel back yesterday it only cost half as much ...

Howdy! This is your sister ... you know the squeaky one ...! Oh well, thank you... I'm not back to normal but my voice is a little bit better ... Are you going to be home today ...? Well, no ... you go ahead and we'll come over tonight. What time will you be home ...? Naw, we'll just go over to Velma's and visit with her awhile and give you a ring later ... Oh, sure enough ...? No, you go ahead and go. We'll just wait till later and drive over. We'll be there when you get home ... No. Don't do that. Somebody might go in there and get something. We'll just ... are you going to Lubbock? Well, here, say hello to Mama and we'll see you sometime this evening ... O.K. Here's Mama."

("She said we better not go over to Velma's until we've had a chance to talk to her. She says Velma stays awake all night and sleeps all day and's under the care of her psychiatrist.")

"Grandmama, I'll try to get back to see you again."

"Honey, I'll try to stay alive long enough for it."

YOU KNOW, CRYSTAL

"You know, Crystal has a very different sense of the old man than yawl had. Her sense of him is that he did a lot more joking and he wasn't as mean."

"Well, he *would* get jolly if the house was filled with *his* relatives and Mama was in the kitchen filling a fourteen-foot or sixteen-foot-long table with baked turkeys and baked chickens and cakes and pies and things like that for Christmas dinner.

"I remember one Christmas ... we had this long long table with benches on the sides for the kids and then a chair at each end for him and for Mama. One Christmas I remember counting twenty-six of his relatives that was there. Mama had been cooking for a week. We had our own turkeys and our own chickens, our own beef and our own eggs, butter and milk, all that stuff. Mama had baked cakes and pies all over the place and a turkey and a couple of hens besides all the vegetables and stuff she fixed.

"You know how kids are. I couldn't hardly wait until we got ready to eat. Of course, the grown-ups always ate first then the children ate later.

"It was always *my* sense of things to feed the children first and then the grownups.

"Anyhow, I couldn't wait till the food was on the table. I'd already picked out just what I was going to have ... a great big drumstick from the turkey and some dressing, mashed potatoes and green beans and cranberry sauce. Then I was going to have a couple of kinds of pie, and so forth. I had it all figured out.

"Then my stepdad took my plate. He just without a by your leave picked up my plate and started putting food on it. I said, That is *not* what I want! I want so-and-so ... So to play Mr. Big he had me get under the table and stay there until everybody had finished their Christmas dinner. Then I got the leavings.

"So you see Crystal got one sense of him and we've got another one. Her view has softened over the years since he died and mine hasn't."

"She was younger."

"She was just a baby at that time. She was ten years younger'n me. And he was her father. I guess that did make a difference.

"She was a lot like him, you know ... but I'm sure....

"He *was* a very talented old man. He would have made a good musician or something. He played a violin beautifully without ever having had a lesson of any kind.

"But the things we pulled on him were really something."

WHEN WE WERE LIVING ...

When we were living in Galveston or San Antone, some-place really hot, there was a lady across the street who had a crazy daughter. She had her living room divided down the middle with floor to ceiling hogwire mesh. Her daughter lived on one side of it and she lived on the other. The radio was on her side and they both had rocking chairs and they'd sit and rock and sew and talk and listen to the radio.

When the daughter was having a good spell her mother would unlock the cage door and they'd sit together in the mother's part of the room rocking and talking. But when visitors came or the girl started to get excited or when she wanted to go outside the mother would put her back and lock the door.

Everyone agreed that the mother had a hard time of it and that it was decent of her to keep the girl at home in-stead of putting her in the county hospital.

Texas mental institutions were really poor and quite re-cently I heard a story about one place where the director only has an MA in psychology, he's not even a psychiatrist. And one girl was brought in there in a state of shock be-cause her father raped her, and his way of dealing with it was to hypnotize her and get her to remember it all and she came out of hypnosis screaming, then zapped into rigid catatonia. The implication was, never to come out again.

But you don't know how much to believe of sensational stories.

We used to visit across the street once in a while. I'd play in the yard and come in and out the way kids do. The funny thing was, you could have the mother looking out her window onto the front yard and the daughter looking out her front window onto the yard and you'd never have known there was a division between them.

I don't ever remember her doing anything crazy. It was more like having that sense of her and her being in a cage was the proof. Otherwise she sat there quietly, joining in the conversation when someone spoke to her. She dressed in cotton house dresses and wore her hair pinned in a roll. She was heavy-bodied, in her late twenties or maybe early thirties.

Her mother had taken care of her like that for about fifteen years so she must have gone out of her head when she was an adolescent.

I remember seeing that she had a white chamber pot tucked by the bed. The mother had to do everything for her, cook her meals and hand them through to her, take the dishes and wash them, empty the chamberpot. The girl kept her part of the room straight and made her own bed.

The mother said she was violent when she got bad.

It must not have been one of those hot places now that I think of it. It must have been a place with a winter because the mother had a fur coat and in one of her daughter's violent spells the fur coat saved her life.

She told my mother that once when her girl had gone through a long sensible period with the two of them sitting and sewing she had suddenly remembered that she had to go to the store before it closed. When the girl saw her mother putting her fur coat on she knew she would be put back in her cage and she grabbed up the sewing scissors and attacked her.

The mother said only her fur coat saved her but it was almost ruined. She had to take it to be resewn.

" ... five hundred dollars, which at that time was a lot of money. They made a down payment on a farm, got them a little house built and got their farming equipment. Beezer was the type of man that could make money on a rock pile. So she never wanted for anything while she was living with Beezer except she nagged him for so many years he finally went to chasing another woman, and she'll *still* drag that up and talk about it and just get herself all worked up.

"I told her Hell! that's water under the dam. Why don't you forget it.

"She was seventeen when they got married and he was twenty-eight. He was eleven years older'n she was."

"I remember when I was a kid Aunt Ethel always snubbed me and I used to get my feelings hurt," I said. "I never could understand what it was about me that made me so inferior in her eyes."

"Honey, she did everybody. Boy, but I tell you I really laid her in the shade out there in that little place ... out there on Byers that Wayne and his daddy built for us.

"You know that night you and Velma went out with those boys and the boys just got a bunch of beer and went to drinking it and the other girls went to drinking it and you and Velma just come home? You remember Ethel was going to let Velma stay for two weeks and when you girls come home Velma told Ethel all that story. Well, *you* had explained it when you come home why you was home so early. And Ethel told me the next day, Well, I don't know whether ... I just don't think I'll *leave* Velma over here for two weeks ... the kind of *friends* Jessie's got ... Boy I let her have it! Man, I mean I fairly let her have it! I said, Jessie's got *just* as nice friends or probably *nicer* ones than Velma's got so don't you throw off on Jessie! And I said, I'm going to tell you another damned thing ... She'd been whining over how when Velma was going to school that the kids wouldn't have nothing to do with her. I said, You dress her up in silks and satins and velvets and half of those little kids down there have to wear cotton and rags. And you made a damned snob out of her. And she's so hateful nobody can't stand her. And I said, That's the reason she can't have friends. And I said, You betcha! I'd be most happy for you to take her home. I don't wantchou to leave her!"

"Poor Velma."

"Well, you know the effect Ethel has on you!

"One day she got me to the point where I was just ready to cut her throat and I told her a few things. She turned around and went in the kitchen and went to washing dishes and humming a tune. Directly she come back in there and I was still just seething and she said (my mother's voice goes prissy and whiny), I shouldn'ta answered you back awhile ago then you wouldn'ta talked to me like that. She said, The Bible says *a soft answer turneth away wrath.* Brother! I tell you the *truth* I'm surprised my hair didn't catch on fire!

"Another thing, she made me mad over there in Albuquerque. She kept digging me about my church. I said, Ethel, why don't you get the Bible out and read in there what it says about people with a forked tongue. I said, You might just learn something!

"And I told her there in Texas one time, I said, If the day ever comes, Ethel, when you realize that *you alone* will never be able to change the whole world! I said, Even Jesus Christ couldn't do that ... I said, When you learn that you alone *cannot* change the whole world and that you're not right and the whole world wrong, then you're going to be a happier person! Because, I said, *Nobody's* going to conform and live the way *you* want them to just because *you* want them to!"

"That piece of information must have been hard on her."

"Well, I think the Lord will be very good to Ethel because she has been so desperate about her trying. She has wanted so much to be a Christian. But Jessie, my idea of Christianity gives this to you. It gives you contentment. Now the year and a half or two years that I lived a good Mormon life, give up my cigarettes ... didn't drink coffee ... Honey, my health was perfect! I didn't have to go to the doctor. I didn't have all these stumbling blocks in front of me. Well, the Bible *tells* you that you won't have them! And I didn't...."

"Yeah, but when you do get the stumbling blocks the Bible tells you how you're supposed to bear with your burdens."

"Right ..." (a musing voice) "I don't mean that everything's going to be made perfect for you. But you *should* have *peace* in your own inner self. You should have some *peace*...."

"Yeah."

"And I don't believe Ethel's ever had a peaceful moment in her life. She was born in misery and she's going to die in misery. And I've got a lot of that in me, but thank God not as much."

(no change of tone she goes right into ...)

"I could go around him but I can't see ten feet."

(a big slow truck in front of us)

"Maybe you better not!" I said, laughing. "I mean ... the way the road is."

"Well, that's what I had in mind too, Mama."

"Get Mama out another cigarette. We'll have to get around him if we're ever going to get anywhere, that's for damned sure! I can't tell whether that car's coming or going but I believe it's coming. Thank you, hon."

Beezer was small and wiry, maybe five seven and maybe a hundred twenty-five pounds. He was in his early thirties when he married Ethel. She was seventeen and a classic beauty, curvaceous but slim with dark hair and black eyes and a heart-shaped face. He caught her at just the right moment between her girlhood when she was so skinny that she wore her high shoes out by knocking her ankle bones together when she walked, and her womanhood when she moved to two hundred pounds and stayed there. Her sisters married when they were fifteen and her brother's wife was fourteen but Ethel had hung a little longer on the vine as a part of her total character which was quietly religious. She came to be a powerful woman manifesting God as her own condition but that was later.

At seventeen she was timorous and even frightened. She ripped a piece of her dress off scrambling panicked through a barbed wire fence running away from the first car she ever saw coming toward her down the road.

She was my mother's oldest sister and my mother told me she wouldn't have had Beezer even then, despite his being a good match, if she hadn't overheard her step-brother Lonny planning with some friends of his to rape her.

Lonny was a shiftless lunk the old man brought with him from his first marriage. He still wet the bed when he was a grown-up man. My mother always contended he was half-witted from the old man beating him in the head. Besides which she'd say, "He couldn't ever think of anything worthwhile. He had his daddy to live up to."

So Ethel, who in a different time and place could have been a meditative virgin all her life, cut her losses and relocated her spirit in power and her person in pride by marrying Beezer.

They were the well-off relatives all the time I was growing up. Beezer owned the land he farmed cotton on and he made good crops year after year. He was a hard-working, hard-living man. His size never stopped him. He kept a woman in town for thirty years, the same woman. When she died he didn't get another one.

Everybody knew about it but I can't imagine anyone ever mentioned it to him, except maybe Ethel, but she didn't have much say over him. She couldn't even prevail upon him to keep beer out of the icebox. Every Thanksgiving we used to congregate at their place and as the women started laying out the cooked meats and baked cakes and pies there would always be a point when the icebox got opened and there would be some beer. Ethel was mortified and shamed to the heart by that blatant instance of sin.

It was sin with a certain amount of work back of it. To keep in beer Beezer had to cross three counties to get to where it was Wet. Most of Texas voted Dry, most people agreeing with my Aunt Ethel.

Dancing and playing cards are also on the devil's list of tools to hook souls with, as are "by-words". I could never say "gosh" or "gee" or "darn" around my Aunt Ethel without turning up in her evening prayers.

Fundamentalism is an up and down philosophy. Think of Billy Sol Estes, another Texan, who used some of the thousands of dollars he bilked his friends and neighbours out of, before they caught him, to build a swimming pool where unmarried boys and girls weren't allowed to swim at the same time. His business philosophy was "Get into a man deep enough and you've got a partner."

Beezer's woman in town and his beer were the cross Ethel had to bear. That and his driving. He drove everywhere he went as close to a hundred miles an hour as he could get. That's not uncommon on the plains with the roads laid out so flat and straight.

Beezer wore out a car a year, but not by just the driving. It was his pleasure to chase jackrabbits. He kept a shotgun over the back seat and whenever a jackrabbit crossed the road in front of him he'd just turn the car into the field after it yelling to whoever was in the back, "Hand me that shotgun!"

Ethel held nightly prayers before bedtime and when we'd visit it always meant we'd gather in her bedroom, standing in a circle around her with our eyes lowered while she was on her knees in the middle. She used those sessions to get back at anybody who had irritated her during the day.

"Dear Lord," she'd intone, "help Mae to shield her tongue. She doesn't know how much harm she does and how many she hurts." And I would give a quick glance under my eyelids toward my mother who would be standing with her fists clenched, biting her sharp tongue to keep from interfering with Aunt Ethel's heavenly conversation.

Beezer was never at those prayer meetings. He always came back from town late. But he was always up early the next day and out in the field.

He died a few years ago and Ethel sold the farm for a hundred and fifty thousand dollars and built a yellow brick house in town. Velma, her daughter, told me that she's loosened up to the point of wearing a little pale lipstick when she goes out to shop.

Getting off the farm is a powerful influence even on a woman in her sixties.

WHEN MY COUSIN VELMA ...

When my cousin Velma was a kid she was skinny and knobby with cottony fly-away hair and a built-in twist to her mouth. That twist always suited what she had to say. She always aggravated me. She grew up to be a thoroughly pleasant woman but all the time she was a kid she was a whiner and a grabber. If we went looking for rocks when the time came to show them, my best rocks would somehow have got into her pile. If we were going out to do something fun just when I started liking it Velma would start whining to go home and we'd go home.

Her mother, Ethel, always gave in to her. She was convinced that Velma was delicate. Really I think she enjoyed having her puny kid being as bossy as she was.

I did have a good two weeks visiting Velma once when she was about twelve and I was about fourteen. She had entered a radio disk jockey contest to meet Eddie Arnold, a famous figure in country music in those days. Every penny she could beg and steal went for postcards to write votes for herself in to the station.

Every afternoon at two we were at the radio to hear. "Well now! Velma Leary is still ahead!"

Or even better to hear, "Well now! Our leader yesterday was Pearl Holiday but we've just received one hundred and eighty-three cards for Velma Leary! That puts Velma back in the lead by one hundred and twenty. Good going, Velma! Keep those cards coming in!"

The two of us got writer's cramp filling out cards. We were certain the station was ethical so we were hung up on disguising our handwriting and changing the phrases around but keeping them short. "My vote's for Velma Leary." "Here's another vote for Velma Leary." "I'm for Velma Leary."

A lot of girls entered the contest but it finally boiled down to three or four who were serious enough to sit all day long writing out votes for themselves.

Anyway, Velma won. And I enjoyed it as much as she did. She was introduced to Eddie Arnold on the radio program and they exchanged two or three sentences and he gave her a copy of his latest record.

The next summer when we visited she had been gloriously saved. She had broken all her cowboy records except the religious ones and she threw away her lipstick, all of which thrilled her mother to death. But I was really bored. All we did was visit a fat country girl friend of hers who had been gloriously saved by the same revivalist. The whole conversation was about how great it was to be gloriously saved and how great it was going to be to go to heaven.

But much earlier than that, when we were kids instead of sensible adolescents, I used to hate her a lot of the time.

One year Ethel wrote that they were coming for a visit and my mother said, "Please don't get in a fight with Velma. I've had a fight with Ethel the last three times I saw her and this time I mean to have a visit that doesn't end in a fight but if you two kids get started we won't be able to keep out of it." She knew how hard it was to get along with Velma most of the time but she asked me to grit my teeth and bear it.

And I did. I gritted my teeth when she took my best rocks. I gritted my teeth when she whined. I gritted my teeth when she tromped around in a little piece of garden I had planted, humming to herself and looking up at the sky like she didn't know what she was doing.

It was a miracle to all of us but we got through the whole visit without a fight. It helped my Aunt Ethel's disposition to be given her way in everything. She got almost sweet. But Velma had just got worse and worse.

The time came for them to leave. Aunt Ethel was putting on her hat. My mother said, "Velma's already in the car, honey. Why don't you go out and say goodbye."

So I went out and climbed into the back seat alongside Velma. As I looked at her all the things she'd done for the past two weeks came rolling up in my mind and I punched her in the nose.

She screamed of course and continued screaming despite my shocked stammering apologies, and the two women came rushing out.

"She *hit* me and I wasn't doing anything to her! She just climbed right into the car and hit me!"

Ethel and my mother were at it then, telling each other off at the top of their lungs, with Ethel clutching Velma and Velma trying desperately to encourage a nose bleed without luck, wailing all the time like a stuck pig.

We stood in the yard and watched the car disappear down the road, dust and gravel blowing up into a cloud back of it.

From Abilene to Lubbock, Snyder, Post: we cleared Caprock and hit the pure flat plains. I can't describe the ease and relief I feel when I see all the way to the clear horizon, all around.

One evening when Velma and I were kids and were playing in the half dark of the front porch it started to look as if there was some big fire in the far distance. The sky glowed red and the glow became larger until it took up half the sky in that direction. And in the wake of the colour rose an enormous full orange moon. Texas full moons have the gift of being seen the instant they surface.

Stand in a perfect half circle. The far line of the horizon is exactly horizontal. That line extends as far as you can see, left or right. Below that line is one colour, above it is another colour. You are standing on the exact line of it. Your feet are on earth and your head is in the air. Roughly speaking you are a 90° vertical line. You are a definite addition to the landscape, that is you *are* holding down that piece of ground and you're human.

That moon rose right up and the colour with it. It became smaller as it rose, becoming finally pure white and brilliant.

And still that horizontal holds. The light from the sky illuminates the flat plain.

"I just don't hardly cook at all anymore. I'm just getting terrible," Ethel broke up laughing at this image of herself.

Her house in town was made of brick, the floors shone, and the fixtures in the two bathrooms. The bedrooms were fully decorated, walls filled with framed photographs of her children and grandchildren. In the bathroom little metal filigree stands held guest soap, round yellow lemons. And there were paintings on the wall that she had made herself. There was no doubt that her lifestyle had changed. There was no cotton bib apron on a hook in the kitchen.

We were in a small restaurant located two blocks down the street.

"Well, this looks like a real nice place to eat," Mae looked around. Formica top tables and chrome chairs with padded backs and seats. The place held mostly middle-aged women and one table of young men, one still had on his straw hat, leaning back against the wall with his chair tilted onto its hind legs.

The waitress was about forty-five and wore glasses with flowers and small rhinestones in a slight upward sweep at the outside corners. She wasn't wearing a wig but her hair was intricately dressed, as good as a French court lady could have done, if she used her own hair.

She stood at the table, her pencil and pad were out and ready.

"Hello, Miz Leary. Yawl ready to order?"

"We haven't made our minds up yet, Eunice."

Eunice pocketed her pad and pencil and smiled, walked away.

We examined the menu. The menus had a border of cattle brands around the outside edge.

"They always have fried chicken here on Wednesdays," Ethel said.

"I wish she hadn't hurried away. I wanted to ask her if they make their chicken salad fresh here. Do you know? Do they make their own chicken salad?"

"Well, we can surely ask."

Eunice returned.

"Is your chicken salad really fresh? Did you make it today? I've just had a longing this whole trip for some good fresh chicken salad."

"No ma'am, it's not fresh. I mean, nobody made any this morning."

"Jessie, what are *you* having?"

"I want the Mexican Plate and iced tea."

Eunice wrote it down.

"They make good chili here, too," Ethel said.

"I'd love some good chili. I feel like ordering that Mexican Plate myself. But I wouldn't be able to sleep tonight. What kind of chili do you put on your Mexican Plate?"

"We usually put red but if you like green better he can put green."

"Oh my, I'd like that. But it would just tear up my stomach. I'd be sick for a week."

"Well, Mama, why don't you get something that won't tear up your stomach."

"What are you having, Ethel?"

"I'm going to have a chicken-fried steak."

"I guess I will, too."

"You both want those cooked well done?"

"Heavenly days, yes! I can't stand pink meat."

Eunice left.

"And they make the *best* breakfasts! I come here two or three times a week for breakfast. There are a few women friends of mine that we meet here and have breakfast together. This place is close enough so I can walk."

"What's the matter with that brand new Buick you've got, Ethel? Dontchew ever get that new Buick out of the garage for anything but to wash it?"

"They recognize me, you know. Everybody knows everybody here. They all know I don't have a license.

"Of course I *use* it. If I want to go to Lubbock or over to Frank's I just get in the car and go. Sometimes they stop me and sometimes they don't. There's one boy, cutest thing in his uniform you ever saw, he'll see me and he'll just grin and wave me on by."

"Ethel, you *must* drive well enough to be able to get a license. You've been driving for years!"

"I was in there about ten days ago getting tested. We drove around with that silly examiner just saying turn right, now turn left. You know how they do. I do just fine when I'm by myself but those old examiners always make me nervous. Well, when we got back to the license place I said, Do I get my license? And he said, Lady, you're lucky to be alive!" She started laughing again.

Marvin answered the door in the bottom half of a set of pale blue pajamas.

"We tried to call you," Ethel said. "There's something wrong with the phone number you gave me."

"Well Jessie! We knew you were due here but we thought you'd changed your mind. We expected you about a month ago."

I gave him a hug and my hands slid around on his bare back.

"Aw, Velma's in the bathroom putting on lotion and she slathered some of it on me."

"I'll go get her out of the bathroom." I headed back through the house.

"Velma?"

"Who *is* that?" her voice came, irritable and suspicious.

"Come on. Get out of there. You can't stay in the bathroom all your life!"

"Who *is* that?"

"Jessie."

"Jessie *who?*"

"Your cousin, Jessie! How many Jessies you got around this place?"

The door flew open. Velma was in a pale pink Babydoll nightgown. She was working on her face, so she wore a pink lace cap that covered all of her hair.

"Oh Jessie." We hugged and she started crying.

"Who'd you come with? Is Aunt Mae here?"

"She's in the front room with Aunt Ethel."

"Oh Lord, is Mama here? I better get dressed. Well I'll do it in a while."

Barefoot and baby dolled, with cream all over her face she started toward the front room, sauntering. She reached out and grabbed a towel as we passed through the kitchen and she entered the living room wiping the cream from her face onto the towel.

"Oh Velma!" her mother wailed. "You'll *ruin* that towel honey!"

"I hafta wipe my face on something if I'm gonna kiss Aunt Mae."

She tossed the towel onto a chair. Ethel snatched it up and looked underneath to see whether the grease had got onto the fabric.

"I've been a practising lawyer now for three years. I've got an office set up in Root."

"He's just turned into everybody that can't pay's *poor* lawyer," Velma complained. "He's so tender-hearted he gets all the people that can't pay nothing! And they hang around all the time. I don't get to see him more than a couple of hours in any twenty-four."

She was sprawled sideways across a chair with her legs hiked and one foot circled back around to let her paint the toenails dark red.

"He got the *highest* score in the whole state when he took his bar exam," she said. "Him and a woman tied for first place!"

"How did you manage to get a law degree?" I asked. "I thought you had to stay home after your daddy had his stroke."

"Well, I couldn't go to Austin. But they put a law school in Lubbock. So I could live here and see to the farm and go to classes, too."

"I just lived for when he got his degree and passed his exam," Velma started on the other foor. "I thought I'd get to see him then, but no. They telephone him day and night and if they don't get him at his office they telephone him here. Or show up. One woman was here almost five hours a few days ago, just bawling."

"Velma, I'm not away that much of the time. Velma likes to have me at home. That was Mrs. Gutierrez. Her husband ran away with a twelve-year-old girl. The girl's parents put papers out on him. The problem was keeping the federal government out of it. He took her to New Mexico."

"What did his wife want? Did she want to divorce him?"

"Naw. He'd been caught and sent back. The kid was back with her folks. The wife wanted him to get out of jail. She got the girl's parents to drop charges. So now they're all back over there working for Mr. Holiday. It seems like everything's O.K."

We sat up talking, the three of us, until three in the morning. Mae and Ethel had gone back over to Ethel's house.

When I was ready for bed and said goodnight Velma said, "I'm going to stay up half the night. I've just been doing that lately. So I tend to sleep late. When you wake up in the morning wake me up and we'll go over and see Frank. But you're going to have to wake me up. Otherwise I'll sleep until well into the afternoon."

The next morning I found the coffee and made some, read through the morning paper and woke Velma up at about eleven.

She had come by a minute toy poodle. It bounced like elastic in the bedroom when I opened the door. There was an elegant arrangement of furniture that let the tiny animal scamper up the side of the bed to where it slept, on a cushion on the pillows at the head of the bed. The poodle slept with its head between the husband and wife.

The night before while we talked, Velma and Marvin had stood the creature on a newspaper and trimmed the fur on its legs with fingernail scissors.

While Velma turned one way and then the other to make sure it was daylight on both sides, the dog ran up and down the "arrangement" with little leaps.

"Good Lord! It feels like daybreak!"

To drive ten miles to see her brother, Velma creamed her face and cleaned it off, pulled her hair back severely so that she looked skinned and stared at herself critically, drew her eyebrows on with a black pencil, (if that's provincialism so's Elizabeth Taylor) used the kind of mascara that makes eyelashes "grow" until they're as good as artificial ones, put blue eyeshadow on so that all the skin between her eyelids and her eyebrows was covered, put on face make-up including rouge and lipstick. End of phase one.

Then she put on a champagne coloured wig with a bouffant styling that made her stand a good foot taller. She intended to be informal and this particular wig had a little neck knot of curls back of and below the enormous helmet effect; the cluster of curls was held by a black velvet clip-on bow.

Then she went back to the closet in her bedroom, the poodle skipping alongside. She put on a new peach coloured silk shirt, a pair of Levi's, hand-tooled boots, and a denim jacket.

We drove over to Frank's in Velma's Oldsmobile; the poodle went with us.

"Frank and Jimmie-Sue haven't seen my new dog," Velma tooled the car around efficiently. "She was *supposed* to be pure apricot. Apricot's really rare. That's why we paid so much for her. See. You can see the apricot here and here. She was supposed to be apricot all over."

The tiny dog watched us as intently as if she watched a tennis match, her quick beads of eyes flicked back and forth and back.

FRANK BOUGHT ...

"Frank bought sixteen pairs of pants today!" Jimmie-Sue said.

"Sixteen?"

"She was supposed to be pure apricot but she wasn't. But we couldn't take her back by that time." Velma was holding the tiny furry face pressed against hers. She put the dog onto the floor and it circled the room, each tiny foot going down like a pin-prick.

"How'd you come to buy sixteen pairs of pants," I asked. "You turning into the last of the big-time spenders?"

"We went into town so he could get a new pair of kha-kis...." Jimmie-Sue started to tell the story.

Frank picked it up. "They're not going to make a hundred percent cotton khaki pants anymore."

"Alice was waiting on us," Jimmie-Sue said. "She said Well, those'll be the last one hundred percent cotton khakis you'll ever get."

"I hate to work in that blended stuff, that polyester. It's no improvement. It gets too hot and sticks to you."

I remember once going swimming with Frank and Velma. Or what I call swimming. I never learned to do more than float. I mean I can't turn my head and breathe as I go, so what I do is I get my arms and legs going with my face in the water and every so often I roll over, totally, and breathe; then I roll over again and go some more. But that doesn't mean I don't enjoy it.

Particularly when it's so hot that even the rocks wilt. That day was that hot. The three of us were in a pickup and going across flat shimmering land. I couldn't imagine where we were going. The truck wheeled right, onto a dirt road and we stopped. No river, no lake, nothing in sight. We walked off the dirt road a hundred yards or so and there was a hole in the ground like a giant well. It measured about thirty feet across. We started climbing down the path, past a small cottonwood. The bottom was a circle of pure blue water, it was so clear you could see rock ledges ten feet below, around the edges. The middle just went on down to black.

"They've never found a bottom to this."

Looking up, the dirt sides were dotted with mud swallow nests and the birds were home. There was a constant chittering from them and at intervals they would cut loose together and fly in a lovely spiral around and around at the top.

We were down about sixty feet. Going down it was like each step moved into a cooler ridge of air. Up above, where the swallows flew and did their quick banking to avoid the walls, the heat shimmered and shook at the lip of the well. It was a magic place.

"So Frank just bought every pair of khakis they had in his size and then we went down the street to *Albertson's,* and he bought every pair of khakis *they* had!" Jimmie-Sue finished with a flourish.

It was a good story. Frank, handsome as ever, that Indian look really paid off, leaned back in his leather recliner and grinned.

"So your plan is to never get fat and never get skinny and never buy another pair of pants," I said.

"That's about it."

When I had to go out to the car for my purse I saw that Velma's dog had deposited a neat pile in the middle of the floor in the next room.

"You better go in the next room and clean up after your dog before Jimmie-Sue sees it," I told Velma in a whisper when I came back.

"The salesman kept bringing them out and bringing them out. Finally she said Well I think I want a Buick that's just like the one Mae's got. So Frank called around and got one just like Aunt Mae's and that's the one she's got now," Jimmie-Sue was saying.

"What does she do that's so wrong?"

"She just drives like she's still on a "country road," Frank grinned. "She moves into the flat middle and goes and nothing can't stop her till she gets to where she's going."

"Well, she's just a menace!" Jimmie-Sue said.

Aunt Ethel decided to cook a dinner for this visit, so we all, Velma and I, Marvin, Frank and Jimmie-Sue, converged on her house, ate, and then Mama and I got our bags into the Buick and kissed and hugged all around and drove off.

A letter from Ethel to Mae says, "Velma just broke down bawling. She kept saying, That's the last time I'll ever see Jessie alive."

EVERYTHING BEGINS AS A DOT ...

Everything begins as a dot at the level of the horizon. The dot gets bigger as it comes closer ... reaches full size and stops ... a farm, a stand of mesquite trees, a humpbacked metal cotton gin with wagons standing derelict around the yard, their insides fuzzy with bits and tufts of cotton.

Or ... a combination gas station grocery store with two or three men in khakis or bib overalls and summer straw hats, hunkered back on their heels talking in the shade of the wall.

They glance up briefly when the Model-A Ford drives in.

"There's some monkies in that cage out back. Why dont-cha take your little girl back for a look."

That cage stood on hard-packed dirt with no trees. A couple of burlap toe-sacks had been laid onto one corner of the top with rocks to hold them down, for a shade.

I broke some cookies into pieces and threw the pieces toward the cage for the monkies to grab and fuss over. Mama stood watching, pleased as she always was when a treat came along. One bit of cookie bounced off a bar and back onto tire ground just out of reach of the small crabby hand at the end of a hairy stick of arm.

I went forward to pick it up, leaning over.

The next thing I knew, I had been got. That hand grabbed my hair and pulled me closer and then the others got in on the game. Cookies forgotten they were all, or as many as there was room for, hands and feet together, in my hair, pulling. I was screaming.

My father came running with a stick he picked up as he came. The station owner came running. They got me loose.

WHEN I WAS LITTLE ...

When I was little the cousin I dearly loved was Billy-Bob. He was my mother's brother's boy and a few months younger than me. He had a sweet nature, really soft and open and, now thinking back, innocent.

My mother was really close to her brother, my Uncle Peter, and even to his wife Maxine, despite the way Maxine had of going to bed during her monthly periods, which made my mother purse her mouth in disgust. My mother figured a fine distinction between womanly weakness and self-indulgence; being really on her brother's side when it really came down to it.

So Billy-Bob and I saw a lot of each other and I took his side in the same way, and carried it a lot farther along than he would have done, him being gentle. When his little brother Curtis was born sickly so Billy-Bob was doubly deprived I hated the new baby for him.

When Curtis could walk and became the classic tag-along I got rid of him at least once by walking around inside the chicken house with the door locked saying loudly, "Look at the little baby kittens. Look at the puppies!"

"There ain't no puppies or kittens in there!" Curtis yelled through the wall.

"Look at the baby giraffes and the baby elephants!"

"There ain't no baby elephants in there!"

And when he was so teased by it that he was pounding on the door I walked out, cool, and he rushed in, triumphant.

"See! See! There ain't no...."

And I closed the door back of him and latched it and Billy-Bob and I headed for the watermelon field.

The bottom fell out of melons that year and made them not worth the picking. We would walk along the rows busting ripe melons and eating only the heart. It was a luxury that took some heroism; the sand was hot as a frying pan and we were bare-footed. We had to hit our feet against the soft dirt with each step hard enough to dislodge the top surface and get into the slightly cooler under part.

We weren't supposed to go into the watermelons at all because what if a miracle happened and one day the prices were up, then that field would be a crop. But that never happened and we went almost daily into the ripening then rotting melons as part of our rounds.

And we played mumblety-peg outside the kitchen door with a pocket knife. And we swung in an old tire hung from a china berry tree.

It wasn't until supper time when we were sitting down and Aunt Maxine said, "Where's Curtis?" that we remembered. I went out and unlatched the shed.

It must have been a hellish day for a little kid, all day long in the hot chicken house. But even now my inclination is that he deserved it.

Until I was ten Billy-Bob and I were "favourite cousins." Then we moved for good to New Mexico and started living with my Aunt Hannah and I came to be favourite cousins with my cousin Bud. Bud would let me choose whether I wanted to wash or dry the dishes in exchange for telling a story while we worked.

One of the running stories was: "What if tomorrow morning we went to the flume and we found the biggest fish in the world."

The flume only measured ten feet across but that didn't interfere with the projection. It was a slightly wider place in a nearby irrigation ditch where a wooden trough covered with slick green moss brought water down from a ditch at a higher level. We could go to the top of the incline and get shooshed along the trough and dumped head over heels into the ditch.

"Well, we'd put it in a tank on a flatcar and we could go all over the country charging dimes to see the biggest fish in the world."

The final image included a lot more. We finally had in mind something like a traveling medicine show, a kind of village of entertainers all living and traveling on adjacent flatcars. We ironed out all the wrinkles like what kind of tent would keep passersby from seeing the fish until we let them. We got the whole theory straight but we never found the fish. It wasn't even a disappointment. The fish was the least of it.

But it was years later when I was a grownup woman with my first child two years old that I made a trip to Texas to my Uncle Peter's. Billy-Bob was over six feet tall and weighed nearly two hundred pounds. We couldn't look each other in the eye. It was truly awkward as if blood and time froze up.

"Well! Ain't you two gonna give each other a kiss?" and we got through a routine of cheek-pecking.

After supper when everybody else was talking we walked out back of the house.

It's hard to explain what the plains look like if you've never been there. The land is totally flat on all sides all the way to the horizon. There's a lot of space and the sky is huge. There was a sunset. Billy-Bob said, faltering and gentle, "I guess it's hard to stay favourite cousins when you move away and when you're playing every day with somebody else." To let me off the hook. As if we're any of us off that hook. Our natural infidelities.

But it breaks my heart to think how he tried to tell me he understood what had happened and didn't hold it against me.

WHEN BILLY-BOB MARRIED ...

When Billy-Bob married he married a girl whose daddy was a sharecropper. They were rock bottom poor and, according to Billy-Bob's mother, a little backward. My Aunt Maxine wouldn't have been satisfied with anybody Billy married and that poor girl had a lot to put up with from her and from Billy's little sister who took the same tone.

When Alvina would come over with Billy for a visit they'd do things like ask her if her breakfast dishes were washed.

Alvina seemed alright to me the couple of times I met her. She was thin and pale with dark hair. Maxine asked Billy once why he couldn't have found somebody a little more healthy.

This is a story about a kind of sorrow and I should really have started it a different way, with some sense of how close country people felt to the radio in the thirties and forties, before television.

Aunt Maxine used to talk as off-handed about Roy and Hank and Gene as if they lived down the road. That was Roy Acuff and Hank Williams and Gene Autry. If you came on it late and think you've got taste in country music you'll probably smirk at the idea of Gene Autry, but at that time he was ranked right in there with the others. The place Alvina's daddy worked had an old wood-frame house that the family lived in. It was two stories high and had a permanent lean away from the direction the sandstorms crossed the plains there. It was really run down, like it could go in the next wind that hit it.

Inside, the house had more rooms than the family had furniture for. They had a table and chairs in the room alongside the kitchen, and everybody had old iron bedsteads fitted out with feather mattresses but that was mostly it. You could go into a lanky old room that wouldn't have anything in it but a rocking chair next to a high bare window that looked out onto nothing but the horizon. And there were rooms that didn't have anything in them at all.

One of the things they did have was a table-model radio.

When Hank Williams died Alvina's daddy took the radio out to the woodpile and smashed it up with his axe as a gesture of grief.

He said that with Hank dead there wouldn't be any more music worth listening to.

"Didn't Billy have a stroke or something?"

"He works for this cotton mill, honey, and that lint got into the bottom part of his lungs and just packed. Of course, you don't use the bottom parts of your lungs very much so you can survive with that easy enough. But what he should of done is sued that mill for an income for the rest of his life, then got disability and social security! He could of got it for him and his wife and all those kids!"

"How many kids does he have?"

"Five. They had twins you know after they had those three. Little twin girls."

"How are they? What are the kids like?"

"That's the *same* damned truck I was behind a hundred miles back! I let him go around me!"

"Mama, you're only going fifty miles an hour."

"Well, their oldest boy's about seventeen or eighteen now. Or sixteen. And he's real smart. Their oldest girl, Hazel, they browbeat her until she rebelled and left home. She just lately started working at the hospital. The little middle one, the little blonde girl, she's a sweet little girl (shift to mournful) but she's growing up too. I don't know ... the little twins are about six or seven."

"Billy-Bob and his wife get along alright now?"

"They'd have always got along alright if it hadn't been for Maxine. Maxine and Pearl was sneaking around and watching her and accusing her of running around with other men when Billy was truck driving. Telling Billy I don't know what. All that stuff ... till she probably did start running around. But I wouldn't of blamed her!

"I better quit talking. My throat's starting to hurt."

BY THE TIME I WAS FIFTEEN ...

By the time I was fifteen I had read enough books to be a common kind of victim. I believed that there was a world I hadn't got to yet that focused on intelligence and wit and graces that were attainable. By the time I was sixteen I had all the grandiose reasoning that let me "choose" in my mind to be an artist. I had rejected being a millionaire as only one of my options and without a look back. My reasoning was that the right kind of millionaires pay court to artists.

You can see how far afield the books had led me.

There was no justification for believing that any of those choices was more than the fantasy it certainly was.

To walk forward in the classroom at school and sharpen a pencil was an exercise in will and drama. I would invent a story to let me cross the floor.

I had already gone through a bout when I was thirteen with chorea. At its easiest it was a twitch in my fingers or a slight jerk in my elbow. At its worst, as my mother put it, Jessie can be walking along a perfectly smooth piece of sidewalk and fall flat on her face!

I was a sore subject. My hemlines were uneven, my socks always worked down into my shoes and my spirit only felt comfortable when it was miles back in me.

I talked too much or too little, too shy to deserve attention or exact to the point of being pedantic, in desperation. I was afraid most of the time.

All of this describes a classic case.

Something was bound to happen internally. The need was finally bound to be past bearing.

My Aunt Maxine hoarded sugar during the Second World War. It was sugar she came by legally. The government gave extra rations to farmers for canning. But she didn't use it all. And, given the shortage, she didn't want to return it.

What if next year there wasn't any? So she "canned" the sugar in glass mason jars. She made a syrup of sugar and water and put it on the shelves in the cellar alongside the peaches and plums and green beans.

That sugar-water turned into the loveliest sight to see. The sugar formed crystals inside the jars. When you'd bring one of those jars of sugar out into the sunlight it could practically throw rainbows.

Aunt Maxine was bothered by the manifest sugar. She was afraid that government inspectors might recognize what was going on. But they never came around. The war did end and the sugar did finally get used up. But while it was being stored....

I feel like I was like that. Something caught in abeyance with a lot of transformation going on and a heartfelt fear of discovery. It felt illegal.

Aunt Ada came from Texas on the Greyhound bus, to visit with Mae. The three of us sat in the small living room watching Zoorama on the television. The two sisters raised their voices to be heard above the sound. Sometimes they would look at each other or at me.

Aunt Ada's voice was wind across miles of plain, a vacuum pulled high into her nose.

"I felt like it was the other mother's turn. I was there for two months and I told Marydel and Duke, It's *her* turn. I'll just go and visit with Mae for awhile. Duke's mother said, Now, are you sure you've got somewhere to go? Just like sugar. Well, you know Marydel! She never would hear a word against *me!* She piped right up and said, Mama has plenty of places to go! Plenty of people want Mama to come and visit! She said, You don't have to go anywhere if you don't want to, Mama, you can stay right here! But I said, No, it's her turn and I want to go visit with Mae awhile."

Aunt Ada's face, all those dry-weather lines, broke into pieces when she smiled. On Zoorama they were feeding the crocodiles.

Mae told about a neighbour's little girl, laughing. "She had her face all twisted up, I'm sure glad I don't have one of those stuck on me. Why doesn't he sit down and stick it between his legs to pee-pee. Why does he just have to stand there and show it?"

Aunt Ada told about Norma-Jean's little girl. When she was three her parents decided she should know how boys were "made."

"Did they show her a little baby boy's?" Mae asked.

"No!" Aunt Ada's voice dropped a pitch. "They showed her Jim's!"

The two women stared at each other.

"They did what?"

"They showed her her *daddy's!*"

Significant looks like pins through the butterfly while the wings still flap.

On Zoorama in Florida the porpoises were trying to talk. There was proof of how closed into aquariums they were adapting their voices, lowering the pitch, trying to form words.

"What would *you* do," the scientist makes his point to the interviewer, "If you found yourself encased in air, held by some obviously intelligent life form, and you wanted to communicate with them?"

Adapt was the gist of that familiar message.

"Isn't that awful! Look at it, Ada! It's just like a little old dried up man! Ooooh! I just couldn't stand to have one of those things near me!"

It was a baby monkey. The head seemed a holder for two enormous eyes, slit for a mouth, wrinkles all over, a little round hairless belly.

"Jessie used to look so pretty when she let me cut her hair and put a permanent in it," Mae told Ada. They looked at me, their eyes weighing what could have been perfect in me, given a few changes.

It was later that evening that I said, "I think I'll go with Axel."

I might still have been stopped if someone had made a joke of it, had let me make a joke of it. The statement sat in the room as black and hard as decision.

"Well, Jessie, if you're sure that's what you want to do."

Later Mae grieved, "I think Jessie got married just to leave home."

PEARL SAID ...

"Pearl said, That first husband of Jessie's ... where was he from? right in front of a bunch of people ... like they *always* do me ...! I said, He was from Denmark. And she said, And the one she's married to now ... he's a writer? And I said, Yes, he is. She said, She sure did marry a couple of funny guys, didn't she?

"Her husband's a real stupe. He's doing alright but he's working *her* to death because he's getting in the business of trying to make money. He keeps them so far in debt that Pearl's worked til she has stomach ulcers!

"So she says, She sure did marry a couple of funny guys, didn't she? And I said, Well, they may be funny but I'll tell you one damned thing. She got herself a couple of smart ones!

"Boy! She just went to bawling!"

"Oh really!" (laughing)

"Yeah! She just went to bawling. Said, Well, I don't care whether anybody likes ... uh ... what *is* her husband's name ... Edward ...! I guess my folks *don't* like Edward. And they think he's dumb. But *I* don't care ... I said, I didn't even know Edward was in the conversation! I thought we was discussing Jessie's husbands!"

"I don't like to go visiting *anybody* that I feel like I've got to fight for my life or fight to be defending myself all the time!"

"She was so shy," Maxine said, "worse than if she'd never married at all."

When Maxine's brother, Boss, married he found that he had a problem. His wife had a muscle that was grown across the opening to her vagina. After a frustrating period of time he saw to it that she went to a doctor and they learned that the "problem" was correctable.

"Well, her first husband took her to a doctor too!"

"She had been married before?" I asked.

"For about three days. Then he took her to a doctor and you know what she did? Of course this was years ago and women weren't so simple about ... women didn't just go in and let doctors poke them unless they were sick. So her first husband took her to be examined ... I guess it must have been the first time anything like that ever happened to her ... and she jumped up screaming off the examination table and cut out for home. She told her Mama that LeRoy had taken her to a whorehouse!"

"The second time around it all must have been simpler," I suggested. "Oh no!" Maxine was positive. "She wouldn't have the operation! She just told Boss straight out that she never meant to have an operation."

"How long did that go on?"

"Oh, for years!"

"I used to love to tease her," Peter repeated. "I come in one time, we were all going to have dinner together, and she was setting in a chair all dressed up and as prim and proper. I just walked over and set right down in her lap...."

"Peter just walked right over and set in her lap!" Maxine started laughing.

"She blushed from her feet clear up to the roots of her hair."

"What finally happened?"

"Aw, she got appendicitis and had to have her appendix

out. So Boss made an agreement with the doctor that while she was under he'd just ..."

"He just took care of that other thing, too."

"And you know," Maxine said, "she never did forgive him for that. It's been years and she still holds that against him!"

"Yeah. They've got a couple of kids and *still* she won't turn loose of that grudge she holds about that."

"How *long* were they married before she got appendicitis," I asked.

"Oh, for years!"

"That was patient of him to wait around," I said, "they were really lucky. She could have gone her whole life long and never got sick with anything strong enough to need an anesthetic for."

CURTIS STUCK HIS FOOT ...

Curtis stuck his foot up in the air at me.

"You don't *see* that kind of boot where you come from, do you?"

He had a right to be proud. It was a handsome boot.

"Sure I do. If somebody can afford 'em."

"Naw, I mean, you don't see these boots with pointed toes and heels like that. Those people where you live, they wear ... the kind of boots they wear has square toes and a strap across here."

"Not all of them," I said. Then I decided to get him. "Curtis," I said, "There isn't a hippy in the world that doesn't want to be a cowboy."

His face blushed fiery red. He could just about stand it.

"Thirty-thirty's what they usually use?"

"Naw, it was biggern' a thirty-thirty. And it come out right over there. And when it come out...."

"A thirty-ought-six? Is that what they call 'em?"

"Yeah, a thirty-ought-six. It made a hole just about *that* big. And it just come through his hip over here. He said, just like you said, he said he just took and got blood and everything out of there."

"Aw!"

"You just think what that did to his ... going through his ... *bowels* and *stomach* through there! And ast him ... said ... You wanna go to a doctor?"

"They can patch that up. That's much easier than ... when it goes through your *lungs* is when you get into bad trouble. That would of tore up his kidneys and everything."

"This time *I'm* talking about ... what I was going to tell you ... see, we don't believe in going to a doctor, you know. So they ast him they said You wanna go to the doctor. He said *No*. He said, Get me down that mountain and *baptise* me. Old Brother Gene said they carried him down the mountain and baptised him. Four days later he was out doing his work. Never did go to the doctor."

"Hmmm."

"You just *think* about that bullet going plumb through just right there ... plumb through ... and coming out...."

"I'd rather not think about it."

For their wedding trip Curtis and Linda drove up through northwest Texas and into Denver. From Denver they dropped south to Albuquerque and stopped at Mae's.

"Curtis's just been eating hamburgers all the way," Linda half-teased and was half-serious. The tone she used was common to lovers, that teasing tenderness.

"So when we got to Denver we was so tired we thought we'd do something different and instead of stopping in a motel we went to a nice tourist home. It was really comfortable. And we decided that night to have a fancy dinner. Well, the landlady was French and she told us about a French restaurant. So we went there.

"Well, the first thing was we had to wait for a table but the place was real pretty so we decided to go ahead and wait. The next thing was everybody there was dressed up in suits and ties.

"Curtis was just wearing one of his cowboy shirts with the sleeves all rolled up. Of course, we were clean and all."

"I told Linda They'll just know a Texas boy's been here."

"We just waited and waited."

"There was these two old boys that it was clear that was the table we would get. I mean they had finished all their dinner when we first got there. But then they *had* to have some kind of dessert. Then they *had* to have coffee. Lord, you'd have thought they could get through that coffee fast enough. You know those little tiny cups? Well, that's the kind of coffee they had. You'd have thought it was a gallon. And they had a little bit of wine in one of those great big glasses. There wasn't no more than two swallows of coffee in those cups. And there was less wine than that! Well, you should have seen them with those glasses! They *made* over that! They took that little bit of wine and they *rolled* it around, and they *smelled* it. And after all that they'd take one little sip. It must've taken them fifteen minutes to get through that two swallows of coffee and that dinky little bit of wine!"

'We walked right past them. There was another table came free just because of the way they was messing around."

"The *next* thing was the menu was all in French!"

"You know Curtis! He wasn't about to ask what it said. The waitress came over and...." The two of them started laughing.

"The waitress come over and Curtis ordered a hamburger!"

"You heard anybody say what cotton pulling's going at, Daddy?" Curtis asked.

I heard old W.B. say some guy told him he'd pull his at seventy-five cents. I said, "You better get him because I said, Most of it's going to be over a dollar."

"You know butane's already twenty cents a gallon? They say by the time we get to pulling it'll be over twenty-five. I tell you something, it's going to cost to pull a crop like this one."

"Aw, it won't be so bad. How about diesel? It depends on what diesel's going at."

"We was setting there," Aunt Maxine said, "and my brother had one of them old watches my daddy bought him with both sides, you know, you have to push a thing to see ... you know how them used to be."

"Them old watches that you'd mash the stem and they'd fly open," Peter said.

"He *ast* for one of *them* kind of watches," Maxine continued.

"But *first* he'd had two men come up there and one of them was on one side of the stage and one of them was on the other side. He give one of them an *orange* to hold ... says, Now you hold onto this and don't let it get away! And he give the other one a *box* just about this big a square and said, Now, you hold that tight where nothing won't get out of there. And *then* he ast for a watch. And I said, Boss, let him have it! Let him have yours! Nobody else there had one or wouldn't let him have it.

"So Boss give him his watch. He just looked at it and said, This old watch dudn't look like it's any good, says, I'm just going to shoot it over yonder across the stage. And he put it in this gun, an old big-barrelled gun. You could *see* it going across, looked like. Going across there. He looks at Boss and says, I'll pay you for that, son, after awhile. Then he went on with his rigamarole, just left Boss setting there. Everybody ... all the boys was ateasing him, you know."

"Lost his watch."

"Yeah, so directly he got a hat. This old boy that I was with he got his hat and busted four eggs in it and stirred 'em around and around, just stirred and stirred and stirred 'em. Put a lid on and set 'em on ... built a *fire* with some paper. Some of those old candy boxes. You know they always sold candy. And he set that hat on that fire."

"Was that hat a good 'un?" Curtis interrupted.

"It was a brand-new Stetson!"

"He wouldn't a got *my* hat. Not unless he taken it away from me!"

"Well, Aunt Bea was just having *fits!*

"Then after awhile he said, I guess them eggs is done! and he picked the hat up and pulled that paper off of it ... that hat just *set* up there on that fire. Never burned nor nothing! And he taken that paper off of there and *four chickens* jumped out! Jumped out of that hat!

"Then he fooled around and said, Son, says, have you helt that box good? He said, Yeah. He said, Well, what's in it? Said, I don't know. You give it to me a long time ago. And he was just a *holding* it. This old man ... it was Hank Utely that was holding the box! So he says, Well, he says, Let me see! He says, Open it up. And he opened it up and there was another box in that box, and there was another box in that box. He just kept opening up boxes till he just had a pile of boxes and got down to a little 'un and that *watch* was in it!"

"Uhmmm Uhmmm."

"Then he said, The *chain's* off of it! Where's the chain! And he says, Son, take a bite of that orange! And he'd give that orange to that guy before he even *got* the watch! And he give this box to this one before he ever even got the watch!"

"Uhmmm Hhmmm."

"He taken a bite of that orange and when he did he *bit* onto the chain!"

"Well, I'll say!"

"I don't know *how in the world* he done that! Boss just swore that watch never did keep good time after that!"

"Well, I'll tell yawl something I don't know whether you ever ... You ever been around Mexkins much?" Curtis asked me.

"She's been around more Mexkins than you have!"

"Well, I don't know. She'd have to be around a whole lot, wouldn't she, Daddy."

"She's *lived* out there in New Mexico."

"She lived in Albuquerque for *years* and *years.*"

"Them's a different breed of Mexkins from what we've got out here."

"Well, they really are."

"What I was going to tell you, every Mexkin in *this* part of the country will tell you that if you know the right man he can take a dollar bill and lay it on a pile of newspaper and draw one off. Then he just starts cutting them out! That size. And he stacks 'em up *that* high. Do 'em like that and every one'll be a dollar bill!

"They say they can *spend* that money. Old Luke said he had often done that and he bought *everything* with it.

"The guy that told him how to do it said, You won't live *long* though, after you start doing it!

"Old Luke said he bought everything! Said he taken that money and do it like that. And old Ben Sanchez down there, said he seen him do it!

"Ever Mexkin in this country'll tell you they can do that. That *somebody* they know can. Old Ben's daddy told me that his brother got to doing that."

"How long did he live?"

"He died when he was thirty-six. Then old Ben got hold of it and started doing it.

"What you got to do is worship the devil to be able to do it."

"Ben?!!"

"Uhmm Hmmm!"

"Ben Sanchez?"

"Yep. And his daddy taken them books, you know he

was telling us about that? His daddy found out about his doing that and he taken them books and burnt 'em!"

"You learn how to do it out of a book?" I asked.

"Yeah. You get this book that tells you how."

"Sounds to me like the guy that's sure to be making the money is the guy that's selling the books!"

"Now this here's the deal though. You can't *buy* the book."

"Yeah?"

"It's got to be wrote, see, by you ... and then you give it to me ... just like him. His *uncle* give it to him. You don't ever sell it!"

"Oh."

"Then his uncle whenever he went to die he give it to Ben. It passes on and on."

"I'd rather be poor and live a long time than be rich and...."

"I'll tell you what ... him and his wife come to see me and Linda whenever we first got married. One night ... Linda has heard this story several times, too. Heard them tell it one night. They was setting on the couch and I said, Ben ... There's a lake right out here called Guthrie. You know where it is, Daddy?"

"Gutherie? I've heard of it. I've never been there."

"Well, I been out there several times. You go out there to Guthrie Lake and that lake stays full of water nearly the year round. Real pretty lake. It's fed by a little spring.

"One night Ben ... him and me was here in town ... I'll just tell you the whole story. And he said, Curtis, go out with me to the lake and let's pray to the devil. He said, Tonight he'll appear because it's full moon and it's right overhead. Said, He'll be there.

"I said, Well where he is I ain't. That's just what I told him. I thought he was crazy.

"I said, You're the silliest thing I ever heard of!"

"He's *still* crazy!"

"Another night or two ... he told me ... I said, Did he appear?

Yeah! Come out there and told me what to do this week.

"So, his wife and him got married. They was over at the house one night and I said ... her name Emily?"

"Eva," Linda answered.

"Eva? I says, Eva, does Ben still pray to the devil? And she said, Yep. Said, I didn't believe him, Curtis, whenever me and him got married. Said, He told me about that before we got married and I didn't believe him. And says, One night he told me he was going out there and pray to him. Said he'd prove it tonight. Said he'd have some *birds* come and appear to me at the door. And she said, Sure enough, while I was washing dishes there was two birds walked up there and knocked on the door."

"*Walked* up and *knocked* on the door?"

"She said they was as tall as a man!"

"That was probably Ben and some crony!"

"Naw! He was in the living room, she said. And ... wait ... did she say they *talked* to her?"

"I don't remember her saying they *talked* to her."

"I think it's enough to have a *tall* bird!" I started laughing.

"Get a tall enough bird and he don't have to do anything else!"

"She said she didn't *deny* his word anymore!"

"I don't believe I could've *lived* with him after that!" Aunt Maxine said.

"I don't believe I could live with anybody that (laughing) has *birds* for friends!"

"It's hard enough when drinking buddies show up!"

"Well, *I* couldn't live with anybody that prayed to the devil! That's *horrible* to think about! Ain't it!" Maxine insisted.

"He don't do that anymore. He told me that he wished he never had fooled with it!"

"Yeah."

"That's like those people raising people from the dead .. You hear of that? They tell me that's going on pretty strong in California! I heard it on TV here the other day!"

"Let's just hope they're making the right choices."

"Who'd be the right choices?"

"It'd be awful to raise somebody from the dead and find out they were boring and you didn't like them after going to all that trouble!"

"People don't think of the *devil* being powerful enough to raise somebody from the dead," Curtis refused to lose his leeway.

"You think the *Lord's* raising 'em up, Curtis? You think the *Lord's* raising them from the dead?"

"Well, he *can.* He *is*! But he's not raising them like the *devil* is!"

"What town were we talking about where you said, Where did all those people come from?"

"They raised them from the dead?"

"New York?"

"In New York I always feel like they've just got people stacked on top of each other."

Idn't there an awful lot of traffic in New York?"

"Yeah."

"I'd like to *see* that town but I wouldn't want...."

"Jessie, you believe in that kind of stuff? Like that raising the dead and all that?"

"Naw. Do *you?*"

"I don't *believe* it! I *know* it's a fact!"

YOU FEEL LIKE ...

"You feel like driving, Mama? You want to drive?"

"Don't make any difference, honey. Whatever you want to do."

"Put your stuff in the back of the car."

"She's been doing all the driving."

"What you got your hairnet on for?" Maxine asked Mae.

"That wind's just whipping around out there. The minute I get over here ... between the wind and the moisture my hair just goes like a bush heap."

"I think it looks real pretty."

"I washed it and put it up over at Ethel's."

"Tomorrow's my day to get it done."

"It looks real nice."

"I'm sure proud of those peas, but I feel bad taking your first...."

"Don't feel bad cause I've had ... Pearl brought us ..."

"Peter said they could of picked a bushel in five minutes ..."

" ... and canned up a bunch ..."

"I wish I'd of known they was over there. I'd of got them to take some paper bags. I'd of took some home and put them in the deep freeze. But these'll make two or three good messes, won't they?"

"Those? I don't know."

"Jessie's proud of that stalk of cotton. As soon as she gets to the California border they'll take it away from her."

"She could put it in her suitcase."

"If I was her I'd put it in a plastic bag and shove it under the car seat."

"Jessie, you better put that stalk of cotton in a plastic bag and stick it under your car seat."

"I just put it in the trunk ..."

"Naw, I mean for when you cross the California border. They'll take it away from you."

'They'll have to fight me for it. That's valuable property with cotton going at three hundred a bale!'

Settling in.

I slammed the door with my left hand and leaned forward to look through the windshield.

Mama arched her back to pull her skirt straight ... then settled, smiled brightly through the glass.

So did I.

We pulled out of the driveway, waved into the vague air at them, still standing there, manipulated a few streets and turned onto the highway, going West.

FRENCHY
AND
CUBAN PETE

FRENCHY AND CUBAN PETE

In I947 Albuquerque got its first stripper club. That was a good year for Albuquerque. The first Jewish Delicatessen opened on Central Avenue right downtown. And a lot of a very different kind of person started going to the University of New Mexico on the G.I. Bill.

The G.I. Bill changed the look of Joe College U.N.M. drastically. A large part of the influx, particularly in the painting department, were Jews from New York. That look blew me over. Every time I saw somebody looking great it turned out later that he or she was a Jew. For awhile I got worried about it. That all my friends were Jews. Then I thought what the hell go along with it.

I sat through evening after evening of conversation so abstract that the only thing clear was that they all knew what they were talking about. And it was fascinating. You have to realize that the talk I had been understanding wasn't worth the effort. A presumptuous snob at seventeen is what I was, out of desperation. What these people were talking about involved rampant energy, arms waving, real anger for intellectual reasons and a dynamic. They were so knowledgeable. One of them who wanted to make love to me, but we never did, gave me a Modern Library copy of Sons and Lovers for my birthday.

I mean I was getting so much sustenance that not being able to follow the mesh of the reasoning and not recognizing the names of the heroes was trivial; hardly to be thought of. And there were consistent small bonuses like eating my first hot pastrami on rye.

Anyway, to return to the history of that city, that was then a growing town, that's supposed to have been the first year the Mafia made their move in on the overall action. It was a stripper club west of town out Central heading for the desert.

The building was a junker; cement block with patterns.

Inside, the room was a huge barn-like square, with a dance floor orchestra section intruding off one wall so the tables were jammed into the remaining three sides.

Every couple of hours there would be a floor show. The exotic dancer was naked on her left side with a little pasty on her nipple and a g-string. Her right side was dressed up like a red and black devil. She was split right down the center and the act was watching the right side get it on with the left side. A lot of the time it really looked like two people, the right side being aggressive, the left side fighting it off, but being progressively overcome, even attracted. Hitting the floor at the same time and working up to a grand climax with all the lights going black to give her/it a chance to get up and walk away. Save the image from a tawdry exit.

And then Cuban Pete and Frenchy would come on for a comic turn.

Cuban Pete was a short fat Greek with a mess of black curls and an accent. He wore a straw hat and a blouse with huge ruffled sleeves. The straw hat worked as a hand prop. He'd take it off with a flourish, give it a shimmy-shake at the end of his arm to make a point, and to enter, and to exit. Frenchy was six feet tall with a high bleached pompadour and spike heels, and almost nothing else. She was a walking example of what was legally allowed. She would station herself like so many pounds on the hoof in front of the band microphone as if she meant to sing. Thank God she never did. Cuban Pete would have a hand mike with yards of cable to let him meander among the tables while they went through their act.

They were really rotten.

The jokes were so bad that the only way you knew when one was over was the band would go *Ta-Taaaa!* Then we'd all break up. *Ta-Taaaa!* was the real punch line. It let you see where you would have laughed if it had been funny.

One of their routines was Cuban Pete would be out among the clientele yelling back, "Hey Frenchy! How you like that movie I take you to last night?" "Oh!" she'd say, her nose like a trumpet, "Clark Gable was wonderful!"

"How you like that?" Cuban Pete would ask us. "I say how you like that movie I take you to last night and she says Clark Gable was wonderful!" He would try again. "Hey Frenchy, how you like that movie I take you to last night?"

"Oh!" she'd answer, "Clark Gable was wonderful!"

"How you like that?" throwing his arms wide in mock despair so the ruffles would ripple.

"I want to ask you just one thing."

"What you say?"

"I want to ask you just one thing."

"She wants to ask me something. O.K. Frenchy. What you want to know?"

"I want to know if you're jealous of Clark Gable?"

"How you like that! I ask her how she like the movie and she wants to know am I jealous of Clark Gable!"

A long pause to build suspense, then—

"You gab-dam right I am!"

Ta-Taaaa!

There was another routine that Frenchy walked or rather marched through with two other women. The orchestra played a rousing medley of *Over There* and *I'm a Yankee Doodle Dandy* and such like songs, and Frenchy would come marching onto center dance floor with a Marine's hat on. The other women represented the Army and the Navy. All three of them wore red satin brassieres and very short blue and white striped skirts. They marched into a triangle with Frenchy out front, all of them keeping a time-step, marching in place. Then the two girls in back marched toward each other and wheeled in unison toward the bandstand where they came by an enormous American flag which they opened out to make a backdrop for Frenchy. They marched around her wrapping her in the flag. The highlight was when all the lights went out and the flag and costumes glowed in the dark.

Ta-Taaaa!

I did have a lover at that time. He was studying acting. I was studying painting. He would talk to me like two artists talking together.

He was also really tender. I had had an abortion three months before and I was basically scared about making love. I also had the Texas Baptist blues riding hard on me ... down the drain ... seventeen and used up ... etc.

It wasn't the idea of getting pregnant that scared me, though that was certainly there. It was more like feeling raw and misused in my spirit and my body, and he helped me over that. It was a real piece of luck for me that somebody that decent and good-hearted happened along just then.

He used to make toasted cheese sandwiches with apple jelly spread on the top for us to eat in bed, talking.

Anyway, sometime along in there I started knowing the vocabulary and hearing the repetitions and one night at two in the morning some type, in the self-righteous tones we all know to our sorrow, said "You've got to qualify your terms," and I started crying and couldn't stop.

For a month or so I couldn't stand groups of people but then I gradually regained my perspective.

You know the brainwash goes that loss of innocence is a one-timer and thereafter you're left sadder and wiser. But in my experience it's cyclical; the place like the San Andreas Fault where your life makes a necessary dimensional shift.

And it's not such a loss, more often it's a trade.

And the pain of it is the least interesting thing about it.

THE BOYFRIEND

I telephoned my mother on Christmas Day and she started right in telling me about her new boyfriend.

"He's another one of them damned Leos! All he wants to do every three or four in the afternoon is get in his old pick-up and tear around town!"

She said she met him when she went with Ed and Ella Lawney to their ranch for the weekend.

"Ella told me, 'You just watch. He's going to be over here just as soon as he sees our smoke rising.' They'd been filling him up with stories about me. We got there around suppertime and sure enough he was there inside of ten minutes. We all talked for half the night. We talked all through supper until four in the morning. I haven't talked like that in years."

I remembered the Lawneys well.

They were neighbours of ours when I was in high school. Ed Lawney drove a Singer like it was a sports car and wore dacron slacks. He was strong on the surreptitious eye. Ella was jolly and very short and very fat. Having a husband with a taste for flashy style must have created domestic problems.

"He's after me all the time to lose weight," she said.

Every day she would come to my mother's house and ride the Exercycle in the living room while she watched her favourite soap opera. For half an hour Monday through Friday the machine would move her through bicycling motions. The electric motor raised and lowered the handlebars like a rowing machine at the same time it turned the pedals around and around. The top half of her body shuttled back and forth, hands holding tight, while her knees pumped up and down.

The machine had two speeds. Every morning Mrs. Lawney pedalled and shuttled at slow speed for twenty-five minutes, then went to top speed for five, a stationary flying finish. She talked non-stop, her eyes on the television image.

"Lots of men take second jobs. Ed could easily work weekends, but no, he thinks it's beneath him!" Mr. Lawney was the principal of a high school on the other side of town.

They had two children, a tall boy of eleven and a girl, four. The little girl was always lost in her clothes with the crotch of her underpants hanging to her knees. Mrs. Lawney made a point of buying children's clothes large enough to be worn-out instead of out-grown.

"Eddy wore his training pants until he was nine years old," she would say.

"He says what if some of the parents came in and found him there selling shoes," knees pumping up and down. "It would *embarrass* him. He doesn't give any thought to me. I can work at two jobs alright. I do my housework and then I type term papers. *That's* not beneath him."

And then she said, "He's worse since he had his head operation. Now I guess I'll *never* be able to get him to take a second job."

"Head operation?" I asked.

"They found a cancer on Ed's head," my mother explained.

"He's so stubborn now. Since his head operation if he doesn't want to do something he just won't even talk about it. I say, 'Let's at least *talk* about it. Maybe we can work something out if we just *talk* about it.' But he won't even *talk* about it. And his temper's just terrible. When he gets mad he'll just yell as loud as he can. He just stands and screams at me. I get so nervous that the only thing that can calm me down is I go in the kitchen and I just eat, and eat, and eat," a dreamy expression on her face, cycling along her private highway.

Now it's years later and in the interim there's been a success story and a happy ending, the cancer a thing of the past, a ranch for the weekends. The kids must have grown into their clothes and worm them out by now. It all worked according to plan.

"What did you talk about?" I asked.

"He said 'I like a woman that's honest,' and I said, 'Well, I can give you that on a platter.' Then he said, 'And what I *don't* like is a woman that goes after a man for what he's got,' and I said 'You don't have a thing that I want.'

"I just told him, 'I've got a monthly income that's as much as I'll ever need and a house that'll be paid off in six months and a three-year-old Buick that's in brand-new condition with only twenty thousand miles on it. Now just exactly what do you think you've got that I want?' And when he went to open his mouth I said, 'Just shut up. I don't want to hear about it.' Ed and Ella just hooted. I knew he was getting set to talk a lot of sexy stuff."

I used to think a time would come when my body would turn me loose. Then last summer my mother and my Aunt Eunice came to California for a visit and got into telling stories on their friends.

"Well, you know how boy crazy Thelma Duvvelton is," my mother said, "She gets a facial and her hair fixed every week and goes to those old senior citizen dances and falls in love with anybody that'll look at her. She was even sillier than that when she decided to get married again. She went all the way to Alaska and didn't come back with a man."

Both of them were breaking up with laughter over the stories.

One woman, when her husband died, wrote off to a man she had met and liked fifteen years earlier. He wrote back and they decided to get married. He wrote her that he was going to buy her a new car and drive it across country for her wedding present. She told all her friends about how she was getting a new Buick and she got a permanent and went girlish, waiting for him. But when he drove up it was a Chevrolet and she got so mad that she just sent him back.

"He knows I'm not interested in jumping into bed with him. The other night he was here and he said, 'Honey, I've just got to leave. You drive me crazy.'"

I can see her at the other end of the line, her head lifted at an angle, a tone of pride and humour in her voice.

"Well Mama," I asked, teasing her, "Are you sure you want to let yourself in for all that trouble?"

She went flat serious. "You ought to see him. He's just as cute as he can be."

A SPECIAL CONDITION

A few days ago driving over the mountain to do chores in Mill Valley Tom Clark said, "When I came back from the hospital it took me just two or three days to realize that I had to get well fast or get sicker." He was talking about walking around shrouded in a "special condition."

"Nobody could see me without going into the state of my health. It was really a drag, you know. It was really dull."

What we had been talking about was Alec and Mary and how you can't see Alec without ... every time you see Alec, even if he's laughing, you know he's miserable. If he's laughing you laugh with him, not to break his attempt at happiness. You're prepared to understand whatever he does. Special Condition Wipeout.

Mary talks more about it and invites a more nuanced conversation, and that's the tone of where *she's* at, and where *you're* at is as if you were knowledgeable, as if you knew Life and could tell her something significant. It's even as if she's asking you to.

With either of them you can talk about anything at all, houses, children, intentions; anything can be as if it were the topic.

Go through all of it. Do it all, everything you can think of.

All that grappling and swaying and the hands holding onto whatever comes in grasp like those comedies where the lights go off and everyone is yelling, "I've got him! I've got him!" And when you look, all that energy disposed into the void, all those confusions paid dues on, and the rewards however fractured and slight now to be tabulated; what have you got but yourself again.

We make a mystique of it, therefore, having it to provide for. We call it some kind of seeking for self-knowledge. We speak of "continuing to grow," as if we'd meant all along that circuitous route to return to ourselves at the end. Not even a return; we say "Ah, now I see I stayed here all along but how the vista did open."

How we variously look for love, all of us, not actively even, rather, we stay prone for its happening. Think of all the religious nuts who waited and wait for God's touch as the "blessing" they can propose forward of themselves in time. That is, their philosophy provides for it. Who better, for them, than God. He sees the sparrow fall.

Longing to have somewhere some thing registering more than its own encapsulation, wanting more than ourselves.

Wanting the abundance we grow given someone else's hands. And we do it too, for the other. We watch the other become substantial. We are each other's proof.

Then, when love "dies," all that flurry occurs, because how can we let it go quietly, what was so significant, without marking its going down.

I DREAMED LAST NIGHT

I dreamed last night that I was living in an amalgam of places I've known well.

The house was at the end of a street, across the street from the Wades who used to live in Placitas. In my dream there was a sign on their house that said "WE'VE TRIED PEACE. NOW LET'S TRY WAR!" Mrs. Wade had asked me earlier in the day if I had noticed the sign. She didn't think it was getting enough attention. It was a reversal as: Peace is what we've called War.

I remembered when I saw the sign that she'd asked if I'd seen it.

I went for a walk, turning right to go into the bigger collection of houses and I was thinking how *happy* I was, really feeling it, to have got it all together at last. Off to my right and about three blocks over would be the Foreshore in Belize with small sailing boats moored and rocking. There's been an improvement. No more buzzards. When they changed from direct current to alternating current all the buzzards were electrocuted during the next rainy season. They'd settle on a wire and rest back, their wet tail feathers would touch the other line and ZAZ.

And *really* the house I was living in, last night, was the house in Bolinas. I do feel closer here than anywhere else to the way I felt in Belize. It saved my life. The ocean is nearby and it's easy to be with people you care for. It's a kind of feeling open and in company in moist air and sunshine.

But the house *looked* more like the house we lived in in Placitas. It was down on the highway with a tin roof, and cramped. I registered some changes we'd made in it. The front porch was fancier and there was a garden with a California feeling to it.

It's hard not being able to pull it together. To drop off those bits of ghost into your history so that even as you think of those places the thought includes yourself, still there in your memory.

Sometimes those memories bounce out at you as if they had got powerful enough to conjure *you* up instead of the other way around.

But *really* you're here, in *real* time. A good thing, too. You can count off one-arm-one-arm-one-leg-one-leg. At least I never left any pieces of myself that stayed there, caught in the story. Unless you count what goes down in time, that we grow older and change, that way. And, of course, there's "I left my heart in San Francisco." And I did leave my tonsils in Texas. And there is a kind of romance about where we left our various innocences. But that was more often than not a trade.

In my dream I was very practical. The cat started having kittens and I got a big bucket of water to drop them into. That's the easiest way, supposedly, to be rid of new kittens. You just reach over and drop them in, never looking. And later you empty the pan into a stand of weeds. If you're tidy you can pick the bodies up then and put them in the garbage in a baggy.

Actually, it wasn't a bucket it was a large pan I boil vegetables in. I regretted not having something more neutral, anticipating in advance that I would remember the kittens when I used it.

The children were excited about the kittens and I hid the pan of water. They weren't to know. A harsh fact. It would all have been easier if they hadn't been home at that particular moment. But maybe I could do it the next day and say they had all died naturally, some disease.

In fact she only had three kittens and I was won over, abandoned my dream murder, thinking: In Bolinas we can easily get rid of three kittens; meaning give them away.

There was one more thing in addition to the kittens, the house, the sign, and the walk that let me have the experience of all my places being one and me in it. There was a really lewd baby boy someone brought by, who stared into my eyes and began to grow, meaning to get big enough to make it right off. I was holding him and in no time he was a child, then too big to hold, but only up to my waist when I put him on the floor. Continuing to grow, looking up into my face.

That's all I remember of that part. There isn't even a confused image of anything further happening. The growth and the intention seemed to be the point of it.

I OWE YOU ONE

Before it gets lost into the void I want to tell about a letter that got written to the Denver Post years ago. It could have been as long ago as 1947 or 1948.

It was apparently written in answer to a letter that had been written earlier and, judging by this letter, the earlier one seems to have been written by a woman who was complaining that when her husband got drunk he'd knock her around.

The woman who wrote the letter I read said that she had had the same problem.

She said she only weighed about a hundred pounds and her husband weighed close to two hundred pounds. She said for years he'd go out on Friday night and Saturday night and get drunk and then he'd come home and beat her up, then he'd fall asleep on the bed with his clothes on.

There came a night when he beat her up and when he had stopped she said, "I owe you one."

When he fell asleep she went outside and brought in a piece of two by four and she started pounding on him with it.

Of course, he woke up right away, and he beat her up again. And she said, "I owe you one."

She said that in no time at all she had him afraid to go to sleep. Then he began to see that it was O.K. to go to sleep if he hadn't beaten her up. So he stopped.

Considering the number of years it had gone on the stopping was really quick.

She said she hoped that her own solution would encourage the other woman to look for a solution because it was not hopeless.

The two principles involved were consistency and perseverance.

FREE STATE OF WINSTON

To start off with I was raised up in a family of nine. I was the *middle* one. That's a bad place to be Boy I tell you! I had two brothers'n two sisters oldern me and two brothers'n two sisters youngern me. I was in a fight with *somebody* ever day of my life.

I was *raised* in North Alabama in Winston County which is known as the FREE STATE OF WINSTON. When the South seeceded from the Nawth, Winston County seeceded from the South! So that whole *Wah*, anybody tawkin about *that Wah*, well, *we* didn't have no part of that wah. *We* seeceded from the South!

There's a big ol *cave* up there, justa little opnin about the size of *that*, well, acourse they sent *reecruiters* up there to git'm. They just shot 'em ever time they showed in that opnin. They couldn't reecruit em; they couldn't take em. They just *fired.*

Man there called Peglag Pike. Lost a lag y'know'n had a peg on. You ever seen a peglag? Ol'Peglag he had a place out of town about five miles, made *whiskey* there'n used to come in to town to sell it. Well, he come in to town one day, a case of whiskey on him, met the Sheriff. Sheriff went to kiddin him, said "Peg, you got a license to sell that stuff?" He was just teasin him. Peg said, "Yeah, I got a license. You wont to *see* it?" Sheriff said, "Sure, I'd like to see that." Ol'Peglag reached in under his coat, hauled out a forty-five with a barrel that long, said, "You wont me to read it for you?" Sheriff said, "Naw, just wonted to make sure you was legal."

Well, two boys took to sneakin into Peglag's still and drinkin his whiskey when he wadn't there. He left a note for them said, "DON'T DRINK THIS WHISKEY. IT WILL KILL YOU." Well, they went on partyin there whenever they saw him head into town. So he left one day'n circled back around'n shot'm both down. One of them was sixteen and one of them was seventeen. So then they just didn't have any choice. Sheriff took a posse up'n killed him.

One of the women had just started using rouge and lipstick. Of course everybody in town, they just thought, well, all the *women* in town just thought she was the *worst* in the world! She'd come into town all painted up and sure enough the menfolk sorta shined up to her.

Well, the women wouldn't stand still for it. They just *had* to go do somethin' about that. That was back in Kew Klux days. So finely the men just had to give in for some peace. They all put their sheets on, loaded up in an old Model-T Ford and went out on a clear bright moonlight night. They went up onto the porch and knocked on the door. Told her husband they wanted in. Well, he didn't mess around. He just took a double-barrel shotgun and let it off right through the door. Kilt the lawyer, wounded the doctor, god knows how many more. All the rest of them lit out straight back to town. Left the car and all.

They had to send somebody out there the next day to get a list of the dead and wounded.

OLD SECURITY

When Sarah started college I started getting mail from insurance companies addressed to "Parents of Sarah Creeley." They were giving me options on Sarah's potential demise as if being a freshman meant life-and-death strikes again, the biggest graph of all.

Ten thousand dollars was the sum most often mentioned. Some kind of mystic choice masquerading as ration -al. Like a number that stands for infinity.

Old Security Life in Milwaukee, Wisconsin enclosed a reply envelope addressed to their "Youth Marketing Division." Their letter started "ACT NOW!"

True enough. Youth flies into the past even as we speak.

The letter said, "Dear Parents: The dollar today does not buy what it bought yesterday."

It's like the math game section in Scientific American.

"The dollar today does not buy what it bought yesterday. However, our Life Insurance Policy is a product that yesterday's dollar can still buy."

That's for those of us who didn't spend yesterday's dollar the day before yesterday.

Under the heading of "Provisions" their ten thousand dollar policy is called *Term* Life Insurance up to the age of twenty-five. After the age of twenty-five it's called *Permanent* Life Insurance. The main difference there is that *Term* costs you $24 a year but *Permanent* costs you $130. I think that's only fair. You get what you pay for. Apropos Life, *Permanent* has it all over *Term*.

"Even in an inflationary environment true values exist," is the way they put it.

Don't make the mistake of thinking that kind of distinction doesn't count. Language can kill you.

There was a linguist named Whorf who worked for Insurance Companies for awhile. His specialty was finding out where accidents were caused by language. For instance, he was called in on one job where a factory was having recurrent explosions.

It seems that when the workers took breaks and smoked cigarettes out in the factory yard they all went to the left side of the yard. The right side was stacked with drums of industrial oil and there was a big sign that said "FULL." The workers were smart enough to not light up around all that oil. So they went to the other side where used drums were stacked under a big sign that said "EMPTY." The fact being the obvious one that the empties were full of gaseous vapours just waiting for a match.

Getting back to Old Security's *Facts to Consider:* "The proposed insured's future is Now!" Which sounds somehow like "yesterday's dollar" turned inside out. The reason "Now" is so important is that Old Security is making life insurance "available to the proposed insured at an age when most can qualify." I guess that's a delicate way of saying that they're as far from dying as they'll ever be.

Those subliminal double plays are endless. One night Sarah and I were in the kitchen more or less watching a medical show on T.V. while I pasted up a collage on the kitchen table and she put together a circular jig-saw puzzle on a foldout card table.

The plot ran like this:

A young woman who is going to be married goes to a surgeon to have a mole removed because Bo deserves the best and when he gets her that's what he's going to get. The young woman's mother, a nervous, fashionable lady, comes with her because she and the surgeon are old friends and she wants him to remove the mole because Cissy deserves the best ... etc. Cissy also needs the standard blood test and a general physical. During all that messing around the surgeon finds a lump in Cissy's breast which is cut into after a lot of by-play and it's malignant.

The big question at this point is how is Bo going to take

to a one-breasted bride.

And he takes it badly. He goes out to walk around the block and think about it. Cissy is pondering keeping her breast by having massive X-Ray treatments. If she does it that way she runs a much higher risk of dying. They make it look like death is desirable alongside being sent back to the store.

"Have you ever seen *one* T.V. show where a *man* facing life and death got hooked on a cosmetic issue?" I ask Sarah.

"What do you mean 'cosmetic'?"

"Where the question of saving his looks was as important as saving his life."

"No, I never have," she said and got on with her jigsaw.

Bo decides to go with the loss and the plot moves into Phase Two.

Mama says she'll only feel secure if her old friend does the knife work.

Enter a young surgeon who has done a heart transplant on the old surgeon.

"Your heart won't stand it," he says. "I won't let you take the risk."

It all starts to function like a variation on that nursery rhyme where the old woman is trying to get her pig over the stile.

The mother is persuaded to use somebody else.

The operation is successful.

Cissy is provided with a duplicate in rubber.

The happy ending is the young surgeon and the old surgeon walking into the sunset down a hospital corridor, both hearts beating a regulation number of beats per minute.

"Huh!" I grunt. "They just mean to ignore the percentages."

"You mean all those heart transplant people have died?" Sarah asked, looking shocked.

"Honey," says I, "It's even worse than that. All the people who don't have heart transplants die too."

But back to Old Security. They have a P.S. on their letter about "the advantages of independent decision, without pressure, made in private."

Well, I'll buy that.

TWICE

ONE:

Barry Hall told me that when they were living in Nassau there was a ship on the nearby ocean filled with a cargo of tapioca that got a fire down deep in the hold. They played water onto it but it kept smouldering, turning the water into steam.

When tapioca cooks it expands to eight times its uncooked size.

A time came when the crew abandoned ship and sat in little boats watching the tapioca pour out of all the ship's openings. Finally the ship exploded.

Barry said that for days afterwards there were gummy wads of half-cooked tapioca washing up on the beaches.

TWO:

A son who was a fisherman and had been going out in his father's boat finally saved enough money for a boat of his own.

The first time he went out with the fleet as his own man they had a fine turn of luck and came onto a massive school of fish. Everybody hauled fish in as hard and fast as they could. The son filled his hold and began to fill the cabins. It was a miracle.

The father radioed that he had a load and was returning home. The son said he thought to stay awhile longer.

The son was piling fish onto the decks.

Part way home the father got a radio message from his son, "You'd better get our position. We're going down."

LITTLE ERNIE

When we came back to New Mexico after the first couple of years in Buffalo our neighbours across the arroyo asked me, "Well, how's about your famous cousin?"

"Who's that?" I said.

"Don't you know about Ernie?"

I have a cousin named after his father so he's always been Little Ernie to me. He was always a bright sharp kid.

For instance, he went along with me and a boyfriend of mine for a drive into the foothills once and while we meandered and did a little mild necking Little Ernie went around picking up tumbleweeds. I just figured he was hard up for something to do.

"I could sell these for Christmas," he said.

It was early November but the sun was bright and clear the way it always is in New Mexico. Even when it's raining the sun shines. It was pretty much of an abstraction, a thirteen-year-old kid talking about selling tumbleweeds in a place where anybody can pick up their own. And getting into Christmas while he's sweating because the sun's so hot.

He filled the trunk and the back seat of the car with tumbleweeds to take home. He went back with other people who had cars to get more. When he had as many as he wanted he spray-painted them gold or silver and hung a few little Christmas balls on them and sure enough, people bought them.

"It was in the newspapers! Didn't you read about it?"

It seems Little Ernie (except this was years later and he's taller than his dad, has been for some time but nobody shifted the names around) had gone into a military airfield somewhere and there was a jet fighter plane warming up on the airstrip. And Little Ernie climbed into it and took off.

He had never flown a plane before.

They got him on the radio and asked him what he had on his mind. He said he thought he'd go to Cuba. They sent two other jet fighters up after him and told him to turn around before they had to shoot him down. When they had explained to him how to turn around he did.

Then they told him how to land and he did that too. Just like a forties movie except that it was a jet.

They questioned him for awhile. He said he was an indigent insurance adjuster who wanted to start a new life.

This all happened before the hijackings or he'd have got a different treatment. As it was they just turned him loose and he went home.

Our neighbours across the arroyo couldn't believe that we hadn't heard about it in New York. It certainly made the headlines in Albuquerque. He was better than a local hero.

That whole family tended to be a little spectacular. Big Ernie looked like Anthony Quinn and had two hobbies. He always went on the yearly rattlesnake roundup in southern New Mexico, and he hooked pictorial rugs to hang on the walls.

The oldest boy, Sonny, saved up when he was about seventeen and bought a big-sized Harley-Davidson motorcycle. His first trip out on it he headed up into the Jemez mountains to visit his girlfriend.

According to his friends who were following in a pick-up he never dropped below seventy-five. And there were cross winds in gusts of up to 40 mph.

The obvious thing happened. He hit some gravel along the road and got slung high into the air and sideways into a cement culvert. The motorcycle smashed into a million pieces, but Sonny went through the only slit in the cement and got off with a broken leg.

They took him to a doctor who put a pin in it.

A week later deer season opened and Sonny went deer hunting in the Sandias. He slipped and rolled down a slope and bent the pin. He fired his rifle so his friends could find him. They took him back to the doctor who took that pin out and put another one in and a couple of days later Sonny got a deer.

When Big Ernie fell in love with a red-headed woman and took off, Little Ernie's mother and sister got their house declared off-limits it was so wide open. It was a kind of expression of grief on Little Ernie's mother's part.

The whole family was headstrong but Little Ernie took the prize.

BATHROOM / ANIMAL / CASTRATION STORY

This is a bathroom / animal / castration story.

Diana and Drummond Hadley have a wildcat that was given to them by the guy that runs the Desert Museum in Tucson.

It stands maybe two feet high and is really substantial if you're used to looking at housecats.

It plays. If you pull a wad of paper on a string it plays. A little languidly but it's playing.

And the wildcat, as it plays, keeps its claws sheathed. And you get a little breathless from not really breathing normally and you get exhilarated with relief because every time the wildcat could jump you he doesn't. He just keeps batting the paper wads, almost politely, with his paws like mittens.

But when you look into his eyes you don't get further than the surface. He looks at you totally blank. No recognition of you, your organism, your species, nothing. When you look that creature in the eyes it's like there's no earthly reason for the two of you to be in the same room. It feels like you've taken off your shoes and socks and gone for a walk on a glacier.

When I went to the bathroom I realized the wildcat was as fast as it was supposed to be. I opened the door and the wildcat rushed to the toilet bowl before me.

Well, O.K.

I decided between two evils.

I decided not to put the creature out. It was a lazy choice.

The cover was closed and as I reached to open it I saw that the wildcat was getting compulsive. It was pacing and jumping and generally acting nutty with all its attention focused on the toilet bowl. It was waiting for me to open the lid for some reason of its own.

I realized that there was going to be a skirmish with a winner and a loser. I knew which one I wanted to be.

I stood between the wildcat and the toilet seat. I blocked its every move while I did the necessary clothing stuff. I reached back of me and raised the lid keeping my eyes on the wildcat all the time. He went frantic. He rushed back and forth in front of me, trying to get past me, trying to look through me.

I won.

After I was seated he went really cool and uninterested. Who needs it?

I stood up, flushed the toilet and wasn't vigilant. It seemed like there was no need to be.

The wildcat hit the toilet. He pounced his two front paws into the bowl after the disappearing water. Water flew to the ceiling. He pounced over and over. Water was spewing up onto the walls, the ceiling. I got soaked getting the lid closed.

He dug the game was over.

We walked out of the bathroom together.

"Why does your wildcat jump at the water?" I asked Diana.

"Oh yes," she answered, laughing, "Men get really nervous."

DOLORES

Bob came home from going downtown in a rage, but keeping it rational all the way home, not screaming at the people in the streets, holding it in like a kid can fall and scrape its knee and run two or three blocks to get to mama before its voice busts out in a fresh bawl. Holding the knee in time to let it go where it counts.

"I was on the elevator in the bank building and I met," he named somebody whose name I used to know but I'll never remember it again, Dick let's say for a tool to tell the story with.

"He was a friend of yours? You went to the University at the same time?"

That was true. I didn't remember much about him except that he was a wild neurotic.

This was nearly ten years later and I couldn't clearly remember what he looked like. All I remember about him is that when he got drunk at parties he used to chase his girl friend around with dangerous weapons. Anything he could get his hands on that was sharp.

Dick was prized for his high-strung bull-shit behaviour. It was like Art. We all felt pleased that we had to accommodate it. It was a forerunner of things to come. We were all going to be great painters and writers and were eighteen up to mid-twenties. Neurosis was our bread and butter. It was as close as we could get. It's true some of those people still keep on but nobody made it big.

This particular party I'm thinking of is notable in my mind for two things: the host made it with four or five girls in the bathroom, one at a time, and somebody turned off all the lights as a way to keep Dick from mutilating his girl friend Dolores with a beer-can opener. Some people grabbed him in the dark, the lights were turned back on and they kept him in the kitchen and talked him into being calmer while Dolores stayed out of the way in the other room.

He only got really eccentric when he got really drunk. We were all intent on getting drunk. A lot of the conversation would be about who was in the bathroom throwing up and a lot of the conversation was about who was fucking who in the bathroom. The bathroom got a lot of play.

The next day I remember talking to two guys who were at the party. One was saying with admiration, "He got five girls into the john," and I say "five?" and they suddenly both look worried and look at me, the eighteen-year-old with a big mouth who tells everybody everything, and one of them says "Don't talk about it. It would really upset Amy." So I said "I won't," and I didn't until now.

"Yeah," I agreed to Bob's question. "He was a nut. He used to chase his girl friend with knives and once he took off all his clothes and stood on a table and yelled that he wanted love and affection and he didn't care if it was a girl or a boy."

That was the only other thing I remembered about him. We were all charmed by that, too. The combination of him stripping and his proposal of a "girl or boy" was more than anybody else could get to.

I don't remember what his painting was like but we all felt that his temperament was exceptional.

"That's the story!" Bob yelled. "That's the story that you told that caused his wife to kill herself!"

It's true his wife killed herself, and it was a shame. She had been really avid to go to school. She worked a part-time job for her tuition and books and supplies, and she waited tables in the cafeteria for her meals. She was pretty tough. And her painting showed a lot of work.

They got married around the time I did.

I left the States, lived in four other countries for six years, had two children, fell in and out of love, learned bits and pieces of other languages and forgot them, and returned to where I'd started for a divorce.

Dick and Dolores were still married. I saw them at

somebody's house. He was working as a salesman. She was acting like a housewife. They had a couple of children. And a year after that I heard she'd killed herself.

Meanwhile, I got a job to support me and my kids and two years after my return I met Bob who, now, a year and one child later is saying to me, "When you were in school together you told somebody that he took his clothes off and yelled that he wanted a boy or a girl and his wife killed herself at the implications."

"It was a party," I said to defend myself, "There were thirty or forty people there. I didn't have to tell anybody. She heard him yell it, too."

But it seems likely I told it to somebody. I loved to be living an interesting life.

Did somebody lay it on her so she couldn't stand the telling, so it was harder than that it had happened, and she mulled it over for seven years, living with him all the time and having two children as a side interest and then ...

I couldn't believe it. I don't believe it now.

I know how, in a lousy marriage, something can become the focus for your misery and it looks more like that.

I liked her and it somehow seemed that I'd added to her problem. I wish he hadn't turned into a salesman and she hadn't turned into a housewife after all those early guts.

Why didn't they go ahead for the splendid and make it come true?

And I realized that I couldn't defend myself in this conversation. I didn't know if I was right or wrong.

Bob was really bugged. This guy had waylaid him in an elevator and told him the tragic history he didn't want to hear, poured poison in his ear and sealed it off, and here he was home. Like a message from Garcia.

"It seems likely I told somebody that story because that's almost the only thing I remember about him," I said. "But I don't think she'd hold onto it for seven years before she killed herself over it."

"Seven years?" Bob was dumbfounded.

Dick had made it sound like she heard the story and killed herself straight off. And my telling Bob the story as my identification of that person kept it all that immediate.

So that held in time too. It was a true coincidence. Everything converging to make this moment be a weird abstraction of who said what, caught in time.

"What did he look like?" I asked.

"Oh ... he was in a suit and a salesman's hat. He's married again."

It was like talking about somebody we knew in common.

BELLAGIO

There is a place in Italy, a small town at the side of Lake Como with white buildings and curved red tile roofs; the doors and windows are deepset so that at certain angles they are black shapes in the white.

In some places the streets are so narrow that persons walking must press flat against the walls to let a car pass. In these streets unless it is high noon there is a black shade and driving along them there is a consistent flicker of the cross streets that extend like tunnels to the lake. At the far end of the cross streets Lake Como hangs half-way up the sides, a sheet of brilliant blue, suspended in perspective, and above it the paler blue of the sky.

This place figures in history. George Sand and Chopin came here, and Liszt with his lady love. Stendhal was a visitor as he could be. And much earlier, high up the mountain, in the very villa we are en route to there is a cliffside where Michelangelo loved to sketch.

The car rises out of the maze of Bellagio to a higher edge of the town climbing the wedge of a hill into sunlight. It is a peninsula. All the edges to be seen from this higher centre touch water. And even from this higher vantage point there is a sense that the lake tilts, its farthest line reaching up.

The history of this place is an ambience of feeling. What caused those others to come here catches at oneself. I feel possessed by the charm of it. This is a charming place.

PITCHES AND CATCHES

There's a gap in the greater American consciousness about the lowdownest level of the magazine business, and I'm going to feed a little into it out of my own true-life experience.

I answered an ad when I was seventeen that invited young women to travel in a chaperoned group and earn while you learn. For me the real hook was New Orleans. They were en route to New Orleans, learning and earning.

I've always wanted to see New Orleans (and I still haven't. This isn't a story with a reasonable progression and an appropriate ending. It's just one more instance of oh, see what fits our foolish hopes.)

I telephoned and made an appointment to be interviewed at the Kiva Motel on Central Avenue. I got the job.

I can't imagine what might have disqualified me.

The job was selling magazine subscriptions door-to-door. That was how you earned and the learning had to do with the underlying principles of salesmanship. Within that simple and usual projection there were nuances so abstract that they could only be the outcome of bureaucratic thought; an inherent growth principle of crummy thinking.

For instance, one word you never say if you're a magazine salesman is "magazine." Pros peddle "Books."

When the lady of the house, that entrenched functionary, opens the door and looks at you and says "I don't want any *magazines*" what you really start to work on is that piece of semantics.

We were handling Better Homes and Gardens *books*, Good Housekeeping *books*, McCalls *books*, Saturday Evening Post *books*; I mean there was just no way in the world to get around it, that we were peddling magazines.

And all we had to come against truth with, our naked faces looking able and our bodies on the line, our only tool against those hostile faces in the knowing world, was our "pitch."

We memorized the "pitch" word for word. It was awful, just on the edge of literate with total non-sequiturs that had to be carried on pure voice alone, the eyes blank as if nothing had just gone screwy in the non-context.

I wish I remembered the damned thing. I'd give you the highlights. It was so eminently forgettable. In fact, that was a problem at the time. Every morning we congregated in one of the motel rooms and practised the pitch. It was so much an applied piece of goods. Take away the screen door and the lady of the house and the mind goes blank. The pitch disperses like gas, like any elective fantasy. So we practised it daily, to remember it, to put it into the day like substance. Then we went for breakfast. Then we were driven to the "territory" and let out with our kits.

Well, I'll start at the beginning.

One morning early three new Mercurys stopped in front of our house on Byers Avenue and I came out with my mother's Samsonite suitcase. It and me were stashed in one of the cars and we headed for Arizona.

I was given a copy of the pitch and suffered the really expectable failing of seeing where it could be improved.

It was like coming up against steel. The pitch was not to be improved. The pitch was absolute. Questioning the pitch wasn't a question at all.

"It works," the lady who had interviewed me said. "We've got experts who don't do anything but come up with the perfect pitch that works and this is it."

I started my training. I memorized the pitch. I went with the top peddler and saw how it steamrolled through objections. There were places that were pauses to let the "prospect" speak. According to the objection made, you responded. And the only point of that little interchange was to get rid of the mounting tension that wanted to resist your salesmanship. The words it all took meant nothing at all.

It hurt me to see how the prospects went under. I didn't at all take it as a triumph. And in my heart of hearts I resolved that when they turned me loose I wasn't going to use the pitch.

I thought there must be a human place where I could stand and leave the person of the prospect unravaged. I believed that there were people who actually wanted to have subscriptions to magazines. And it was true that the rates we offered were the lowest going. I figured that with whole towns turning over under our crew I could depend on ratios.

That's how I learned at the age of seventeen that you can't underestimate human nature.

Straightforward and bare-faced I would start to outline the magazine subscriptions I had to sell.

I didn't achieve any one-to-one relationships. What I did was I gave a lot of people the opportunity for long overdue revenge.

You know the kind of expression you see on the faces of satisfied lynch mobs who mean to have their picnic now that the action's over? That's the look that followed me away down the sidewalk.

I was a magazine salesman who handed my body over. Boy, was I soft.

So then I started hating them, sitting smug, and me on my way back to the crew to hold down low man on the totem pole.

I started using the pitch. And it worked. I got a reputation among our little group.

It looked like I'd make a book salesman.

What I couldn't bypass was the moral torque. I was into an increasing anxiety. I was a hotshot acceptable criminal and the vanishing return on it was how I was tucking away subliminal guilt into bits of myself where I didn't have to pay attention. There was an accruing factor that earning money didn't touch.

We got to south Texas, still en route to New Orleans.

One morning our boss gave us a pitch of her own on the value of poverty. The sense of it was that poor people are pushovers. They don't have muscles.

"Don't let the territory mislead you," she said. "I've had some of my best days in territory just like this."

Because I was still new and it was another moral jog to be gained they sent me along with someone more experienced and I watched her talk a thin, ruined woman in a shanty into three subscriptions, complete with the first payment. The woman took three dollars out of a coffee can where they didn't have much company.

They put me out on a dirt road and the Mercury went flashing away leaving me standing in the swirl of its dust.

I sloped off across a sandy lot to a shed standing by itself in the blistering sun. It was the kind of arrangement where the top half of the front raised on hinges and stayed up with a stick, opening the place into a counter.

There was a stool and an old kitchen chair standing on the ground in front and I sat there all afternoon with an old-ish Mexican woman, drinking Coke and learning Spanish.

"Hello."

"How are you?"

"Good morning."

"Good afternoon."

"Good evening."

I spent that hot afternoon rejoining the human race just outside of Houston.

We were supposed to have a treat that night. The Director for that area was going to take us to dinner at the Emerald Room in the Shamrock Hotel. We were going to hear somebody named Nat Brandywine play for a singer named Dorothy Shay. She was sub billed as the "Park Avenue Hillbilly."

I missed that reward, spent the evening packing, feeling alone and floppy. The bird had split the cage.

I didn't feel noble or even relieved. I just felt undefined.

I was really young, but of course I didn't know it then.

CURRY

I've been thinking today, planning a curry, of the sad little wife of the Major, ex-Indian Army, who did not cut her wrists when a very usual sexy female arrived to apply for an American visa and on that visit devoured the little Major as if he were a dressed-out partridge, but on the lady's *second* visit when the visa was ready and the woman rejected the Major in favour of the fat-assed U.S. Vice-Consul.

It was having her husband handed back as cast-off goods undid the Major's wife.

They were such dowds.

They could never have anticipated such a *romance* as that; the Major short and balding, his wife only one more of those incredibly dressed women once to be found in multitudes living their lives out in backwater British colonies.

The malice of that woman's choice, the dowdy major; and the ridiculous pathos of the later known stories, that the wife had bedded down on the couch to save them all from gossip.

In her happier or at least more felicitous days she taught me to make curry, and the last time I saw her (we were due to leave the following week) was at an official dance. The Major and his wife were in the Governor's party which meant standing, having to stand, at attention just inside the door while the band to announce the Governor's arrival played "God Save the Queen."

That arrival, her wrists taped so neatly it was decorative, and herself with her eyes straight ahead of her, herself standing at attention facing out into the room that faced back, a roomful of people who knew the story to some extent.

I went home from that dance alone, Axel having many young ladies to say his goodbyes to.

At the club Saturday nights I could say, "Do you know who the most beautiful woman in the room is?" having watched him ogle the lot.

"That one?"

"No, that one over there, in the far corner, in the white dress."

And he would look, as if hypnotized, to agree that yes she was the most beautiful woman in the room and move to join her company.

Poor Axel, he had almost no imagination.

For my own part, insofar as I remember it, my behaviour had something to do with an exaggerated notion of what passed for worldly. I was only twenty and it stands to reason that I believed myself to be sophisticated. It was a value in my mind.

A letter from Gordon says, "How long ago it seems and I have no nostalgia left for those Belize days. Belize was too broken after Hurricane Hattie it was awful. We were not sorry to get away."

And he says, "Where you lived stood. Lindstrom's house was totally down and Sir Alfred was laconic and Lady L. mental, I thought, and quite funny and pathetic."

And he says, "Belize a monumental ruin."

The only friends in my life were there, perhaps forever true, coming as I have to be so ambivalent that I must weigh every piece of cheese pro and con.

Still, if I exaggerate, the place and the people have changed. No one left to contradict or distinguish between the memories I stored back even as they happened, knowing I would want them later, *that* sadness in forethought, I loved it there, a kind of homesickness *in situ* as if I walked backwards. And the memories of *now*, rising up, that I didn't know I had. As that when I touched the Major's wife's wrists to say "Did you hurt yourself?" she winced so deeply I was struck silent, remembering only then the bit of story I'd heard that afternoon, why her wrists were bandaged. Wondering, shocked, how I could have forgotten.

How could I have forgotten?

OLD VIVVY

Roosters bring the day up, poor scrawny things to sound so splendid. Before the first show of light their racket begins. They excite each other to hysterical effort.

The dogs are also infected, that in the day's heat will have as much as they can do to move from the sun into the shade. They bark and howl until they feel they've done enough.

Old Vivvy, wearing a dirty rainbow of dresses goes into Mrs. MacVeitche's prized garden, a shadow among early drawn shadows, to pick the flowers.

"When that woman was a child ..." she owned the first piano in the colony. Her parents meant to make her a concert pianist. Both parents were killed in an accident and the child's guardian took the money. That was the story.

In the local voice, a calypso swing to her speech and with the drawn-out, pulled-out rhythms of any storyteller dealing with a myth, Rita says to me, "Whan dat whomahn wass a chile ehveryting she touch wass gol'!"

Who stands now in the palest gray lift of early morning at Mrs. MacVeitche's door, a mahogany door polished to a high shine, and drops the brass knocker repeatedly on its sounding brass panel until the door is opened a cautious crack then wide by Mrs. MacVeitche herself, in a pink dressing gown, who looks in shock to see her treasured darlings, all the flowers from her garden, in a crushed mass, a madwoman's bouquet, held toward her as Old Vivvy simpering says, "Fi'cents!"

Mrs. MacVeitche pays the five cents and brings her fresh-picked flowers indoors, to the kitchen, where she puts water in the sink and the flowers also. Flowers, she would be the first to say, are best picked in the early morning while dew still clings to the petals, as it does to these.

Vivvy takes her five cents and turns down Queen Street to go to the market.

The rising sun finds the day already begun in that small colony of houses. The roosters have crowed and stopped. The dogs have barked and stopped.

Old Vivvy, having been raised to be clean, comes to the Fort Square sea wall to bathe. The cast-off dresses she has been given, layers of filthy faded print, are laid across the wall. Wearing, on different mornings, one dress or two, or nothing at all (her body is younger than she seems with her tangle of hair and her lunatic face) she goes into the water among the floating garbage from that morning's slops.

Light pours horizontally over the flat still water and the day's heat begins.

PIECE OF TRASH

He was a piece of trash from the first, not to be taken seriously. He arrived in the colony together with his wife, a heavy woman, and two daughters who were, one later learned, twins but not the identical kind.

They seemed good enough girls, quiet and formless, pre-adolescent. But the parents were, each in their own way, impossible.

The mother was graceless, with a raucous voice and a continuous line of harangue. She seemed never to stop. She had only to start again to erase any ease of quiet that had fallen since her last speaking. Peace was such a rarity in her presence that there was no enjoyment to it, one simply waited for the accident of it to be corrected.

But that was no justification for his being such a squirmy stick. He stood back of his wife's vulgarity inviting understanding. Now, what kind of man is that? The complacency of that immense self-pity of his, he believed himself to have deserved better.

What he believed he deserved was clear all over him, a kind of slime. He ogled all the girls from behind his wife's back. He was immensely capable of changing his expression whenever she had reason to turn his way. On and off he flashed according to the direction her head was turned. For her eyes he was proper and insignificant, gone quite into the woodwork. At her back he was wormy with pink edges around his eyes and mouth, as if his lips hung open, as if he panted.

It was no compliment to be looked at by him. One felt glimmers of his fantasies, ugly and trivial. A rotten kind of Hollywood sex-dream like those ads that say "Learn to be a Hypnotist" and show some man looking potent and evil with his hands hovering over the unsuspecting breasts of some swooning female.

Anyway, there was a relief in knowing they weren't to

stay in town but were almost immediately to go up-country. He was some kind of functionary for the Stann Creek establishment.

But before they could properly leave he wrecked his jeep on the one-lane road between the town and the airport and his wife was thrown right through the canvas roof and killed. One of the girls was badly hurt and had to stay for awhile in the hospital.

What was difficult was the necessity to show him sympathy for what so clearly was not a tragedy in his life but a release. He had believed she was the anchor that held him back. He was rampant to get on with what he thought was now open to him.

It's possible that in the way of fantasists he had convinced himself that all the women he lusted for reciprocated his fancy.

Instead of staying decently at home with his unhurt daughter he showed up at the club any evening he wasn't invited out to some commiserative dinner.

There were two clubs in the colony. One was very proper and almost exclusively white. Its only black member was a judge whose wife was now a faded lower-class white he had married in London while he was there as a student studying Law. The other club allowed anyone who could pay its fees. All the whites in the colony belonged to both and the good family mix-bloods and blacks belonged to the second.

It was the second club that the new-made widower frequented. He had a dated idea that the mix-blood girls were there for the taking, which wasn't true. In most cases they were strictly chaperoned, while the English or South African or Australian, in short the daughters of white colonizers, were let go almost casually and were endlessly boating or dancing or playing tennis or whatever without any supervision.

The more generous minded women interpreted his feeble attempts at lechery as "Poor man, he can't bear to be alone. He simply haunts the public places for company."

But even their good-heartedness was stilled when his need for company stopped showing itself at the clubs and he began to go nightly to the local dance halls.

His frustration, the frustration of at last getting into his imagination's Eden only to find no fruit fell to his hand shifted his search.

You must realize that this move on his part at that time constituted what could only be called going to the dogs. "Men go *bad* in the Tropics" was one old English saying.

If his wife had lived he would probably have come and gone in proper order. As it was he had no sense of behaviour.

I don't mean who he took to bed or whether he did, I mean he had no notion of how to maintain appearances.

The prevailing notion was that all the whites owed it to each other not to go to pieces under the colonial strains. Pukka-Sahib was not a literary joke.

Of course, one only had to pay attention to such a sense of things if one wanted to maintain relationships with the other whites.

He hadn't much imagination but even so he realized quickly that his communication with the women-folk of his fellow civil servants was suddenly nil. All dinner invitations and the little attentions that showed he was one of a group stopped.

His daughter fortunately was not made a pariah on his account though it's hard to know how much she was aware of anything. She spoke almost not at all and was clearly in a state of grief for her mother and the sudden changes in what had been until now a quiet and usual existence.

The sister in the hospital got better and the small family left for upcountry but were back in a matter of weeks. The father had got amoebic dysentery and was himself hospitalized briefly in preparation for being shipped back to England.

They left on a Saturday afternoon on the weekly plane

to Jamaica and my last sight of them was the two girls who didn't look alike going quietly and straightforwardly into the plane. Their faces then appeared, placed and ghostly, back of the round glass windows.

The father halted at the doorway and looked back, waved his hand as if to many friends, his fantasy still holding to that extent. He had no altered sense of his own worth though physically he had lost pounds and was as pale as if he had been washed in bleach.

Then he entered the two-motor plane to join his daughters and that was the last of him.

WHY DOES ANYONE ...

Why does anyone write except to speak of those things that conversation will never elicit; what is closest to the heart. And to speak of the personal with some accuracy, in the proper setting. And to have finally and for once the statement of the thing, dear thing, caught out of the void, caught onto paper; to be there at least as real as what usually happens, namely that we are so often misshapen by event, obscured by misunderstanding.

I know how those papers flutter in every breeze, ephemeral. They are so fragile. Statement is fragile. It only exists as its record.

But the records of the heart return to the heart as information.

And we are so hungry for it.

Why does anyone write except to say what presses closest to them; what matters.

How has this nightmare come to usurp my life. Where did all that thought go that was so fine and as if life were available. Oh, of course it is. But once it seemed so simple and now it's so complex. I find myself in the middle of it and the mess of it as if I were another item in the chaos of it. No life at all.

It used to stem forward and I was the root of it and my life grew out from me and was my own.

It is true that too much despair for too long a time deprives the sensibilities of their assumption of hope. Discouragement strikes in the most trivial places that required no courage at all.

There is living in one's skin. The skin extends to include sunshine and those etceteras of daily pleasure. And just inside and within that coat of apparent daily possibility there is the great gaping torn thing that is life gone wrong. There is the thought as one is suddenly caught back from thoughtlessness, there is the thought that is a feeling that somewhere it has all gone wrong.

If there's a place I know not of, that is a place where I want to be. Does that necessarily mean that there is no place for me. And so we keep on. Just that fantasy, that one can think of a place for oneself, makes it as if it is there and waiting.

No wonder we go crazy. Not out of our heads but into them, where everything is provided for. Where we imagine the shape of our lacks and fill in the gaps and bring the furniture in and live there.

One wants finally to destroy the world as a mercy. How to be rid of the pain of it.

But in pain it is as hard to imagine simple pleasures and uncomplicated days as it is to remember pain during happiness.

And the rest.

THERE'S AN OLD ...

There's an old Texas saying that I think I may be the only one who remembers it.

It goes "I've enjoyed just about as much of this as I can stand."

It's a magic formula that lets you head for the door past all the frenzy of any minute now it's going to get significant. It's a way to say that whatever you had in mind this ain't it. It lets you stop eating slop that needs a palate and a vocabulary.

I've enjoyed just about as much of this as I can stand.

IT'S A PHONY

It's a phony surface but who's to know the difference. Not enough time. All that flash.

Hey, it's as good as real. Like living a life.

"Who said that?" drawing back and centring. Let's show a little muscle here.

"You saying this ain't my life?"

Naw, I never said that.

"I know what's real. I feel it."

Yeah, we all do.

GOT FROM YEATS' 'CELTIC TWILIGHT'

How Columcille cheered up his mother. "How are you today, mother?" "Worse," replied the mother. "May you be worse tomorrow." The next day, "How are you today, mother?," and the same. The third day the mother said, "Better, thank God." And the answer, "May you be better tomorrow."

(of Paddy Flynn) "He was a great teller of tales, and unlike our common romancers, knew how to empty heaven, hell, and purgatory, faeryland and earth, to people his stories. He did not live in a shrunken world, but knew of no less ample circumstances than did Homer himself."

(a weaver said) "… for there are three things that are the gift of the Almighty—poetry and dancing and principles. That is why in the old times an ignorant man coming down from the hillside would be better behaved and have better learning than a man with education you'd meet now, for they got it from God."

THE DISMAY OF:

Outside the glassed door, looking through, being on all fours, not to be seen; looking through the merest corner of the door, just an eye of mine and a corner of my upper right face in that lower left corner of the door; there I was hidden insofar as to be seen the other must be specifically *looking*. And the occasion was this, that she was going to come down the stairs and I meant to see just when, and how, and maybe follow the direction she went, or, perhaps it was *time* I was after, I wanted to know *when* she came down the stairs and went.

But what I saw was, at the point where the lowest stair pushed beyond the corner wall that concealed all the rest of the staircase, the corner where she would appear, walking past and down the one last step, leaving the stairs; there where her feet and lower legs would have been had she come walking, there was a corner of her face and one eye and a bit of vivid blonde hair and she was also crouched beyond the wall, on the stairs to look toward the glass door.

We laughed but it was a despair. It had been important that the concealment and the watching work.

TAKE LOVE, FOR INSTANCE ...

How can it be desirable, that flurry of feeling that if it continues and maintains intensity we call Love?

How perverse we are relative to our own good to have that in our feelings that from the age of thirteen or so, younger all the time they say, until seventy or whatever, no end to it they say, we give over or are given into the "divine emotion."

Divine mix of anxiety, insecurity, longing that drives us until if we are fortunate, lucky in love, we have a brief relief that shines like fulfilment.

The constant fool's miracle, like fool's gold, but inherent; an inherent miracle. Passion brought to bear on eyes that shine back.

And then, or somewhat later, downhill all the way.

From here to there. Remember *there.*

Caught in the clutches of a one-way ticket. Express.

We are poor.
We are poor.
There is nothing here.

And we sling our everything into the void of it, to be caught.

What is that appetite that pretends to sustenance and ends with all the colour gone from the day and no one funny anymore. The appetite that carries veils and obscures our memory.

And can you in that moment's tender voice say No to it? How mean to refuse it, this little miracle that does so want in. Feel it knocking at your heart.

Poor heart.
See what followed me home.
Can I keep it?

PLAN

or—do it with colour and light
a clear spot for the actual
voice, one colour for the
"definitive" voice, one colour for the
narrator. go black on return
after intermission—"if you were
a desert bird"... to ... "mother ship"
colour rises overall *rose*

what about a tape with itself a
second time just off so the voice
is a stutter or echo throughout

circle those four statements
between the two screams

then *she* says, "Son, I see ...

SOME BITS

"Sweet dreamland faces, passing to and fro
Bring back to Mem'ry days of long ago.

Ted Berri-gram

Joanne's *range* as wide
as spread out on a table
and herself with a first-rate
boarding-house reach
grey eyes
GREY EYES
(her) grey eyes

She shrugged her shoulders and abandoned the personal side of the subject.

Actually we cannot put ourselves back into the spirit of those days.
A punitive spirit entered into our subsequent negotiations.

Soft and slow cartwheel of yourself sheathe your tongue walk in the true hot sunshine.

"You're so human ... You know what I mean, you always put your hand out to see if it's raining." *Sido*

NEW
STORIES

THE ELEVATION OF TERRE HAUTE IS 50 FEET

When you come to Terre Haute's city limits there's a metal sign, a shape like the state of Indiana. And stamped into the metal you can read:

"Terre Haute Indiana pop. (so and so) elevation 50 feet. The birthplace of Paul Dresser who wrote The Banks of the Wabash."

Terre Haute is one of those cities that flourished and grew a hundred years ago. Coal and steel exploded it outwards and surfaced the fronts of the main street buildings with a variety of fancy cut stone facades. The end of the First World War marked the turn. The city began to dwindle as its nourishment lessened. And now the beautiful stone faces that are still distinctive all have blind eyes. The windows have white or black or dark green painted on the inside of the glass.

Not enough people walk the streets. The women are in cotton house dresses. The men are in overalls and khakis. It looks as though this story was meant to be about a small farm town, and the set man got it wrong on the false-front buildings, too grandiose.

In the very middle of town the bulky courthouse and its lawn use up a city block. On one corner of the lawn on the mainstreet side there is a large statue, a memorial to the Civil War. Have you ever thought of that pun, the Civil War. There are four pedestals marking the four corners. On each pedestal is a representative warrior. There is a Confederate soldier, a Confederate sailor, and a Union soldier and a Union sailor. Steps climb between the four pedestals to the plateau that holds a tall column with a man on horseback high overhead. He is holding an unsheathed sword. He is a specific hero with a name. Metal chains drape between the pedestals to keep people off the steps. And from the exact middle of each chain hangs a small cleanly painted sign that says "Please Do Not Spit On The Monument."

When we were driving across country a couple of times a year I came to love Terre Haute Indiana. I decided to make a movie of it. Every time we went through I planned to take some footage. When we stopped in the business district to let me get a long shot of the street a man came out of his store, glared at me and my camera and conspicuously made a note of our license number. He was not to be fooled. When the caper came off he wouldn't have been slack.

Terre Haute was also the birthplace of Eugene Debs and Theodore Dreiser. The city made some choice to forget about them. Debs was too radical and Dreiser was indecent. He wrote dirty books and seduced young girls and got ruined by his excesses. But when Dreiser was born at 8:30 a.m. on August 27, 1871 "three graces garbed in brightly coloured costumes" entered the room and circled the bed. They were witnessed by his mother, his father and his sister.

He was the ninth child in a poor family in the poorest part of the town. His brother Paul changed his name to Dresser during the Great War. Dreiser was too German. Paul Dresser wrote My Gal Sal. He dressed in plaid suits and bowler hats and was a fine figure of a man.

But for the sake of the record it was not Dresser who wrote *The Banks of the Wabash*, it was his brother. The twisted lecher who could never look the other way, whose birth was attended by the graces, Theodore Dreiser wrote the words Terre Haute still holds in memory.

Oh, the moonlight's fair tonight along the Wabash
From the fields there comes the breath of new mown hay.
Through the sycamores the candle lights are gleaming.
On the banks of the Wabash far away.

SALAMANDER

The tilt of a delta valley; this place is the Salamander, the great dish of the alchemist's, shelving to let its downward edge rest at the ocean's edge.

Where they meet there is a small line of beach. The sand reaches unevenly at the townside; there is seldom a clean line. A slow motion falling away of the cliff that is the dish tilting up and away from the beach causes landslides that dump downward to messy shapes.

Some years the beach grows to an almost impressive width as if the ocean brought sand from other places to give us a grand gift. Now there's real room for frisbee, more privacy for lovers. The children move farther from their parents. Things are more peaceful. There is more room.

And other years the sea takes it all away. One day it's there and the next day we find that overnight, in one great bite, our beach has gone into the sea, taken away elsewhere. I wonder, sitting on the few high bits that are left, who is using my beach now? Where did it go and where did they wake up this morning to find their world expanded. Or, that stupid and mindless thief of an ocean could as simply have piled it in places where no one has any use of it, the lee side of bridge pilings, islands where there isn't any water and no one goes.

Meanwhile, we are all on top of each other in these shrunk places, usually half-moon shaped, the result of earlier landslides higher and deeper into the land mass. The children are falling over each other, crying. The bullies have emerged and are feeling threatened that the territory must be redealt. They are solving it by winning. The losers are filling the beach with themselves as victims. The lovers have gone elsewhere or are modifying their behaviour. The great number of dogs that live here have become pests. When there was room for them they could take long romping gallops and come up to be with people as a place to lie down and snooze or simply check in before going back to their distant places. Now they shake water over us, throw sand on us.

Rats go crazy in congested space, and us, we also go crazy in it. The parents scream at the children to insist that the children stop. The children scream at each other. The winners are looking so disgusting I want to kick them. The victims are wailing in their dramas. It is intolerable.

Of course it is really not this bad. I am describing the bad part. And this is not a year when the sand is away. This year the sand is here, the beach stretches into distance like a Fellini movie. And this year the sun is shining and has been shining since May. It is so unlikely. We are blessed by a drought.

It is never *too* bad. It is quite tolerable, actually.

I have lived here for six years now. That is longer than I've lived anyplace since I grew up. When I moved into the house I'm living in now I had moved 23 times in 15 years.

This is my home.

I can't bear it. The notion "this is my home" and my heart quakes inside me. My immediate reaction is to begin packing. But I hate packing. I will do anything else. I'll stay here and not call it home.

A SENSE OF HUMOUR

I don't remember who said it but somebody said, in fact wrote it down in a book:

Sober people can't take humour seriously.

And it's true. If you're a writer you should know that you lose genius points with one whole set of people every time you make them laugh. And if you really get to them and make them laugh a lot they may just give you up as hopeless and not to be counted on.

Critics of that persuasion will say things about you like "not to be taken seriously!"

Mark Twain got the short end of that stick. Saul Steinberg. Make up your own list.

Those guys who opt for the miseries as what they can understand never have to worry about laughing in the wrong place.

Take that story we all know about the man who overnight turned into a giant cockroach and now he spends hours on the ceiling with his friends and relatives shoving garbage through his bedroom door. Not a laugh in the carload. That cockroach and his clan were humourless. Remember the endless why why why throbbing like an undertone. No sweet young thing to kiss that trapped piece of misery and turn it back into a dull and humourless young man.

It didn't have to be that grim and it didn't have to be to the death but dying comes easier to people like that than a good belly laugh. Killing off that poor cockroach was their kind of happy ending.

Mark Twain would have put a saddle on it, joined the circus, and made the family fortune.

I don't want to belabour this so I'll just close with something somebody else wrote:

Gravity is a mysterious carriage of the body intended to conceal defects of the mind.

ROSARIO

One problem with intelligence is that when it's thinking about something it thinks it's knowing something. And if it's mistaken and learns the difference then it starts thinking about it the new way and thinks it's knowing something.

When I was living in a little village in New Mexico where most of the people were Mexican and interrelated there was a man I'll call Rosario Rodriguez.

The thing about Rosario was, he was a crook. He was also a really good plasterer and bricklayer if you were strong enough to make him come through.

Everybody knew he was a crook.

When I moved to that town the word came all the way from Panama where a lady who had heard of the move wrote to say, "If you get Rosario Rodriguez to do some plastering for you don't pay him until he has finished."

One curious thing about that village was that a lot of the Mexicans there were Protestant. It stemmed from a really early time when that village had an argument with the priests in Bernalillo. The argument got so hot that the whole village went Protestant despite the fact that most of them had never even seen a Protestant. For a long time that village was known as the "Pueblo de los Protestantes."

Later on some of them turned Catholic again but a lot of them stayed Protestant.

Anyway Rosario was a Protestant. And at one of the church's business meetings someone brought up his case, that is, his being a crook. The gist of it was, "Rosario is a crook because nobody trusts him. He has no pride in himself because he knows that everybody thinks he's a crook. If we gave him a reason to know that we trust him he would be a changed man."

They decided to make him the Treasurer for the church.

When he stole the money everyone said, "Of course, it was foolish to give the money to Rosario because Rosario is a crook."

"I got the house, and I got the car." (Which she tooled expertly out of the parking lot, holding the steering wheel with the pads of her hands, fingers extended, nails too long to be curled under.)

"Well, I *needed* it. I couldn't go looking for a job or go to school or do anything without my car! I sure didn't intend to just sit in that damned house and go loony. Not with *him* off on a honeymoon in *Bermuda!* And I got alimony and I got child-support. Me getting the house means the kids get to go to their same school. But that house really takes some keeping-up! And if I decide to sell it *he* gets half of the profit. How about *that!* I can *see* me doing *that!*

"Well, I never would of let him have the kids! He would have had a *fight* on his hands if he'd tried that!"

Her ex-husband had married his twenty-three-year old secretary and they had returned from Bermuda to live in a "swinger's" condominium. Fighting for the kids seemed to me to be remote from his plans.

I asked her whether she wanted to be a writer. We were returning to the city from a reading I had given at the local University. She had attended with a group from the University's writing workshop.

"Oh yes. I don't know yet what kind of thing I want to write so I take all the writing courses. And *grammar!* I've been doing a *lot* of grammar. And *psychology.* I do a lot of psychology. Do *you* do a lot of psychology? I mean, *did* you do a lot of psychology when you were beginning? To get the motivation straight and stuff? It seems to me that your work has a *lot* of psychology in it."

"No, not much. I like William James. And some Jung. Not like studying it."

"*Carl* Jung!"

"Yes."

"My *favourite!* I take from this professor that loves Freud.

Sigmund Freud. He wants me to go to Europe with him on his sabbatical. That's next year. Vienna and Switzerland. What do you think of Switzerland and Vienna?"

"It sounds exciting. I've never been to Vienna or Switzerland."

"You've *never* been to Europe?"

"I've been to some places in Europe. I've never been to Vienna or Switzerland."

"Where've *you* been?"

"England. Holland. Germany. Denmark. France. Italy. Does he want to go to the Eranos lectures in Switzerland?"

"What's that?"

"The Jungians get together and deliver papers to each other on some topic."

"Oh no. He just likes Freud. He wants to work on ... you *know* how Freud said everything is sex? You know about that? I mean, the *creative impulse*. Freud says that if you don't have enough sex it interferes with your *creative impulse*. Of course, there's two streams of thought on that. Well, this professor's interested in how it is the other way around. What happens to the creative impulse when there's too much sex? Well, maybe just *enough!* But does it interfere or what? What do *you* think? Do you think too *much* sex would interfere with the creative impulse? Or do you think it might help it along?"

"Hard to say. There are only so many hours in the day."

"Yes, well *that's* true. That's an interesting way to think about it. So *we're* ... he wants me to help him research this *other* angle. The *too much sex* angle. He says that *nobody* has done hardly *anything* on *that*."

ROOTS

Roots! That cry goes up that wants *My Story*! Where's *mine*? Where's the cigarette machine I was so casual about and the drug store that had a counter and how a gang of boys look on a gang of bicycles out for mundane adventure?

Where's my story?

How did it get cut loose and drift away down time and nobody even noticing it like continental drift across ocean floors and somebody takes wrong steps along the shoreline and falls into the water because the land has gone away ...

Just like that the stories went away and people are getting hungry for them like a vitamin deficiency, that subliminal. And will the stories ever come back? The ones who want them are gathering like ancient tribes gathered when they saw they had lost their gods and now must call them from the shores.

There's a sense that that's why psychiatrists have proliferated. That's where the stories are let out now in bits and pieces and everybody's a learner, looking through the mystery of the bits to recollect them into entity and come by meaning. Poor Osiris, and all those daily dispersions, and all the disassociations we experience moment to moment now that war has made geography general. Now that home got stuck in time way back there with childhood and adolescence and yes sometimes I remember those long summer evenings in the half-light of late day returning home across grass lawns punctuated by driveways, eating, if I was lucky, a cone of raspberry ice cream.

The trees were large and old and went down when they widened the streets across this whole nation. Part and parcel with when the cars went big as a value. Big streets for big cars. That kind of trashy thinking where the exterior was suddenly the winner and got all the goods.

What in God's name did they think was going to come down those streets that needed that much room!

Forward thinking like the cargo cults put their little piece of landing strip in the middle of their home place and wait for the great silver gods that have gone into the sky and pass over their heads to notice. See, we have made a place for you dug into the body of our place and we wait, see we wait.

And the trees went down. And the houses that had been dappled with shade and private, each one a thing, they got dumped onto the street and stood exposed and naked and now you could see things about them as that there had been only three patterns the builder used and seeing the same house repeated cheapened it. And the houses shamefully acknowledged their new condition by becoming whatever sign was nailed to their fronts. Realtor. Sunshine Insurance, Inc. Massage. Artistic Framers.

And the gods never came. The streets never justified their widening. And the cars got smaller, shrank as the years passed. They had lost their chance. The cars were finally not what they had tried to be in the Greater American Imagination.

Remember how we deplored it. Think how long we hated the growing cars and it kept continuing to be just the same. Remember we were deploring it even as they were putting the sharp fins on the back that literally killed people by stabbing them, when all the driver meant was to back up.

That was when the cars were fighting back. And they lost. And in the wake of that war, a lot of litter and ugliness. And we got left with all those streets.

HER NAME

It was 10:30 or 11:00 in the night, dinner finished long ago and since then the five or six of us had sat around the big square old time dinner table in the big square old time kitchen with coffee and beer and wine and smoking some dope. Another usual Northern California late at night stoned out brilliance, or so that's the feeling. The conversation like a dog that's good to go walking with, trit trot in one direction trit trot in another meandering circle, intent, nosing.

And in the midst of no reason for it that I can remember a bell rang very gently deep in my mind, a sweet sound for me rising from the valley floor. A reminder. I had missed something. I was short exactly one item on my list that had nothing else on it. I went mindless except for waiting to recognize it and my thinking went onto automatic scan and the only advantage I had was knowing it was in this room. My eyes moved as lightly as that bell had sounded, moved around the large room not quite lighting on anything while I waited to see if the memory that had announced itself would make a show.

In that kind of float of letting it happen I got up from the lighted island of the table and my feet carried me to a darker corner, to a stack of discarded newspapers that waited in their place between the fireplace and the kindling. I took up the top paper. I didn't have to read it. I looked consistently at the upper left corner on the right hand pages. I picked up the second paper. I found what I wanted on page three. And I still didn't know what it was I was after.

The article was three or four paragraphs about how police were looking for a doctor who had murdered his mother, his wife and his two adolescent children in one berserker rage. Blood everywhere. There were pictures of the two half-grown victims smiling off the page the way victims often do, and the doctor was smiling too, alongside them. All of them looked pleased. The doctor was wearing a cap with a bill as if he were playing golf or set to go on a boat.

When I had read it through the first time I had wondered how they knew the doctor was the murderer and not a victim taken elsewhere. But really, that's probably, in that kind of no-cover-up, just the thing that would be known.

I reread the piece, following whatever that questing bit of my mind was and I found what I hadn't paid enough attention to.

The given name of the doctor's mother was Lobelia Amaryllis.

She must have been the only one ever with that name. Her mother loved flowers and passed on the sound of them to this infant she held in careful arms dressed in white lace to be named forever, the dress hanging down long, a cross made in holy water on the infant's forehead. A click of the camera and that placid infant gaze is held, printed in fading sepia, thrown forward in time to be dead on the floor in a pile of newspapers dated 1978; her name en route to oblivion invoked this one last time by its own insistence.

THE CHILD

After the child had been taken from the water. After someone had said it that the pool cover should be taken completely off to see whether he might have slipped through he was so small and the cover was removed and there he was in that strange element. There was a question of shock and something like discretion that could not let them use one of the long poles with nets on the end to reach into the water and manipulate the small body toward waiting hands at the poolside. That expedience was so possible. The poles were right there but. The owner jumped into the pool fully clothed and gathered the dead child to himself as if he hoped to save it back into life. As if it still might be that he would be in time. And the awkward moment was past. It had been dealt with humanly with an implication of hope and salvaging against the grief that was now all that could happen seeing the child's blue tinted face.

And the knowledge they all possessed had no hope left now. They all knew. Still they called the fire department and the ambulance that couldn't possibly arrive in less time than an hour and they laid the child in different positions and expelled the water from its lungs with pressure and breathed breath from their mouths into it and pressed that breath out again and breathed more useless air into it and pressed it out for a long time it seemed forever before the fire truck arrived with a resuscitator. And still no one said it, that he was dead. And when the small body was tidily on the bed in the ambulance and whisked away with tubes taped on the arms and injections still continuing and the ambulance attendant not looking at the mother, it would be so complicit what they knew together and no one would say now, not yet.

After all that and the inevitable outcome, the statement, and the clatter of true life drama when shocked eyes cannot understand the world that looks just the same.

After all that the young woman was alone again as if the child had never happened, as if death had annulled the child instead of ending it. And with the final drama faded and she felt the emptying there was also a fading to the earlier drama that had been happening before all this.

That earlier drama had begun with herself enamoured with the child's father, a young man of eighteen. She was also young, in her middle twenties, older than her lover therefore, significantly. It was her decisions that mattered.

She adored him, his eyes that were a light blue of clear skies, chestnut hair that sprang wiry around his face. She loved his laugh. He was beautiful and caught at her heart-strings so that it could never occur to her that he was not her own true gift. And she was tired of being alone.

She said when she became pregnant that she wanted the child as her own choice and that it was her responsibility. Her lover told her that he didn't want the child, that he was too young to be a father. He said that he wouldn't marry her and he asked her to have an abortion. She said the child was hers, it was her choice and she chose it. In her heart of hearts she thought the child would turn him. She carried the child and bore it, meaning to have its father.

It was true that she caught him in the wake of her decision. He trailed after her looking more and more sheepish. He daily looked less the man and more the boy. He was ashamed to be seen with her, with her great belly that laid such a claim to him as if his most private name were written there. He followed her shopping to carry the bags now that her belly was so big and he dawdled behind or walked swiftly ahead to the pick-up he had paid for with his own money made at his first real job doing construction work. He had been so proud of that truck. It had felt like a statement. A proof. And now it meant nothing. He cringed and ducked when his friends were in the store or on the street like an adolescent boy ashamed to be caught shopping with his mother.

For her part she suffered also. She had the bulk of her body and she could see that she might have made a mistake. She could see the ramifications resulting from her choice. But she would not acknowledge it. She told herself it was her lack of a figure that embarrassed him. It would all finally be the way she wanted it. When she was attractive again and they could go dancing, when the baby was here and a sweet thing to point up her femininity even more, when she would be outdoors in sunshine with the darling at her breast he would melt. It would be too much for him.

But she was simply wrong and found herself with the child she had insisted on and all the work of it. And the child was flawed, had a heart problem that must be operated on at a later date and until then there were things she must do about it. Her life was altered. Even with a figure she didn't get the response she had got earlier from men when she had been carefree. Men don't get turned on by women with kids, she thought.

She could get bitter about it. She felt more alone than ever, and let down. She felt jilted and resented it that her baby's father continued to live his old life almost untouched, while her life had changed so drastically. She would remind him that little boys need to know their father and he would be seen with the baby on his back in its little backpack that it travelled between the mother and father wearing, like a snail made of canvas cloth. She began to worry about the baby's heart, poor baby. Oh, the poor baby. And her face tightened up with it. She began to feel that her life was ruined, that the baby was an invalid, that she didn't have enough money. She began to ask the baby's father for money. Then she began to ask his father and his mother and even his grandmother for money. The money was never for herself. The money was for the baby. The baby needed money.

At first the father and his father and mother and grandmother gave her money when she asked but they realized over a period of time that the money went for dresses and babysitters so she could go dance at the bar. She longed for her earlier life.

The child got to be three years old before it was missed, then found, then treated ritually and finally allowed to be dead as if the statement was what killed it.

And now the drama was of herself bereaved. She was a mother who had lost her baby. It was true she felt it. She wished she had been a better mother, more loving to the poor baby.

She went to the bar now but seldom danced. She would sit in intense conversation usually with a man, with tears on her face. She would rehearse some aspect of the child's short life. The man she was talking to would have his arm around her shoulders or be holding her hand and she would be telling him her story as if she pleaded and when she would begin to cry he would hold her until she felt better and if she was too unstrung he would offer to drive her home and they would leave the bar together with little murmurs of farewell to and from the people they passed leaving as if they were leaving a graveside.

For awhile it looked dangerous, as if she might let the story carry her over the edge. She had a history of getting stuck in her own machinations, her imaginings. But at some point she did make the turn and she began to be more normal.

And after a couple of years had passed she could talk about how that time was without the complication of playing her role.

She was talking about her parents who had come to be with her for the memorial service. She had wanted to please them. She had borrowed a car for the time of their visit to drive them around in and she stocked the food they liked. She wanted it to be alright for a change. She thought for a visit like this one they would surely want to make it work.

"I took them up to Fort Bragg. I drove them all over.

And for the whole drive my father never looked out of the window. All he did was look at a map of California he had on his lap. Oh, he did look up once. My mother said, 'Look Harry, there's a Mercedes,' and he looked at the Mercedes. And that was it," she said, laughing.

She thought about it, how parents are, and looking very pretty she said, "Can you believe it?" and laughed.

A MORAL TALE

I was more than overdue to leave that job by the time it and me parted company. I wouldn't have been there in the first place but for desperation. Me and my two kids had been scraping by on forty dollars a week and that's the bottom of the barrel. You know how kids go through shoes and there's no way around it that they've got to have new ones.

I paid in close to sixty hours a week to get that forty dollars so when they offered me three hundred a month guaranteed against a percentage at the town's lousiest television station to be an Account Executive which is a piece of semantics that tries to make you sound like something more than a salesman I took it.

I think they thought I was "hungry" enough to be a natural but I didn't live up to it. Get a hungry enough salesman and he'll get out there among his prospects and dig the money out with his teeth. Something like that. I just don't have the teeth for it.

Anyway I had enough accounts already on the air to justify my three hundred and I kept their copy and film and slides straight and told them when there was something they might be interested in but I wasn't a go-getter.

They got a new sales manager and it didn't take him more than a few days to see that my particular "hungry" lacked the verve so he called me in one afternoon to give me my last chance.

He said he understood I was some kind of "artistic" person and he translated that into "Bohemian" without a look back. The next in line was "free-love" in the sense of not caring much who you went to bed with and he stressed it that he didn't exactly mean "free."

He said I was a good looking woman and there were plenty of high ranking accounts that would throw to our side if their account executive was a willing good looking woman. And also, how did I feel about making extra bucks when out of town bigwigs hit the place and needed to see some night life. He was sure it was okay to discuss this with me having as I had a larger Bohemian sense of things. And needing the money as he knew I did. It looked like an arrangement that could work out all around.

It's always been a flaw in my moral makeup that I just don't get indignant and righteous and brain people and feel insulted when they come up with something interesting. It really interested me to hear this businessman laying out his kind of goods. Maybe I really do have a larger Bohemian sense of things. Anyway, when he finished his sales pitch I explained to him that being poor meant there were lots of things I couldn't afford. But I could keep on affording the luxury of only going to bed with somebody when I cared for them a lot and probably not even then.

"That doesn't cost me a dime," I said.

We didn't bother mentioning that it had just cost me a lousy job and without further ado we were quits. We didn't bother shaking hands on it.

I went home and came back late that night, ten or so, to clean out my desk when I could be pretty sure nobody else would be there.

The television station sat at one end of a parking lot half a block big. The other end of the lot was held down by a giant orange like Peter Peter's pumpkin only this orange was big enough to hold half a dozen wives with their kids all seated in groups around little white plastic tables drinking Orange Julius and eating whatever their hearts desired. But not at ten o'clock in the night.

I went from the deserted office to the deserted orange.

Inside, the place was set up so that you always sat in bright lights in a window like a showcase ad for a customer in the process of being satisfied. I celebrated my newly departed job over a chili dog and a Pepsi with the bright overlighting bouncing back up into my face from the white plastic table.

The door swung open to let in one of my ex-colleagues. It was a hot night and his plump face was flushed red above his red necktie, white shirt and blue plaid sports coat. He would never be asked to enhance the station's hopes with a little night work. In fact gossip had it that he no longer had access to his own bed when his wife was in it. She was an athletic red head who spent her days playing golf and tennis and her nights whooping it up at the neighbourhood cocktail lounge with anybody but her red-faced husband.

He brought his cheeseburger and coffee and joined me. There was a certain amount of embarrassment in it, almost a kindness, as if he wanted me to know I was still okay in his books despite my being a loser.

He had that kind of face that works its way back to babyhood as jowls and chin and cheeks fill in and the hair falls out.

"I was thinner," he said with a gesture toward himself, telling me this story, as though I might now see through him into that earlier person he spoke of. And it was true. I did see it. I saw him younger, thinner, more fresh, with the same slight bewilderment on his face that then, in a younger man, did not necessarily foretell as it did now that he would go to his grave bewildered and wondering.

We had never had any particular inclination to talk so it must have been my imminent departure that created that old atmosphere of ships passing in the night. However it came about it did and he told me this piece of himself, something sentimental to haul forward into a late night un-likely conversation.

After the war he had been stationed in Paris. He was a young officer and probably good looking. His face still held traces of that possibility.

The Opera had resumed and officers of the Allied Armies were given free passes. He and his friends went often. It was clear he had loved the spectacle. It was a place where the grand old world fought to regain itself. The women bared their shoulders and wore jewels if they had been able to keep them.

It is such a cliche this story. Throughout time in all the wars young men have been made seemly and acceptable by their uniforms. This story would never have happened to a man dressed in the jacket he now wore. It would never have occurred to him, it didn't occur even now to him, that he had been a valid fraud, costumed and glossed over, a sincere trap who meant it for the young woman he met. Naturally he described her as being from a "really good family."

My eyes must have shown the scepticism I felt. He described the young woman's mother, father, the style of life they maintained and gave him entry to. He was right. She had been from a good family.

When she knew that she was pregnant she told him and told him that she must tell her family.

Her young officer assumed that they would solve it by marrying.

"I'd have had to look a long way to come up with something better," he said.

She tried to make him understand that she would never be allowed to marry a man capable of seducing her. Her father made it quite clear to him.

"People like that have a different kind of standards," he wanted me to understand. It was another instance of their superior condition in his eyes.

"It's a different kind of morality," he said. He was awed by it. Being snubbed by it proved its reality to him.

"I asked her to just run away with me, just go off and get married. She wouldn't do it."

For as much longer as he was in Paris he spent long hours on a park bench near the house, hoping to see her. He did it in all kinds of weather. Finally he was transferred.

He had seen her only once after her parents laid their injunction down. She had come out of the house and he had seen her from a couple of blocks away. He had rushed to follow her. She went into a department store. He ran along the aisles and almost crashed against her.

They faced each other frozen in place.

He said her name, yearning towards her. He said, "Her face was very tender."

He said, "She looked so young."

"No," she said softly.

While he begged her she looked into him, miles of it between them, and said, "No," again. Then, without buying whatever she had come for, she turned and left him there and was gone.

But not quite.

Years later, years gone by, water over every dam, and it's night in the Orange Julius and here she was, invoked into being among the plastic tables, and here he was, aging, innocent and vulgar, his face forever bewildered.

He never knew what hit him.

THE SANGUINE
BREAST
OF MARGARET

ONE

A woman, twenty-nine, slim, dark hair in a braid down her back, dressed in faded soft Levis and a red shirt faded to pink, sat on a wooden chair at a kitchen table.

She was reading the newspaper, the Help Wanted section. She and Patrick wanted help, needed help. And there it was—someone in Guatemala wanted a tutor for five children of various ages from two adjacent coffee farms. The tutor would be provided with a mail order teaching kit. The pay would be negotiated.

Outside the kitchen door two ancient tamarisk trees shaded the house from the afternoon sun with a shadow that was lacey at the edges. When Margaret Dougherty raised her eyes to look through the windows she saw a hard packed yard, a chicken house with chickens scratching bare dirt, a long narrow garden extending toward the Sandia Mountains on the horizon.

She was thinking of leaving this place.

"Hope," the saying goes, "springs eternal in the sanguine breast." Margaret of the permanently sanguine breast went for scissors to cut the ad from the paper.

At very nearly the same moment three of the boys Patrick Dougherty was supposedly supervising made off with the ball during gametime. They chased around the playgrounds, collecting boys from other games as they passed.

The three and Patrick were invited to the office of the headmaster. They stood in a straight line in front of William Wepsey's desk and waited to be told they had done badly.

The boys were dealt with quickly and sent out. Patrick stood alone.

Patrick, thirty four, tall and thin with the trimmed dark beard he had had since he was twenty, looked at the floor, didn't look at William Wepsey (called Willy Wetseat by the boys).

Latin teachers were rare in the American southwest. Patrick was one of three in a thousand square miles. He had no degree, had left Harvard six weeks short of graduation when it was suggested to him, quite kindly, that he might rather have withdrawals on his records than failures. Patrick was perfect for Wepsey who introduced him to parents as "a Harvard man" while underpaying him as if he were being generous. When the French teacher dropped dead in harness Patrick came to school the next day to learn that he was now the French teacher as well as the Latin teacher. He might come to school any day and find he was also the janitor.

"I think you'd better be taken off active sports altogether," the seated headmaster announced. "You haven't any talent for it."

To Patrick who had no depth perception and the muscles of a scholar the slur was a potential blessing.

"Do you know anything about archery?"

"No," Patrick answered, "I've never..." (arched?)

"Neither does Hansen. I might as well put him on soccer. You can handle archery. It's only a beginning class." Wepsey waved his hand to indicate that Patrick's lacks would do well enough for beginners.

When Patrick left Willy's office to go to his next class he found two of the boys waiting for him in the hall.

"Sorry about that, Patrick," one of them said gruffly, man to man.

Margaret went out to feed the chickens, a notoriously excitable breed. She left the house, whistling and singing, slamming the screen door, banging on the pan she carried, a procession of one accompanied by racket. It wouldn't help, never worked. We can but try, she thought, whistling and banging. When she opened the mesh door to the chicken pen the hens flew shrieking into the air, trying to escape the daily dangers of being fed.

Next she carried a five-gallon kerosene can to the fifty-gallon drum, braced it in place, turned the spigot handle. She carried the filled can into the four room house, emptied it into the space-heater. Five gallons would see them through the next twenty-four hours. She wiped up the kerosene that had dripped from the rim of the can onto the cement floor. In the small bathroom she scrubbed at her hands. The kerosene that had spilled onto her pants she left there.

That night the couple read the ad through, talking it over. It seemed, given their limited resources, an option.

Patrick drafted a careful letter for Margaret to mail the next day, with the proper postage, from the post office.

A poured chalk line marked the parameters of the newmade archery field. In Wepsey's mind the chalk lines were invested with a mystic power. Any arrows that flew were expected to take notice.

Patrick had not expected willow boughs and string but it had not occurred to him that his new archers, outfitted by affluent parents, would be rigged for bear. One boy had a cross-bow.

"Is that legal?" Patrick asked.

"Sure," the boy answered. And smiled.

All sixteen eyes of these eight beginners glittered, or so it seemed to Patrick, at finding themselves loose in the schoolyard with justified lethal weapons.

Two of the boys knew more than the others, spoke knowledgeably of recurve bows, wheels-and-levers. The group was shown by these two how to stand, how to string and unstring their bows, how to seat the arrows. Patrick watched, relieved that they emphasized safety.

A line was formed.

The plan was that each boy would shoot three arrows along Willy's corridor into the targets stretched over bales of hay at the far end. Then, while the others waited, he would retrieve his arrows to give the next boy a clear target.

Predictably, the third boy got off a shot too soon. The arrow stuck in the hay near the second boy who was still pulling arrows out of the bale. It was a great joke, particularly to the boy who had been mercifully missed, who could not stop laughing, whose teeth almost chattered with the humour of it.

Thereafter the next boy in line was not allowed to raise his bow until the previous boy had returned and tapped him on the shoulder.

At the end of the line, bored, a boy shot an arrow straight up, as if it were into nowhere. It fell back to earth, the weighted shaft gaining momentum as it fell, to bury a part of itself into the ground near him. It was a sobering moment. Patrick saw that Willy had given him life and death to be responsible for, a definite upgrade over who had the ball.

Two months later, letters having been exchanged, Margaret and Patrick sat at the kitchen table calculating the salary Patrick should ask for. They based their figures on what it had cost them to live in Mexico. They would learn later just how wrong they had been.

A final figure was arrived at.

"Three thousand dollars."

"Three thousand dollars?"

The next letter Patrick got from Barney Shaw agreed to the sum and the job was a job.

The Job Description:

On two adjoining coffee farms (called fincas) lived two families: Barney and Mildred Shaw at San Felipe with three children; Helen and Antonio Grisanti at Los Cedros de San Juan with two children. The school would consist of those five children and the Doughertys' two older daughters. There would be four first-graders, one third-grader, and two fourth-graders. A mail-order plan of education, ordered from Baltimore, Maryland, would cost eighty-five dollars per child (which the Doughertys would also pay, from their three thousand, for each of their two daughters) and would provide textbooks, paper, pencils, together with a day by day guide for the tutor to follow.

Patrick's salary would be divided between the families. In addition the Shaws would provide the school building and the Grisantis a house where the Doughertys would live.

Patrick told Willy he wouldn't be returning the next year.

"Enrollment is up," Willy cleared his throat. "I think I can see my way clear to offering you six thousand."

He saw that his generosity made no difference and that Patrick was leaving for more reasons than they would either admit.

He sniffed.

"Well, I suppose we'll have room for you when you come back. You'll have lost seniority, of course."

Patrick's fellow teachers, particularly the ones who had complained the most, were critical. "You're giving up a real job to go tutor kids for a year?" One even said, "There's no future in it." Patrick looked around this drab connivance of a school, this future, contrived by way of William Wepsey's sex appeal. Whatever Willy was as an educator and despite his being lantern-jawed and horse-toothed, it seemed he was a very devil with the ladies. He romanced wealthy women who were so reassured when he made no attempt to marry them for their money that they were quite open-handed. In exchange, they were given their names on small metal plaques, scattered over the grounds and the buildings.

"Are you taking your children?"

"Oh, yes." Those poor hostages to fortune with no other place to be, of course they must go.

And as the final proof, someone asked, "How does your wife feel about it?"

"She found the ad."

The others couldn't be expected to sympathize. They recognized an enemy by his back—an enemy could get away and did it. For right thinking people any day anyone set out to drive to Guatemala with a wife and four children for less money and a questionable life style would be a frivolous day and too sudden.

No resources, no way to make a move that matters, the belief that large things must happen, and over the edge is the only way to go.

Take the poor amoeba that wants to make a move. Every peripheral bit is a potential leg. Outshoots on three different sides—each thinking "Excelsior!" Then they haul back in while two more shoot out elsewhere. In all that jiggling does it think it's moving right along? No, no thought— just another creature dependent on all that interior destiny stuff that moves lemmings to the edge of the cliff and over. No thought needed to go all the way down to splat.

What does the human mind do that's any different? Not what it thinks it does. The mind goes along for the ride, explaining all the way.

For four years Willy and been Patrick's "boss." It would take too much space and time to describe Willy in his beastly entirety. He belonged in Dickens and you know how wordy that can get. He was self-indulgent, alcoholic, mean in heart and pocketbook and a sadist.

After Susie was born, the first time Margaret drove to the school to pick Patrick up, Willy walked over to the car, looked in and said, "So this is the new baby." His mouth was fixed in a rictus grin and he said, "Well." And then again, "Well."

Margaret had grabbed the sleeping child into her arms for no reason and Willy walked away.

For four years Margaret had been wistful and surprised when she saw poverty guidelines issued by the government and realized the amount they should have to qualify as poor was more than they had.

Who knows how long it would have continued without the newspaper ad. A cattle tick can hang on a twig for as long as thirty years, suspended and apparently lifeless, until a whiff of butyric acid signals a nearby mammal, springs it into being, and it slings its body out into the void toward its one main chance. If it lands on something solid that registers a temperature in the vicinity of ninety-eight degrees the cattle tick plugs in, mindlessly. It is, despite the thirty years of suspended animation, a quick and immediately resolved little story.

For human beings only fairy tales try to solve life with one large leap—"happily ever after." In real life we hang and leap, hang and leap, hoping with each leap that it is a forwarding. For each next effort we gather together our latest fund of enough courage, enough hope, and we leap. And being mistaken takes as much effort as being right.

For four years the Doughertys had lived on next to nothing, with no hope for improvement. However unlikely, this new job was the first whiff of change they could call their own.

They just held their noses and jumped.

A storm of intent blew through the adobe house, stripped it clean of their lives. Every item the family owned came under Margaret's eye, was judged and dealt with. The dog was left with friends. The chickens were sold, carted away to scream for their lives in someone else's care.

The summer was almost over. Time to leave.

Opened side doors on the VW Combi showed a horizontal sheet of plywood holding a double bed mattress halfway between the floor and the ceiling.

Under the plywood, solidly massed, was a patchwork of cardboard boxes. Margaret had solved every inch of space by cutting boxes to fit, taping them together again with duct tape.

"What are you doing with those boxes?"

"Making boxes."

All their worldly goods were fitted into place in the custom-made containers. More immediate necessities lined the length of the mattress on the far side: sweaters, comic books, a pan to vomit into, canned tuna, a box of crackers, canned milk, water in gallon wine jugs, diapers and a diaper pail with an airtight ("ha," thought Margaret) lid, towels and washcloths (including two washcloths wet and wrung out in a plastic bag for quick hand wipes.)

A baby bed mattress was fitted over the motor casing in the far back. An accordion folding gate stretched across the van between the two mattresses to keep Anna, the baby, secure and also let her be reached when Margaret wanted to bring her into the larger bed.

There was also, under the double bed mattress, a five gallon Army Surplus khaki-colored can filled with water, provision against breaking down in the desert. The manifest organization was reassuring. They both believed it would always stop short of disaster.

They had exactly one hundred dollars for food and gasoline. Forty dollars was in Patrick's pocket, sixty dollars was in an envelope tapped under the dash panel.

Their plan was to drive almost non-stop, taking turns (the one not driving could climb onto the mattress with the children and get some sleep) through southern New Mexico, a bit of Texas, the length of Mexico, and half of Guatemala to arrive at San Felipe. With luck they could do it in a week.

They thought of everything they could think of, provided for what they could provide for. The gaps were disregarded, a kind of faith. All else was the ongoing truth that disaster and the real world can crush any plan that was ever made. Who can provide for that? No one.

The moment came when they were ready. Set to go. They added the four children to the goods. The old woman who lived in a shoe had nothing on them.

Anna solemnly examined her new place, took the wooden gridwork in her hands and pulled. Susie, two years old, who knew fun when she saw it, looked at her two older sisters with a flaring grin of mischievous joy. Alix, eight and knowledgeable, tossed some picture books into a heap against the moment to come when Susie wouldn't be so pleased. Lucy settled in stalwartly, looking toward the house they were leaving.

Patrick climbed into the front seat through the left front door.

Margaret walked the traditional one last time through the emptied farmhouse, locked the door behind her, reached high to put the doorkey into the crotch of the tamarisk tree and walked back through the heat to the van. Small faces were framed by the windows. She joined them, slammed her own door shut.

The overloaded van reversed heavily over ruts onto the dirt road that would take them away from here, dug its wheels in and they were en route, dry dust rising in their wake. They passed the length of the abandoned garden where tomatoes still flourished on the drying vines. Someone else would have the good of them.

When they reached paved road Patrick turned left, south. Margaret sighed a deep sigh of satisfaction. They weren't, after all, to be stuck here. How beautiful it looked, all they were leaving, poplars and cottonwoods and flowers

BOBBIE LOUISE HAWKINS   219

glowing with the season's reds and yellows and golds in the vivid finale of late summer. How easy it was for Margaret to love this place now that it had let them go.

She put her hand on Patrick's leg and squeezed.

"Oh boy!" she said.

Patrick grinned back at her.

They were exultant in their escape.

And now you see what they had recognized in each other from the very beginning. They were compatible. Driven by thwarted self-esteem and by lack they both would opt at the first opportunity to join the flagpole sitters, the goldfish swallowers, all those misfits with aspirations who have too high an opinion of themselves and won't take no for an answer.

· · ·

From Margaret's first sight of Patrick she was bound to him. She was partial to tall, bony faced, high strung men, eyes all over the place to see everything at once, or caught still in an intensity of looking, for the same reason—to see everything. Patrick laid eyes on Margaret and went dead still, looking. And Margaret couldn't quite look back, he threw such a shake into her. She kept talking to his friend, Sam, who had just introduced them. At intervals she'd give Patrick a quick glance. Between one glance and the next she would forget what he looked like he already mattered so much. Every time she looked he was watching her.

He was lean and dark with a beard when beards were meaningful, when a man with a beard was expected to have something on his mind.

They could have been brother and sister in their colouring, their intensity. Pictures of Margaret then sometimes caught her looking like a beauty.

• • •

Margaret worked as a disc jockey at a fifth-rate radio station. The "psycho-shift," midnight to six, when every stressed-out insomniac who turned a radio on realized that out there in the blank night was another real live person: awake; with a telephone.

She had half a dozen regular callers, a drunk who always wanted Mahalia Jackson at three in the morning, a woman who had a new white Cadillac she thought Margaret might like to drive. And the Party Guy:

"Hey! Listen to this!"

A sound not easily interpreted.

"That," the Party Guy said, "is ice cubes rattling in a pitcher of martinis for just you and me! Howzabout it?"

"I don't get off work till six. By that time ..." By that time all she wanted was to get to bed but saying so didn't seem wise, "... all I can face is bacon and eggs."

"Naw, we don't have to think about breakfast. I can just strain these martinis into a thermos and come over there and we can get acquainted."

"I don't think so."

Another time the sound was two steaks on the grill. The martinis were already in the thermos. The Party Guy was coming over.

She saw him through the glass front door when he arrived. He was a dark silhouette carrying bags. He could see her at the far end of the darkened lobby, sitting and working in the traditional glass-windowed control room. He knocked and waved to catch her attention. She looked toward him and made no move. He made large gestures, miming that she should come and unlock the door. Margaret stayed put, continued playing the station's collection of the world's worst records, with every tenth selection taken from a small pile on the mixing-board. That week's top-ten.

After a while he left, taking his cooling steaks and his warming martinis.

The telephone rang.

"You didn't let me in."

"I know."

"I came all the way there and you didn't let me in!"

"I told you not to come. I told you I wasn't going to let you in."

"Well," he said sadly, "You really looked good."

"Thank you."

"Are you sure ..."

"Don't come over again I won't let you in."

When she applied for the job the station manager said, "We don't want any personalities." Desperate for work she reassured him that she was no personality. She did a straightforward audition, reading the news—pulled in a long sheet from the machine—flawlessly, with no inflection he could construe as an attempt to make herself interesting. She got the job. Seventy-five dollars a week, before taxes.

Every night she arrived at the station at 11:45, stood while the announcer ending his shift signed off to the "listening audience" or "all you good night-people," and set a record going. The music gave them three minutes to walk to the front door, let Margaret lock it behind him and return, ready when the song ended to say what it had been. She would announce her own first record (always pre-ordained, the new owners had shelved all the stations holdings [male vocal, female vocal, instrumental, male vocal ...] and wanted them played exactly as they were shelved) and settle in to eight hours alone in the semi-darkened station.

Early mornings she drove home, slept four hours, went to her mother's to pick up her two daughters for the day. Twice a week, to keep herself human and pretend she had a future, she went to the University for a writing class. The other students were younger than Margaret, were not spending the long nights at a job.

She was in a weakened condition, prone to destiny.

She and Patrick sighted each other and froze. There was an almighty relief in it. In the vast wash of all the world here was a lifeline. Time stood still. It is so noteworthy it is notorious, that fraction of a second. Commonplace uniqueness has made it a cliché. Time stood still, then flashed past, unnoticed by Sam who introduced them, who continued to talk about Israel.

Margaret asked whether there were kibbutzes that took non-Jews. She said she was fed up with the life she and her two kids were living and she wanted to get out of the country ... something like that, like she knew what she was saying. But she felt as if she had got halfway across a tightrope and forgotten how to walk. And she couldn't remember his name.

She left the two men, trying to move casually with their eyes on her. She thought she had been babbling like a damned fool. She couldn't remember what she had said. When she pulled her car away from the curb she wrenched the gears into place with an almighty racket, knew the two could hear it, looked straight ahead and drove away from so much awkwardness. Empty with the loss of leaving him there.

"Damn men!" she exploded.

The next few days were spent waiting. She didn't know where or how he'd do it but she knew he was on his way.

Four nights later, Sam and Patrick were out on the town. The bars closed at two-thirty in the morning and Sam called the radio station.

Margaret opened the door for them. Quite casual.

"I should have told you to bring some coffee," she said.

"Is there someplace nearby?" Patrick asked.

It was January. It was dark and cold.

"Go get some coffee," Patrick told Sam. Sam grumbled, but he went.

Topics are often the least crucial thing in a conversation. Sometimes the fact that the conversation is happening at all is the topic. At last he is here, I am here, we are talking, that was the topic.

It was not the case that nothing got said.

"I never want to get married again," Margaret told him and meant it.

"You'll never be a writer," Patrick, who was a writer, said. She had mentioned the class she was taking. It was something to say. Anything.

"Why do you say that?"

"The way you talk, I can tell."

When Sam returned, shivering and miserable, he was an interruption. Patrick, irritated, told him to go get some more coffee.

"I just got coffee! We haven't even drunk the coffee I just got!"

Patrick asked, "Do you have a couch or something? A blanket or something? A place for me to sleep?"

Sam looked back and forth at the two, not understanding what was happening.

Margaret knew what was happening. She was taking Patrick home.

A dilapidated wooden house on Griegos Road with almost no furniture. In the living room two single bed mattresses on the floor with cushions against the walls were couches. A table and four chairs belonging to Margaret's landlady were in the dining room. The kitchen was sloppily painted blue and white, Margaret hadn't had the time or the money to repaint since she moved in. There was a stove on legs, a refrigerator (also on legs, with a circular cooling unit on the top) a built-in "nook" with a yellow and blue table, and blue benches. There were two bedrooms with beds. Margaret's two daughters slept in one bedroom when they weren't being cared for by their grandmother. Margaret slept in the other when she had the chance.

Daylight was another hour away. Margaret turned lights on, made coffee. They talked, the air around them as charged as filament in a lightbulb.

It was light out when Patrick said, "I have to teach today. I should try to sleep."

He stretched out on one of the living room mattresses, rolled over to face the wall, lay there. Margaret brought blankets and covered him. Playing house.

He wasn't asleep. He kept looking toward the wall. Margaret went to her own bed. She stretched out there, looking toward the ceiling, fully dressed, awake.

They hadn't touched.

When the alarm sounded Margaret got off the bed, went into the living room where Patrick was sitting up on the mattress.

"Good morning," they said to each other, as if a night had passed instead of an hour.

He followed her into the kitchen. She made eggs and toast and more coffee. They ate. Saying almost nothing, as if they had been married for years. As if there were time.

Margaret drove Patrick to where he lived, four rooms attached to the end of an old adobe house. They were both living in the valley north of Albuquerque. The Sandia mountains glowed in the early morning desert light.

Patrick said, "Can I come back when I finish teaching?" Margaret said, "Yes."

She watched him walk to his door. He gave a wave. She left.

They still hadn't touched.

It was only a matter of time.

When Patrick came home from that day's teaching Margaret was waiting for him in her car.

"I didn't know whether you'd remember how to get to my house."

"Let me just get some things. I'll be quick."

When he came out again he threw his bag into his own car. It was more sensible.

They went home to Margaret's and went to bed with all the shynesses of the first time, all the sweet places, and a vast feeling of luxury as if the bedroom and the bed in it were cradled and rocked as if they'd finally found the universal King's-X.

Then years passed.

• • •

In the desert of northern Mexico the van, the cheapest of its kind, no insulation, was a moving oven. They cooked. Opening windows only caused the heated air to rush around them in a gale. The children stripped to white cotton panties, pulled tops on only when they were nearing towns. Diapers reeked in the "airtight" pail.

When Margaret opened the ChapStick it had melted.

Alix and Lucy watched telephone poles passing. Their heads swung back and forth in the rhythm of the approaching pole, the passing pole.

"Count them," Lucy ordered.

"Where should I start?" Alix's head was swinging towards the next pole to come.

"Start with ONE!" Lucy exploded in a giggle.

Alix turned away from all of it, reached for a comic book.

Lucy's face fell, too smart for her own good, won the battle, lost the war.

Early mornings they would stop in whatever small town they came to and Margaret would use her limited Spanish to buy fresh baked bread, fruit that could be peeled. Once a day, in the late afternoon, they stopped at a cheap eating place for their daily meal—stringy beef or chicken, eggs with chili. Margaret and Patrick drank beer. The children had Pepsi or Coke or bottled fruit juice.

Halfway to Mexico City they could see that their drinking water would get them there.

The overloaded van was slow. On any upgrade the motor laboured. They began the long climb to Mexico City. The van's motor racketing, losing power in the higher altitude. The air turned cold. The earlier heat could hardly be remembered. Extra clothing and sweaters were pulled on. It began to rain.

In Mexico City, eating in a cheap restaurant, Susie vomited onto the table. The waitresses seemed honestly to be more concerned with the child than they were with the mess as they helped Margaret clean it up.

The city was left behind.

The van, an enclosure of air in non-stop rain, rushed downhill toward Puebla. All the roads were running rivers. The windshield also ran a river. Wiper blades could only clear a thin line in their immediate wake. In the lower altitudes warmth returned bringing with it the returning stench of diapers and soured milk.

Anna began to have a yellowish diarrhea.

Susie vomited onto the double bed. They stopped, wiped the vomit off the blanket with wadded newspaper, rolled the blanket and stuffed it underneath the platform to be dealt with later. Its smell was added to the stifling air.

• • •

In the rational light of day, sitting over a cup of something soothing, Margaret would be the first to acknowledge that her night vision was bad. The rain made it worse. Exhaustion made a triple play. Driving in the darkest small hours of the morning oncoming headlights would splay out across the wet windshield like exploding stars. She would have no idea of whether the vehicle coming at her filled the entire road or only its appropriate share. She would solve her fear by slowing almost to a stop until they were past. A bicycle with a strong headlight could bring her to her knees.

Her eyes longed to close but she resisted—just one quick flicker of rest against this dark rush—but she resisted—Oh, we're dancing here in Idaho—we're all dancing here—a band of dancers in sunlight with long streamers of flowers, arriving so gently she hardly noticed, filled her head. She was jerked back into present peril by a crashing lurching of the front right wheel over a pile of boulders.

"Whatsat! Whatsat!" Patrick yelled, jerking to sit upright on the mattress.

It was all right.

The Idaho dancers had come and gone in a split second. The rocks were somewhere behind them.

"Nothing!" Maragret yelled back. "Go back to sleep."

She reassured Patrick, thinking, We're not dead. We're not damaged. She sounded confident. Patrick rearranged himself among the arms and legs of the sleeping children.

Margaret was shaking, shaking.

The van ate more miles out of the wet night.

When her grandmother said, "Honey, I know you'd like this," and threw a round rock over the cliff into the valley below, smiling a sweet smile at Margaret as she did so. Margaret was faster, stopped the van, rolled the window down to put her hand through and get it wet. She washed her face over with her wet hand.

Mexico in the rainy season. Pitch black night. She continued to drive, five miles an hour, wheels grinding and slipping in the rubble washed down into the road.

• • •

"What does he say?" Patrick asked.

The grinning face of the border guard dropped lower, looking into the van to see the man who had spoken. Looking into Patrick's face the guard raised both arms high above one shoulder and dashed them downwards in a diagonal across his chest.

"Whoosh!" he said.

"He said the border is closed," Margaret said. "It looks like he's saying there's been a landslide."

"Quando es la frontera posible?" Margaret asked. Posee-blay. Is that Spanish, she wondered.

"Martes," the guard grinned.

"Tuesday," Margaret said.

They drove back along the southern tip of Mexico, going the wrong way.

As if it were a consolation prize they saw farther, moment by moment, into an expanding world. The rain was giving them a rest. A weakened sun began to shine.

By the time they were sitting on pink chairs at a pink table in the patio of a small hotel the sun had become strong enough to cause the yellow and blue tiled floor to gently steam. Soon they would have to take their beers and move to another table in the shade of the nearby small orange tree.

"Como gente," Patrick said into the drowsing afternoon. That and "y pues" were almost his total store of Spanish.

Like people.

They had arrived at the border with thirty-nine dollars of their hundred intact, enough to let them sleep in beds until Tuesday, to drink beer and eat cooked food.

The two oldest girls were playing across the street in the plaza that centred the small town. The baby was asleep in a bed. Susie was in the kitchen, watching tortillas be made by two Indian girls who played with her as they worked.

Patrick and Margaret lazed in the sun.

Como gente.

And, walking into the enclosure, one of their girls holding each of his hands, came an obviously American man in pale blue canvas shoes with crepe rubber soles and the faded blue denim pants that were not faded at all but a commercial colour. His boyish and knowledgeable face was predictable. There he was, no help for it.

Chance encounter is one of the joys and ruinations of travel.

Margaret sighed.

They watched him cross the brightly coloured tile floor. He introduced himself, Henry something. He had come to save them from their social ignorance.

"Only Indian children play in the park," he said.

"You're a writer, aren't you?" he asked Patrick as an afterthought, recognizing his name.

"Is it dangerous?" Margaret asked, wanting to get the terms straight. "Can they get hurt?"

"Well, no." Henry's concern was for appearances, some notion of status.

Margaret told the girls they could go out again to play in the park.

"And don't talk to strangers." she added. Too late.

"I've read some things of yours," Henry told Patrick, showing himself to be a reader of significant and obscure literary publications.

He was a tenured professor of Creative Writing. He stressed "tenured" with a wry look to show he felt his shackles.

"Good money in it?" Patrick asked, his eyes half-closed, whether because of the sunshine, Henry, or exhaustion it was hard to tell.

"Oh, yes. Well, the going rate."

Henry was on sabbatical which meant that he was currently being paid to not teach Creative Writing.

He invited them to his house, saying their children could play with his children.

"Have dinner with us," he said. "What we laughingly call *comida*."

They gathered the girls and strolled along the street, around a corner, through a heavy wooden doorway into a central courtyard with doors opening around the squared sides into rooms.

The courtyard was filled with children and a woman with grey hair, introduced by Henry as "my wife's mother, Charlotte."

"Charlotte, have you seen the small tortoise-shell box that should be on my table?" Henry's domestic voice had the clear, hard tones of a boss who would brook no argument. Charlotte went off to find his tortoise-shell box.

The two oldest children, a boy and a girl, were distinguished from the others by being the children borne to Henry by his first wife.

"I married the first time for love," Henry said bitterly. "I never made that mistake again."

He took them through dark rooms into a medieval kitchen, rotting and damp, to meet his second wife, the mother of his five most recent children.

She was washing clothes in a tub.

"This is where the servants stay," Henry said, and laughed to show it was a joke. Mrs. Henry didn't laugh, didn't stop washing clothes, didn't look up when Margaret tried to chat. Margaret was not to be an interruption in her career of being Henry's unloved wife.

Charlotte returned, carrying a small brown box.

"I didn't want the box, Charlotte. I don't need the box. I simply wanted to know whether it was where it was supposed to be."

"It was." Charlotte said. "It was right where you said it should be."

"Then will you please put it back." Charlotte left again.

Henry's menage also included a pimpled, plump young man named Charles, introduced by Henry as, "... my *star pupil*," who would, "be a really good writer, someday." The implication was that Henry's tutelage would be responsible for moulding Chuck's pathetic clay into a finer form.

Henry reintroduced the issue of the children playing in the park. It had to do with the prestige of persons like himself in the outback nations. He had come south a few thousand miles and found himself a nation of peons. It suited him, this poverty he was remote from. Now all he need do was maintain the status quo. Born to be free and own it. He lived in a house that cost him twelve dollars a month, could hire servants for five. Though it seemed Mrs. Henry could not keep servants. She was not firm enough, Henry said. They despised her. And who can work for someone they despise.

He brought out two glasses, poured red wine into one of them from a green bottle. He reached past Margaret to give the glass to Patrick.

"I find this wine is too harsh for women," he explained, bobbing his head in agreement with himself.

"I've been married to a writer for four years now, Henry," Margaret told him firmly. "I can drink almost anything."

Henry, inconvenienced and obligated, went all the way across the room, fought the latch of a cupboard door, bore the weight of another glass the distance back and poured it half-full of wine, all for Margaret.

She wondered whether he might pour it on her, an accident, his hand too weak, finally, to hold it all. But he didn't. She sat, como gente, drinking the wine she had fought for, listening to Henry describing the servant problem with no doubt in her mind of where the problem lay.

That bottle and another bottle went quickly.

Comida, which Margaret had thought would be lunch, was not forthcoming.

Enough bad wine on an empty stomach equals rhapsodies. Rhapsody.

Darling Patrick.

Margaret smiled at him. My life has been blessed by a various man. Patrick smiled back.

The party of three was becoming jolly. Chuck whose function seemed to be to stand on the sidelines and swell the throng was sent for more wine.

"If these marks aren't on the label," Henry said, holding an empty bottle for Chuck to look at, "don't let him sell it to you. He'll try to tell you it's the same but it's not."

"I'll go with you," Margaret said, and stood up. Good move. She could do with a walk.

Chuck was looking toward the bottle he had been shown, his brow furrowed with the act of remembering.

Margaret said, "Why don't you take the bottle?" and his brow cleared.

"You don't need that," Henry frowned. "You should be working on your Spanish."

"I need it, Henry," Margaret reached for the bottle.

The thought of Margaret nurturing her ignorance caused Henry no conflict. Margaret, the bottle, and Chuck walked out into the street which opened expansively after the strictures of the patio.

"Why does your husband call him Hank?" Chuck asked Margaret, "Henry hates to be called Hank."

"That's probably the point, Chuck," Margaret answered.

"What?"

"I said, 'You said it, Chuck.'"

"What?"

At the wine merchant's the shopkeeper looked puzzled while Chuck, prepared to kill for quality and his master's voice, earnestly examined the labels. The marks were there. Chuck treated it as a personal coup.

It was getting late, then later.

Henry borrowed ten pesos from his mother-in-law and

sent his wife to buy coffee. He specified green beans, only enough for two pots of coffee.

"You can't send servants for the coffee. They'll give them trash."

Seeing the door close behind Henry's wife Margaret wondered how expansive she found the street. Did it occur to her that she was out? That she could run?

Mrs. Hank returned with coffee and change, gave the change to Henry who insisted he had given her twenty pesos. She turned to leave, to go back to the shop. It was Henry's idea that she had left them money lying on the counter.

"It won't be there now!" Henry hissed. "Stop making a scene!"

"You only gave her ten pesos, Henry," Margaret said. The couple didn't hear her. "You only gave her ten pesos, Henry. You borrowed ten pesos from Charlotte, that's all you gave her." The couple wouldn't hear her.

Mrs. Henry went into the kitchen to start the green coffee beans roasting, after which they would be ground and coffee would be made.

"This is all much too much trouble," Margaret said to Henry, "We could come for comida another time."

"I know she's slow," Henry chided Margaret's impatience, "but she does only have one servant to help her."

Mrs. Henry, who had come from the kitchen for further instructions, glared at Margaret then turned back to her husband. She stood near his shoulder, her eyes on him as intently as if he were the cliff she hung from.

"This is something I assigned my freshman class last year." Henry passed Patrick a sheet titled PRINCIPLES OF ENJAMBMENT.

"You use enjambment?" he asked as Patrick blindly scanned the page.

"I do enjamb, Hank," Patrick said seriously.

In the buzz got from sharing three seventy-five cent bottles of wine did Margaret worry that her fine Patrick had a recognizable gleam in his eye, might well be in the beginnings of one of his notorious bits of drunken behaviour and might, in all likelihood, direct it toward ghastly Henry? She did not. Every move Henry made defined him as deserving a very different treatment than he was given by his defaulted household.

Comida was beans and tortillas, wilted lettuce, potatoes, watery coffee. It was not laughable.

"OK, Hank," Patrick rose with the finality of a brown bear rearing onto its hind legs, "it's time for the cantina."

Before they left Henry added a thirty-one page poem, (romantic theme, ballad form, personal innovative method), to the stack of items given over for Patrick's consideration. Patrick being caught here until Tuesday meant there would be time to discuss all of what was close to Henry's heart. Patrick turned the pages in quietly increasing despair.

"Lots of enjambment there, Hank," he said.

Henry smiled, then frowned.

Margaret stopped at the hotel to see the children to bed, told the young Indian girl watching over them that she would be at the cantina, three doors away, walked through the darkened patio, onto the sidewalk, into the caressing night air.

The cantina was one room, three wooden tables, a dozen rough chairs, a jukebox, a light bulb hanging at the end of a cord. Every table had a lighted candle in the depths of a tall glass with a religious image decalled on the outside.

The three men were at a table lighted by the Virgin of Guadalupe. The candle had burned down far enough to be a glow in her belly.

Chuck was nervous. He licked his lips and looked

around the almost empty room, telling his story to Margaret in a babble. He had had bad experiences in Mexican bars. "... just picked up a beer bottle and broke it on the bar ..." He wished the lights were brighter.

"They'd just see you sooner, Chuck," Margaret reassured him.

Patrick was also looking around, gleeful. He was looking for the action. If there was any action to be had Patrick would find it or it would find him.

In Vera Cruz, the second summer after they married, Margaret quickly learned she hadn't the energy to follow along on Patrick's night-time adventures. Besides, there were the three children and the fourth in her belly. Daytimes were spent with all of them at the beach or sitting in the plaza. Nights, Margaret stayed in the little two room apartment, swinging children in hammocks, reading to them or to herself, falling asleep. Patrick would go to the central plaza and come home with stories.

He had gone around restaurants with an armless beggar who drank beer by holding the bottle to his mouth with stumps. Patrick had somehow, he said, come by a violin and he had fiddled and passed the hat while the beggar danced. Margaret knew that Patrick was truthful but she gave his stories a grain of salt. He had been drunk. She was sure he had found a fiddle and played it, but when he insisted his childhood lessons had all come true, that he had played it well, she was inclined to doubt it.

"That's where the Japanese man with the two children lives," he could say as they drove through the streets, pointing up to the third floor of a derelict building, and Margaret would look up toward where that man, worried for Patrick, had taken him home and fed him soup. There had been two small children there who were left alone all day while their father worked at his job. "He ties a rope to their ankles and ties them to the bed so they can get around the apartment but they can't go out and get hurt. He came home one day and his wife was dead on the floor so now there's just him to take care of them."

Another time in the early morning, still dark, Patrick waked her to say, "The car's gone."

"What?"

"I've lost the car. It isn't anywhere. Somebody stole it." His voice was mournful. How could they live and go on without a car?

"You just forgot where you parked it. We'll go out in the morning and look for it."

"They stole it. Somebody stole my car."

"If they stole it, we'll report it. If they didn't steal it we'll find it. Come to bed. Get some sleep."

"That's it, is it? Just go to bed! Go to sleep! That's the best you can think of when they steal the car!"

"We'll find it, Patrick. It's too dark now to go looking for it. When it's light we'll go looking for it."

Patrick was hurt. A man does the best he can do and a woman can't even be bothered. He grumbled himself to sleep.

Margaret lay awake. A woman who couldn't sympathize with a man who's lost his car.

The car was parked where they usually parked it in the block nearest the Plaza, near a streetlight. Patrick wanted to say, "They brought it back," but he knew better.

Henry, who had specified his wife as the woman he need never love, still had notions of romance. He began to wall his eyes in Margaret's direction. He caused a lugubrious rendition of "Quando Me Tiquieros" to play on the jukebox."

"I like Rancheros," Margaret told him.

Ah, he had known she would be cruel.

Chuck scattered his chair sideways, crashing against Margaret. His fears had been proven justified. The space he had cleared so adroitly was filled by a drunk who had crossed the floor, intent on their little group.

The man's body kept a slow roll of motion as if the floor were in heavy seas. He leaned forward against the table and looked at Chuck, his lip snarled and ugly.

"Gringos!" The "s" spewed spit over their heads as the Mexican continued his glare around the table.

Chuck was crawling into Margaret's lap, his head turning to look back.

"He means trouble," Chuck whispered as he crawled, "He's going to cause trouble."

The Mexican continued his sneering way around the table until he saw Patrick.

There is a vast understanding among drunks. Like dogs and small children they recognize one another across all barriers and their faces tighten to attention. All else fades into the background.

Patrick waved one arm in a splendid gesture.

"Y pues!" he announced to his newest long-lost friend.

"Y pues?" the standing drunk was understandably confused.

"Y pues!" the seated drunk insisted.

The Mexican reached to the next table and dragged a chair across the bit of floor to put it in the space so recently vacated by Chuck, who sat shivering and terrified beside his new neighbor.

They made a charming picture, Patrick and the Mexican. The Mexican's arm was laid over Patrick's shoulder and left there while the Mexican, his face screwed into a villainous expression, talked. There faces were a scant inch apart. At intervals the Mexican would wave his free arm at the other three and glare and Patrick would also look at them, his face angelic and delighted. A friend at last. Whenever the Mexican stopped talking as if he had asked a question Patrick would say "y pues" and bob his head sympathetically, and after a moment of puzzlement the drunk would continue.

Margaret's ears were being hissed into, Chuck on one side, Henry on the other, an ear apiece. They were telling the same story, catastrophe in stereo: "... he just picked up the beer bottle ... hadn't done anything ... straight for the face ... three men to hold him ..."

The Mexican stood.

His chair fell over behind him, crashing against the floor. Chuck and Henry flinched as if it were a gunshot. They were ready to go under the table.

The standing Mexican glared at them with venomous intent that stopped short at murder but who could guess why. He leaned toward them, putting his hands on the table. They were transfixed. Their faces registered horror Hollywood would have paid for.

"Gringos!" he accused them, spewing them with spit.

He took a long time straightening up, his eyes still on them. Upright, he glanced only briefly at Margaret. She wasn't in his argument. He looked at Patrick. His face melted into a tender regard. He lifted his right hand at the end of its arm in a soft flourish of farewell, a gesture as pure as an entire ballet. He turned and left, a shambling creature.

Chuck pulled his chair back into place.

"Why did he like you so much?" he asked Patrick jealously. It was a burden to him that the Mexican nation went for his throat on sight.

"Well," Margaret stood, "I'm for bed."

She felt no pity for Henry's obvious anxiety at whether he was being left responsible for Patrick. Life in the fast lane, Henry.

She said good night to the duo, gave Patrick a kiss, and left. She walked through the warm air to the hotel, gave the girl who had watched the children some money, changed the baby's diaper, went to bed.

"He threw me out of his house!" the wail of Patrick, misunderstood. "He told me 'leave!' He said, 'go home, Patrick Dougherty!'"

The room was semi-dark with a seepage of light around the door. Patrick was on the floor in a sprawl, as he had fallen.

"I said," the dark lump moved as if toward a more dignified position, "I said, 'You understand this means that the next time we meet I must kill you!' And he said ..." Patrick gave up any attempt at dignity, laid flat and chortled, "He said, 'then I must do my best to avoid seeing you!'"

The next day the Doughertys gathered their belongings. They had decided not to wait for the highway to be cleared. It was all too possible that while one landslide was being repaired others were happening elsewhere. They had decided to drive back down the mountain, cross the Pacific coast, put the van onto a flatcar and be carried across the border on a train. No landslides to contend with. It would be more trouble but they could depend on it.

Patrick decently laid the manuscript to one side before he ripped all the other things Henry had given him to pieces.

"What that son-of-a-bitch has on Charlotte," Patrick hoisted a filled suitcase onto the floor, "is that she didn't know she was pregnant when the man proposed and she wanted time to think it over and he went off to war and got killed. Henry blames it on Charlotte that his wife is a bastard. Henry's bit with Charlotte is he asks her why she didn't say yes right away. And Charlotte tries to remember what she had in mind and then she tries to explain it to Henry."

Margaret and Patrick were sitting in the patio for a last cup of coffee. The older girls were having a last run in the park.

"I looked at Hank's wife and her mother waiting to be told they could go to bed and all I could think of to say was 'Hank, enjambment is shit.' That's when he threw me out."

Chuck, his face lined with fear of failure, came through the patio entrance on his latest fetch and carry errand. Patrick went to reclaim Henry's manuscript from the owner of the hotel.

"I've never seen Henry so upset!" Chuck told Margaret.

"Would you like some coffee?" Margaret asked.

"Oh, no!" Chuck backed away. He would be asked for an accounting when he returned. Hank wouldn't take kindly to his having fraternized.

Patrick returned, handed over Hank's epic. Chuck was free to go and did, in a hurry, relieved and sweating.

Margaret said, "I wish I had a couple of borachos with busted beer bottles to see that boy home."

Patrick was out in the van hoisting the bags around when Chuck returned.

"Henry wants the examples of enjambment," he announced, firmly righteous, the voice of Hank coming through by remote control.

"Patrick tore them up," Margaret said, smiling and friendly.

"He tore them?!"

"He tore them up."

Hank disappeared from Chuck's framework, leaving him floppy and soft. "It was the only copy Henry had with him!" Chuck wailed, "He's really going to be mad!"

They drove down the mountain into the heat and the rain, across the narrowest part of Mexico, the curving tail of the gigantic comma, to the Pacific coast, to the dirty, cluttered, small town where putting cars onto trains was the major industry. And were stopped again; it would cost fifty dollars to put themselves and the van onto a flatcar and they only had twenty-three.

They found a room in a junky pensione.

They walked along the town's central dirt street to the telegraph office and sent two telegrams, one went north to an old friend of Patrick's to ask for a loan, the second went south to tell Patrick's employers they were delayed.

• • •

Margaret carrying the diaper pail (again) went into the current bathroom (again) to begin (again) to wash diapers.
Theme recurrent to the point of boredom. In Greek myths,
those women always at the creeks? They were washing
clothes. Even the princesses.

One small baby and a two year old child means endless diapers. Margaret stretched rope clothesline between
chairs and doorknobs. Rain kept the two adults and the
four children caught into the one room where the diapers
hung, dripping, making the air more wet. Moisture ran
down the walls.

Margaret of the sanguine breast kept it to the forefront
of her mind that this sloppy hell was temporary.

They were en route to a place, a life, something other
than what had become too intolerable to bear. Hope sustained them. They would arrive elsewhere and, like Alice
down the rabbit hole, they would learn where they had
come to.

T W O

In that place that was the Doughertys' destination, the Grisantis were gathered. They had eaten Sunday dinner and were relaxing in Antonio and Helen's living room.

"There are two people lost in the desert," Don Cesar was putting a riddle to his family. "They have exactly enough water to keep one of them alive until help comes. What should be done?"

Coldly handsome with vivid white hair and pale blue Sicilian eyes he looked around him. He had left his armchair to stand near the centre of the open floor. They all looked up at him from wherever they sat.

"It is the moral law I mean. It is the moral law I ask you to consider."

He pointed to his youngest son, whose house he stood in. "Tonio, you first."

Antonio's face twisted in a pantomime of thought; he wanted to please his father.

"Is there more water anywhere nearby so that the two men can get there by rationing the water they have?"

"You miss the point!"

Don Cesar's finger circled the room.

All the answers were questions. Were wives and children involved? Was one man much older than the other? Could one man take some of the water and go for help?

"If the two people are a man and a woman," said Salvatore, who had arrived two weeks earlier from Italy to make cheese and to court Dolores-Rosa, and now walled his eyes at her, "then the man should give up the water to the woman."

It was clear that Dolores-Rosa agreed. Small and plump as a roasting chicken, her dark hair lifted into a great bulk of intricate curls, she approved of him, smiling.

Don Cesar swung his glare away from the couple. He was intent on the right answer.

"You must put the saddle on the right horse," Don

Cesar would say to his sons in Italian. For himself he meant himself; for them also it seemed he meant himself. There were always mistakes in what he entrusted to them. They would never reach his measure. It saddened and reassured him simultaneously.

"I won't be here to see it," he resigned himself to the disaster they would make of his holdings when he was dead.

The thought that they would live on beyond his own death made him want to strangle them.

"There is no hope! There is no way out! The situation is no more and no less than I have told you. There are two men," with a look toward Salvatore, "in a desert, with only enough water to let one of them live. What is the moral law to be considered?"

More weak mumbling. The Christian and Democratic consensus was that they must die together. It was not good enough. Dominick, the eldest son, conceded that given a fair way to draw lots and an agreement between the two to abide by the result, one of the two, the winner, might live. It was not good enough.

"The law of survival! God's law! The first law!"

The old man's finger was a hammer.

"God gives you life! It is criminal not to fight to keep the life that God gives you! The man who is strong enough to get the water for his own must do whatever is needed to survive. He would be going against God to die for a sentiment."

His riddle ended he sat in the large chair that he expected to always be there and to be his own.

Don Cesar Grisanti seized the first opportunity to prove his worth when he was still a young man—he suggested to his father, Don Sebastiani, that now, between coffee crops, was the time for him to have the visit home that he had spoken of for years.

Don Sebastiani went to Sicily, to visit with his old mother

and to see his sisters and his brother. Within days of his departure he had inadvertently retired. His son, Cesar, wrote to tell him that he no longer owned what he had owned. Also, damaging correspondence found in his desk proved that during the most recent revolution his sympathies had been with the wrong party and if he were to return he would be arrested.

Since that promising beginning Don Cesar had quadrupled his worth and had never taken a vacation. When his wife went on her regular visits to Italy Don Cesar stayed where his holdings held him.

He had slipped away to Italy only once, to bargain for the cheese vats that were necessary to his latest venture: he had gone and returned before telling his own sons about his plans. Not that he thought they were a threat to him. They had no such moves in them.

Don Cesar owned two fincas, a house in Guatemala City, and the lives of more than two hundred Indians. In his own domestic life he owned, just as absolutely, his three sons with their wives and children, an unmarried daughter, and his own wife: they all looked to him for their imported clothes, imported appliances, imported food, and imported fiancés.

And, apparently, imported tutors. Antonio was talking about the American tutor who was expected to arrive within the week.

Don Cesar watched the others listen. They would think that they must have tutors. They all had to get their gouge in. It was their sense of fair play.

It seemed to the old man, lean to the point of being thin, that they all ate too well. They were cushioned and plump. They grew fat eating into him.

Even now Cosimo, his second son, the dandy with the thin little moustache for tickling the girls, was on his way home from a buying trip in Mexico City. Don Cesar had been told of a new stove, an automatic clothes washer, dishes. And when the others saw his haul they'd be off to Mexico City, to keep it fair.

My and Mine, they ate it like bread.

Antonio could not have said "my father's money," "my wife's jewels" as if he spoke casually. But he could say "my children's tutor" as if he spoke of the weather.

As the tutor had value he must have standards and in his absence Antonio had them for him. Antonio listed what had been done and would be done to make the tutor snug. He believed his father would acknowledge his efficiency.

"... next Thursday," Helen was joining in as her husband's chorus. "But we haven't heard from them since they left the States."

"Barney had a letter to say they had left," Antonio said.

"Why does Barney get the letters?" Don Cesar exploded. "Why does Barney have all the correspondence? Does Barney own him? He is your tutor as much as he is Barney's tutor. Let Barney pay all the salary and supply the house as well as the school! Then he can have all the correspondence!"

Don Cesar's eyes canvassed the room. Salvatore and Dolores-Rosa were smirking at each other. They would not have thought of it but now they would expect a tutor for their snot-nosed darlings.

He could see them arriving in ever increasing numbers, his grandchildren, with teeth to eat his money and stupid heads that must have tutors.

And what of this one here? This one no tutor could teach. He looked at the idiot Helen had given Antonio for his first son, this one who would be four years old forever.

"It is a bad idea, this tutor!" Don Cesar flared in anger at the roomful of people. He turned his cold face to Helen. "What can this tutor teach your idiot, Señora? Will he teach him to drop his turds in the toilet bowl? Will he teach him to keep his fingers out of his nose?"

Helen, rickety in shock, left the room in slow motion, her mouth twisting.

In the room she had left her oldest son was looking at a picture book. His forefinger, stubby and wide, was buried deep in his nose. Antonio walked to him and slapped his hand away from his face. The boy wailed. Helen rushed back in, grabbed him into her arms, left the room carrying him, soothing him, her burden.

• • •

Six mornings a week a broken and mended blue bus stood in Tapalapa's central plaza, loading passengers and their belongings for the long looping drive north and west and back again. An assortment of badly wrapped cargo was piled on the roof tossed there by the driver's helper who then climbed the side of the bus and stood kicking and hauling the lot into a more secured shape. Inside the bus wooden planks were laid across for passengers.

When there were fiestas and on market days the Indians were packed row by row according to their destination. A row of passengers would be settled onto their plank and the next plank would be slid into place, pushed against their legs.

Three different times the bus had broken in half and been welded together again.

The driver's name was Teodoro. He was short and broad with grey beginning to show in the black of his hair. He sweated heavily whenever he did any physical labour. He had the helper for that.

He was more than he seemed to be. The government paid him to keep an eye on the territory he covered. He noted anything unusual that he saw or heard and he reported regularly to a bored clerk in the city who practically yawned in his face and never expected to hear anything of interest. He was, in his own imagination, a secret agent. He carried a gun he had paid for with his own money under the dash panel of the bus. He also had a smaller gun which he sometimes wore in a shoulder holster made for him by a leather worker in the city.

He was gratified to see the Mercedes-Benz driven by the wife of Don Alessandro Klaag pass the office on its way up the hill to the yellow brick house as he exchanged identical leather mail pouches with Don Antonio, giving him the incoming mail and receiving the outgoing mail. He returned to the bus and in his notebook he wrote, "Señora Klaag visiting Grisanti," and the date.

Teodoro was keeping a particular watch, for reasons of his own, on Don Alessandro Klaag and his family.

In the office Antonio read the telegram which had come in the mail pouch. It was from the tutor who was, apparently, still en route.

DELAYED AWAITING MONEY THURSDAY EARLIEST WILL PROCEED TRAIN REGARDS STOP DOUGHERTY

Antonio was relieved to have a telegram of his own. This was not news he would have to hear from Barney. It would show his father that he was not excluded from the correspondence.

He laid the telegram on the desk at different angles, testing its effectiveness. He wanted Don Cesar to see it when he came into the office.

The bus wheezed, backfired, and departed. In the quiet aftermath Antonio closed the office door and climbed into his jeep to drive up the hill.

He drove past the pulpe, a high mound of mush discarded in a wash of water, the pulp of the coffee berry that was cleaned away from the bean and carried along a metal conduit to be dumped into this perpetually rotting pudding.

One of Don Cesar's complaints when he checked Antonio's bills from the Puerto del Sol in the city was the number of air-freshener sprays bought by Helen, his American daughter-in-law.

"It is an American thing!" he would say in disgust.

"Perfume for the garbage can! Perfume for the bathroom!

How much can one family stink!"

Antonio's house sat directly uphill from the pulpe. When Don Cesar smelled the pulpe he smelled money. When Helen smelled it there was nothing so redeeming.

Airsprays were a part of Helen's continuing attempt to make this place, this marriage, be all she had hoped. The house had been built from plans ordered through Better Homes and Gardens. It was ranch-style with an attached double garage. It was yellow brick, with a yellow brick planter under the picture window. The front door had a small diamond-shaped window set into varnished pine and a doorbell that glowed in the night.

The house was so specific it made a volcano on the adjacent horizon seem unlikely and artificial.

• • •

In Antonio's living room Inez Klaag was weeping. Helen sat, making little cooing noises in her throat.

Don Alessandro had shot himself in the leg again. This time the bullet went into a bone and stripped the marrow all the way down as it went. It was more serious this time. He was again in the hospital, his leg in a cast. Inez had come to Helen to be consoled.

"The children were with me," she was saying when Antonio came into the room, as they were now, two small boys, round-eyed, watching their mother cry, "and still he stuck his head from the window and screamed at me to go home. He screamed, 'Go home, you whore! Go home, you bitch!' and the children heard it all."

She had saved her husband's life twice now, dragging him semi-conscious to a jeep and driving him, pouring blood, to the doctor in Tapalapa, and from there to the city, to the hospital.

Don Alessandro was a German but he should have been a Latin. He carried the burden of machismo. He spoke loudly because of it. He carried a revolver in his hip holster.

If one carries a gun one should be proficient with it. He practiced quick draws in his bedroom before the mirror and shot himself in the leg the first time. And was saved by his wife.

And if one wears a gun and has shown oneself to be a fool with it, shooting oneself in the leg, there is then the further problem. One wants only a proper respect. Drinking beer in a small shop in Quixaya if one wants the radio turned down and the shopkeeper dawdles about it one must wave one's gun in the air and with a proper flourish shoot the radio off its shelf. As Don Alessandro had done, successfully.

But the finger should not be near the trigger when the gun is returned to its holster or one is again, as he found himself, shot in the leg.

"It is hard to be such a man," his wife said. And then "There was a woman in the room with him. They won't leave him alone." She said it sadly but gave her head a lift of unconscious pride.

Antonio was abrupt with "poor" Inez. He had begun to rethink what his telegram meant. It seemed the message was brief to the point of insolence. The tutor thought he was a fool who would put up with anything. He went to his room to change his shirt, prepared to leave.

"I'm going over to see Barney about that damned tutor."

"What's the matter?" Helen turned from one crisis to the next.

"I should have listened to my father. Nobody worth his

salt would work for three thousand dollars a year."

"Has something happened?"

"Just he's such a prize he can't get here without being carried."

Antonio stopped at the office to retrieve the telegram. Thank God his father hadn't seen it.

Barney's whiskey bottle was a female torso moulded of foam rubber. It was pink with a pronounced belly button in the plumped stomach and bright red nipples on exaggerated breasts. It had been a Christmas present from Antonio. Since being given it Barney had kept two bottles of whiskey open in the liquor cupboard. The torso-covered bottle was brought out whenever Antonio came to visit; he was always pleased to see it.

"There's no reason to worry, Tony," Mildred said. "The books still haven't come. If he was here right this minute he couldn't be teaching."

"But he'd be here!"

"Relax, Tony. Have a drink." Barney poured, a nipple sticking out between his fingers. "Ella?" he asked, swinging the bottle in invitation toward his mother-in-law.

Ella Purvis sat with her lips closed tight over her teeth. She had hated the whiskey bottle on sight. "It's just vulgar!" she had snapped at Barney.

Ella Purvis didn't like Barney either. They made a pair in her eyes, Barney and that bottle. He had never deserved Mildred and things like that foam rubber female proved it.

Mildred was intent on ignoring all the dramas being played around her. She would not take Tony's fears seriously. She would not help her mother feel righteous about Barney's failings. Mostly and above all she wouldn't watch Barney act like a besotted simpleton with his damned bottle.

She was ordering books. The marbletop table Barney had given her for her birthday was covered with back issues of the New York Times Book Review and bulletins from the Book-of-the-Month Club. She sat turning pages, reading reviews and advertisements, writing down titles onto a sheet of a paper.

She was not too involved to know that Barney had drunk his first drink where he stood officiating at the sideboard, and that it was his second drink he brought to the couch.

She would not look toward her mother who grew heavily significant, waiting to catch her daughter's eye.

"How's the cheese factory?" Barney asked.

"Eduardo lost two fingers in the new mixer. We had to throw out a whole batch," Antonio said glumly. "That sets us back two weeks."

"Here's to health."

They drank.

Barney's catch phrase was "Let it happ'n, Cap'n," the punchline from a long since forgotten dirty joke. He could mean almost anything by it, an irreverent prayer, a message to fate to do its damnedest.

He drove in a headlong rush, roaring around the finca and in and out of the city in his jeeps, trucks, cars.

"That's the fifth one this year!" Mildred had said hysterically when she heard of his latest accident.

"Ricardo!" Barney yelled toward the kitchen, "bring some ice."

"No more for me," Antonio had had enough. "I'm going home for supper." He felt a slight spin to his head when he stood up. Barney toasted him on his way with an empty glass, walked to the table to refill it when the door closed. His fresh drink in his hand he turned toward his wife and mother-in-law.

Ella Purvis's lips were in a hard straight line and Mildred's lips were in the same straight line.

• • •

Cosimo, Don Cesar's second son, the one with the moustache, was stopped at the same border that had stopped the Doughertys. He was told, as they had been told, that landslides blocked the road.

Slighter than his brothers and more deliberately elegant, he usually drove something more splendid than this pick-up truck with its mass of lumps covered over with a tightly tied tarpaulin.

He waited in a red tile hotel for Tuesday when the road would be passable. On Tuesday he returned to the border and learned that the slide had been cleared and he could continue.

The road was saturated and the rain which had stopped just long enough to let the repairs be made was turning it to soup. Driving had not been made easier by the repairs, it had only been made possible. Cosimo drove slowly along the road, a ridged wound of bleeding red clay. The tires of the truck were forced deep into the wet clay by the weight of the load. With each turn the tires added a thick layer of clay. When the accumulation had grown enough to be unwieldy it would slough off and the truck would jolt sideways. Cosimo drove as carefully as he could but it was fortunate that he met no other cars, the narrow road could not have supported more than one such uncertainty at a time.

He realized he was approaching the site of the earlier slides when he saw, through the windshield made almost opaque by rain, a road grader stopped directly ahead of his truck. Stopping was an exercise in mundane engineering, momentum times the weight of the loaded truck complicated by the mud that glued the tires to the road or caused them to slew. Cosimo slid to a stop.

The driver was sitting in his high cab drinking from a jar of coffee and eating a sandwich. He had been oblivious to the threat of Cosimo's approach and was now oblivious to his presence. The rain had the effect of cotton batting and kept him from hearing the horn of Cosimo's truck. Finally, seeing it was hopeless, Cosimo left his truck and with the rain sluicing him through walked forward to the side of the cab and banged on the metal with his fist. The driver, complacent, opened his door and looked down at Cosimo with the interest of a visitor to an aquarium.

Ah, of course, he understood without needing to hear what Cosimo was saying. He had not expected a car so soon, he explained, soundless as a mute in the sounding rain. He looked toward Cosimo's truck as a polite conversational gesture, bobbed his head at it. Of course he would move instantly to let that little truck ... which as he looked began to move sideways, riding the road which also moved sideways. Cosimo, seeing his face, also, turned to look. They watched a large piece of mountain move, at first slowly then in a great sliding mass.

The angle was steep enough to let the truck fall away into open air, freed from the earth, to hit farther down, to bounce and hit again.

Making their own ways went a refrigerator, sliming over with mud, a bright pink clothes dryer, losing its colour, and a number of smaller unidentifiable objects.

· · ·

On the other coast, with no idea of the disaster that might have been theirs had they had waited until Tuesday, Patrick and Margaret and the children walked along the main dirt street of the southernmost Mexican town. They were walking, as they did every morning and every afternoon, to the telegraph office. Alix was holding Susie's hand, who trotted to keep up. Margaret carried Anna. Alix and Lucy were talking about horses. They had somehow come to the agreement that Lucy, who was five, knew about horses.

The family's progress was slow. The sun was shining and they had come out of their cell. They circled around small puddles and larger gullies. This time the money was there.

They returned along the same street circling the same puddles to the room they could leave now.

Margaret took down the maze of thin rope that had stretched for days between the doorknobs and the furniture. The walls of the room had run with damp for the whole four days in the need to keep Susie and Anna in clean diapers. She stuffed the damp wad of diapers washed that morning into a plastic bag, collected the rope into a coil.

They were, all the family, exhausted and practical, experienced. They gathered their goods together like migrants the world over.

By midday the sun had established itself, blistering the sky and making the ground steam. At the train yard Patrick paid the precious fifty dollars, drove up a ramp and across two rickety, clanking metal plates onto a flatcar which they would have to themselves. The yard crew set to work nailing wooden chocks around the wheels of the van.

Margaret took two cheap striped rugs and spread them over the splinters to make a place where they could sit out and take the breeze.

There was no breeze.

They were hauled along the track to join other flatcars also holding automobiles. The string of attached flatcars were pulled onto a shunting to wait.

And wait.

They sat in heat made fierce and abrasive by the sun being absorbed into the cindery ground and rising again, as if the ground burned, had been burned and still smoked from it.

The flatcar waited adjacent to a siderailed string of freight cars that housed families. Maggie and Patrick and the children and the van and all their possessions, which Maggie felt had suddenly multiplied, were stared at by women and half-naked children who sat in the semi-shade of opened freight car doors, eyes staring out of a permanent insolvency. Ruined and poor, the eyes watched them until an engine arrived and joined itself to the flatcars with a crashing jerk and they were drawn away at five miles an hour, no faster than a walk, to another part of the yard where they were again left to wait.

Margaret took wet diapers from the plastic bad and spread them on the flatcar. By the time she laid down the last the first she had laid down were dry. Anna was crying. Susie was whimpering but bearing up. The family, wilted and miserable, waited for three hours, eyes and mouths dried by the heat. Finally, with great jerks that made them grab for something to hold onto, the train began to move.

• • •

Deepening jungle. Swamps where white lilies were vivid in the rich, oil-coloured water. Wild orchids bloomed in the crotches of unapproachable trees and white egrets, at the train's passing, gave a thrusting shove of their wings that lifted them in a slow motion haul into higher air.

On splintery wood the family rode in an unlikely grandeur.

Vegetation and water cooled the air.

Along the way, in the middle of jungle, small villages sat beside the rail track. No roads could be seen. Some of these people had only seen automobiles on flatcars. They had anticipated the train's passage, making fresh tortillas and boiled tamales to sell to passengers during the train's brief stop. With a jerk the train would begin again to move. Five miles an hour, through untouched jungle.

Margaret felt placed just right, content. Those egrets are my kind of sparrow. All I need to be happy is a whole jungle and a train to ride. A whole family looking all right enough so I don't feel like a shirker. And I need Patrick. Other women solve it more simply. I'd be a lot better off if I could feel like this by just buying a new refrigerator. She wouldn't have been better off. Besides, they couldn't afford a new refrigerator.

In the early evening the train came to a long shuddering stop, metal scraping, at a trainyard near the Guatemalan border.

The cars would not be unloaded until daylight.

The Doughertys tidied the van. When it was dark Margaret laid down on the mattress with the girls. Patrick stretched as he could manage it on the front seat.

The small side-hinged windows of the van were open in the hope a breeze might pass through.

There was no protection against the noise that went on all night as boxcars and flatcars were shifted around the rails, got into place for the next day's action. The flatcar they were on was hauled from one truck and set free on another, over and over again, to roll until it hit flatcars already in place and came to a crunching stop with ricochets echoing.

Finally, even the noise and the mosquitoes could not keep them awake.

In the small hours of the night there was a time when everything was as it should be. The racket stopped. It was possible to sleep.

• • •

A small jerk of the flatcar, hardly to be noticed.

Margaret roused, semi-awake, waited to sink into sleep again. Her left leg was at a distance, wedged between sleeping children.

The effort of withdrawing her leg brought her more awake. She saw the windows as pale squares. It might be four or five in the morning.

She turned her head and saw a face, malevolently formed, floating over her face, the eyes huge and staring down. She jerked upright as if wires had jerked her.

The thing floating above her fell, lifeless, onto the mattress.

And she saw another face, very much alive, staring at her through the window.

She tried to cry out, "What are you doing?" or, "Go away" or, "Help." The old dream came true. Her tongue twisted in her mouth, caught in meaningless garble.

The van jerked with the two or three running steps it took the man to reach the edge of the flatcar and jump.

"What?" Patrick came awake.

The girls roused slightly.

Margaret explained that a thief had tried to steal Susie's doll. She picked it up, the face was still frightening.

"Are you alright now?" Patrick asked.

Of course she was alright. Nothing had really happened.

There might be an equation for it. Direction plus enough distance equals driving from poor to rich. They had driven far enough south to be wealthy and attractive to thieves. They would have to pay attention, to see that they had changed however much they were the same. If they didn't pay attention to what they had turned into they could get into trouble, be victims of their new description.

That's an old story. That's the same old story.

The others, not having had the jolt of adrenaline that coursed through her system, went back to sleep. Her heart was pounding.

She felt it must be pounding in unison with that of the thief who was crouched somewhere, waiting to see whether he was to be chased.

His face had been a white oval in the night. He must have seen her as the same, a white witch face, raised up to stare, a mouth caught to animal sounds.

She couldn't quiet her heart by thinking.

The body throws the mind away and runs.

Take deep breaths. She breathed.

She breathed.

Take deep breaths.

She breathed.

Where are the manuals and How-To books when you need them? When you're at the bottom of Mexico. Lashed to a flatcar in a railroad yard. When hands and arms and faces are coming at you in the dark heart of the night. And all you meant was to get to the job.

Thought of "the job" sustained her. The mundane reality was that they were en route to a job. It was not un-understandable however exotic the description might, for these few hours, be.

The thief had come and gone never to return. He might be their only thief ever.

Margaret breathed.

She breathed.

Finally, she slept.

• • •

"We've still got twenty dollars," Margaret said. "Do you think they'd take ten?"

"Not a God damned penny!" Patrick raged.

The yard crew in this place where they had arrived also wanted fifty dollars, another fifty dollars, to unload them. Once again the Doughertys were short fifty dollars. When they tried to talk to the yard boss, to tell them they only had twenty dollars and needed ten to cover the last tank of gas, the last day's food, he wouldn't listen. More gringo bullshit. He walked away. The flatcar they were on was pulled to an adjacent track and they watched all the other cars be unloaded. Then their flatcar was pushed back into place.

The workmen lounged and joked, watching them. The crew couldn't lose. They had these gringos nailed down.

The large metal plate was in place. Only the chocks had to be removed to let them go, let them drive off and away.

"I'm going to do it myself," Patrick said.

He jumped off the flatcar, onto the ground. The group of men roused, laughed, they thought he was coming now to pay them. He walked toward the stack of tools and took a crowbar before they understood what he intended. Two of the men jumped up, came toward him. He held the crowbar like a weapon and they paused, confused about what this meant. One of the men still lounging in the shade called out, "Let the gringo do the work." The others laughed. There was no problem. The pair returned to their shaded spot and watched Patrick circle the van, prying off the blocks of wood. As he freed the last wheel the same two men walked over, grinning, and shoved the large metal plate so it slid away from the open space to lie on the ramp.

The metal plate was more than Patrick and Margaret could manage between them. They were caught. Patrick wiped sweat from his face with a cloth Margaret had wetted and wrung out. Wiped his hands. He climbed back into the driver's seat of the van and they sat, hopeless, not knowing what to do.

As if to compound their problem a car and then a pick up truck came through a far gate of the trainyard, bumping across tracks toward them. The two vehicles drove to the foot of the ramp and stopped there. They were waiting to be loaded for the return trip. Another car came through the gate.

The crew of men looked disturbed, then sullen.

Patrick and Margaret sat taller, slowly, looked at each other. The arriving cars must be loaded from this ramp where the van was being held hostage. They must be loaded onto this flatcar that had only moments earlier seemed an unnegotiable trap, fixed in place forever. The tables had turned. The yard crew would have to let them go.

They watched as the men grumbled among themselves. The two who had shoved the metal plate away shoved it back into place. Patrick started the motor and, with both of them looking straight ahead, drove over the sagging plate, down the ramp, across the train yard and out the gate onto the road that would take them to the Customs office. They had held their breath but when they passed through the gate they whooped and hollered.

And now, as they had thought, today was the day when they would arrive.

The rain began again, to show that one success at a time was as much as they could hope for. At Customs they were asked to open a suitcase, a paper bag was poked into and they were waved on.

• • •

Sometimes two volcanoes could be seen, once there were three, there was always at least one. The land of the perpetual volcano.

Groups of Indians walked along the side of the road protecting themselves from the rain with large candy pink and sky blue plastic squares.

The night, when it came, fell quickly, intensified by the opaque rain.

Patrick would stop next to a group of Indians, each mounded with pastel squares shining and Margaret or Patrick would call out "Tapalapa" and wait to see an arm emerge and wave them forward or back. When there was no one to ask every road they passed might be the one they should have taken. However real their maps were, however much the coloured paper implied there was a place where in time they would arrive, Tapalapa was still a miracle when it appeared, shining in the night. They learned too late that they should not have turned into the first of the town's two streets. The street had been paved with round stones, rain through the years had floated the stones into groupings and gullies that made the road impassable. Patrick reversed the van before it was too late, turned, went forward to the second street and drove along it.

Now when they asked directions they were asking for San Felipe.

There was a last small hill hedged by poinsettias ten feet tall.

There was a driveway.

They turned and stopped.

There was a house, a screened porch.

Patrick turned off the motor. He turned off the lights. He and Margaret sat, stunned, in the quiet, in the dead car.

A screen door was thrown open. A man stood silhouetted there. Light from the porch threw his shadow toward them along the long shape of the doorway on the ground.

It was Barney.

He called out. "It's about time."

THREE

Mildred had assumed the tutor and his family would arrive at a decent time of day, that they could be shown the way to their own house and left there to settle in. This grubby couple Barney led into the dining room and deposited at the table had never entered her mind.

"Where are your children?" she asked Margaret.

"You brought all four of your children?" Mrs. Purvis said.

Margaret heard the disapproval in that apparently simple question.

There are too many children.

They have been brought here.

Tongue-tied by exhaustion and the shock of arrival, Margaret said, "They're sleeping in the van."

Barney called to servants to bring plates and cutlery and wine glasses. When the glasses arrived he poured them full.

Imagination fades before solid fact. Reality is more various and there's more to it. This dinner table with crystal candlesticks and silver laid on white linen had not figured in the Doughertys' expectations of their arrival, nor these two stiff-faced women with their lips pulled into welcoming smiles that never reached the eyes.

And Margaret saw there was something more. The two similar noses had a slight twist at the nostrils. On Margaret's mother that crinkle around the nose always preceded her saying, "I smell something!"

We smell, Margaret realized. Days and nights among diapers, soured milk, and vomit in the van's dank warren had perfumed them. They had come so far. So tired. To this table. Candlelight. Roses. Collapsed like bags of grain into their chairs, but trying. Making smiles. We have arrived and we are stinking. Barney seemed oblivious but those two noses wouldn't be fooled, registered the Doughertys' aroma absolutely.

Mildred began as she meant to continue. Manner slightly remote, she said, "You can sleep in the big house tonight. Barney will take you over to your house tomorrow."

It was clear that they were not guests.

In Margaret's depths her backbone stirred. Easy to look good when you've got money, Money cleans the house. Buys the clothes that give you a figure. Keeps the car running. Money buys the flatcar and keeps you from having to arrive stinking. To people who don't have the jaundiced eye of personal poverty people who have money look like they've got talent. But when you've come to be poor and you stay poor and you don't see any future but poor it can impact on your disposition. You can lose your compassionate regard and fellow-feeling for people like this bitch who means to make it clear that she's the gracious employer being put to trouble by the employees.

Smiling across the table at Mildred, Margaret laid a classic curse on her, thinking. "My stink is temporary but your nose will have that twist to it until you die."

"Thank you," she said, "that will be just fine."

Barney sensed crisis, spooned more food onto the newcomers' plates, topped their wineglasses. Went for brandy. He would see these strangers carried from the table dead drunk before he'd see them snubbed.

"Barney!" Mrs. Purvis wailed, "they don't want brandy now! They're still eating dinner. They haven't even finished their wine."

"Ella, they've just driven three thousand miles in the rainy season on bad roads and we're going to drink to that."

He poured brandy into his glass, into Margaret's glass, into Patrick's glass, downed his, asked "Another?" "Oh, yes. Thanks." Patrick followed his example.

Margaret stayed with her first, drinking it slowly, feeling the warmth curl in her stomach. She felt the improvement. Every few minutes she would remember that they had arrived.

The driving was over. They were here. This was it.

She wondered whether her two hatchet-faced detractors were capable of seeing just how tired she and Patrick were. She wondered whether they were wondering whether she was some kind of drunk. I just might be, she thought, if Barney keeps pouring.

Barney, Mildred and Mrs. Purvis resumed the conversation interrupted by the Doughertys' arrival. The dinner table topic was death and dying. It seemed people died in wholesale lots in this place. Mildred and Barney were comparing how many had died so far this year with how many died last year. At Los Cedros de San Juan, where the Doughertys were to live, twenty-three children were counted in the most recent epidemic of whooping cough.

"Our kids have had their shots for whooping cough," Margaret said. Relieved.

The conversation moved smoothly onto the current typhoid epidemic.

Mildred, it seemed, was convalescing.

She laughed, "Tony thinks Indians get typhoid because they're Indians. He says it isn't a 'white man's' disease. I don't know what he thinks that makes me." Seeing long faces on the Doughertys she added, "You won't have any problems. I let my booster shots get out of date."

"We didn't get typhoid shots," Patrick explained. "We thought we'd get them here."

And here they were.

It might already be too late.

Barney stood. He was unsteady on his feet.

"I've got plenty of serum in my office. You want your first shot now?"

"No." The couple declined in unison. However mindless they had been, this happy host and this hazy moment was not their idea of a solution. They would begin the shots some other time, tomorrow maybe, when they were not so tired, when it was not so late, when Barney was not so drunk.

And imagining their arrival Patrick and Margaret had never included Barney insisting that Tony and Helen must meet the new tutor immediately.

"Mildred!" Ella Purvis knew there was no appeal she could make to Barney who had no better nature to be appealed to. "You can't let Barney drag Mr. Dougherty back out into that weather when he just got here! He hasn't even finished his dinner!"

It was true that Patrick's plate was still more than half filled, given Barney's ministering hand. The wine and brandy glasses were empty.

Mrs. Purvis looked at Margaret and, in a crooning tone of voice, added. "I can see you're both just half-dead!"

Margaret, her mind on typhoid, unobtrusively knocked the wood of the chair she sat in.

Barney shoved away from the table. He meant to go and he meant to go now, Patrick also stood.

"Mr. Doughertys' a full grown man, Mama," Mildred said. "He's able to tell Barney if he doesn't want to go."

They all knew better.

The room was quiet when the men had gone. The three women sat looking at the door. They heard the jeep start, gun its motor, pull up the incline onto the road. The women looked at each other and smiled for no reason.

Lucy and Alix, wakened by the racket of the men leaving, came through the rain, barefoot, into the lighted house to stand, dazed and blinking, in the doorway of the dining room. They came to lean against their mother.

The time Margaret had spent breathing untainted air had cleared her nose and what she had suspected was true. The two girls had a smell as ripe as an overdue cat box.

"You must want to get the children to bed," Mildred said. And Margaret saw that she must.

. . .

"That's a Harvard man?" Ella Purvis asked her daughter. "Did you ask him for any proof or did Barney just take his word for it?"

She knew some Harvard men. They wore three piece suits and made good money at respectable jobs if they had to work. They didn't drag their families into the wilds for a salary a decent man would spit at. Not waiting for an answer she continued, "I don't trust a man with a beard. When a man had a beard it's bound to mean he has a high opinion of himself."

"I wonder how long it's been since they had a bath," Mildred said.

•　•　•

Barney drove fast with no regard for potholes and rocks lifting out of the mud.

Patrick, warmed by wine and two large brandies, crashed against the parts of the jeep nearest his body and felt a sweet reassurance at having a driver who knew the way. They would miss no crucial turns.

"That's your house there!"

Patrick swiveled to look back at a vague shape in the darker night and was thrown against the side of the jeep when Barney made an abrupt left turn around a larger vague shape. A church? They began the climb, the twists, up a hill toward an improbable vision shining in the night. Helen and Antonio's brick house with its glowing picture window, porch light, and the rest.

"Here he is!" Barney announced with the fanfare of a conjuror.

Patrick stood, slightly loop-legged in the overheated room, feeling himself markedly less than Barney's tone implied. Feeling his face gape in a silly smile. Not a good smile. The family, lined up and looking at him, smiled back. Maybe his smile was alright. They seemed to think it was alright.

Patrick stood until he was asked to sit. He looked for a chair. The room was entirely too warm. It was entirely too warm. Exhaustion and drink swirled by the warmth set Patrick's head spinning. He found a soft chair to sit in and sat in it without stiffening his backbone to the appropriate bend—he slid in a continuing flow onto the floor.

"Whoops," he said, grinning up at them all, a good natured, conciliatory grin. What the hell. Happen to anybody.

The boys laughed. Barney laughed. Helen's smile faded. Antonio's smile was replaced by a frown. Three out of five. Not too bad. Patrick climbed the chair to stand, tried again. Did it perfectly, by God! Proved himself an experienced visitor who could sit in a chair.

Now that he was sitting the room stopped spinning and he saw that he had died and gone to Sears Catalogue Heaven. A Mama, a Daddy and two boys, the Mama a dumpy Doris Day in a polyester pants suit, the Daddy a plumpy Valentino with a greased curl falling precisely in the middle of his forehead, the two boys in matching pajamas with feet, the cloth covered with little Mickey Mouses, Donald Ducks and Plutos.

"How was your trip?"

"Would you like some coffee?"

"Would you like a drink?"

"Ev'body die!"

The boy with the ancient face, his eyes goatlike and slanted, had come to stand in front of Patrick, to make his apocalyptic statement.

"He always says that," Helen said, a note of motherly exasperation in her voice. "The funerals go by on their way to the cemetery," she waved her hand vaguely in the direction beyond the fireplace. "They ring the bell when they leave the church and when he hears it he watches for the procession. I don't guess it's good for him," she said wistfully, thinking perhaps of her own childish pleasures in Dayton, Ohio.

"Red and blue and yellow," Antonio said firmly, giving the words the importance of terms in quantum physics, wanting them to sound and be more than they were, "and count to ten."

Patrick had known that one of the two boys had Down's Syndrome and wondered what he would be expected to teach him. The child stood listening to his father, looking at Patrick.

Patrick heard himself assuring Antonio that he understood the ramifications of red, yellow, and blue, and counting to ten.

· · ·

"Did you know he had a beard?" Ella asked Barney when he came home. She didn't expect him to give her a real answer. "Those people are not going to know their place!" her forefinger pointed at Barney's heart. If it had only been a gun ... she felt it twitch.

"What do you figure their place is, Ella?"

"They're employees but they're going to think it's all just one big family because you're all Americans. They're going to expect those grubby children of theirs to play with your children."

"We had that in mind as a benefit, Mama," Mildred snapped. "It'll help their English. It's not something for you to worry your head over."

"So I can just mind my business. Well, I will. But don't say I didn't warn you."

"Mama, I'd never say you didn't warn me."

"I don't see why you won't let those children stay with me while they go to school!" the old woman exploded. "The schools in Kentucky were good enough for you." It was an accusation to her daughter, gone so far beyond her reach. "Those children would just blossom with a decent environment." She stopped, seeing Mildred and Barney mirror the same cold glare.

Ella Purvis went to her room, to her bed, to lie awake, power-less and unhappy. She had had her yearly visit and was due to go home. She felt it keenly that when the weather turned fine, dry and warm, Barney's mother would arrive and be in the big house on the other side of the swimming pool.

When Barney and Mildred married the two mothers met head on. Mrs. Purvis had been being decent about it that Mildred had married somebody who wasn't Southern when she realized that much of what Elizabeth Shaw said had the underlying implication that anyone who didn't live in New England wanted to and envied those who did.

"Well, it's true enough," Ella Purvis said haughtily, "that there's been some people immigrating from my part of the country to your part of the country since the War," both women knew which War was meant, "mostly our worst class of niggra and all the white trash."

Thereafter the two women fought the Battle of States in an outright fashion, the field of battle being the persons of their respective son and daughter.

"Your grandmother never sat down in a room with a Yankee till the day she died."

Acres of lawn, a houseful of servants, a swimming pool and a stable full of horses meant nothing to Ella Purvis, awake in her bed, alongside what really mattered—Mildred had gone too far from home and stayed there. And look at the consequences, Mildred did everything she could think of but still had three babies who talked like a pack of little spics.

You'd think they'd have some thought for the raising of those poor children, the only flesh Ella Purvis had in the whole world. It broke her heart to go away and leave her grandchildren in this misinformed mess, living their lives in the middle of a houseful of Indians with a drunk for a daddy.

And now this tutor. Leave it to Barney to think it was an improvement and a solution to hire in somebody anybody else would pay good money to keep away. She knew that everything she hated was going to be reinforced by that "Harvard man." She knew Barney had hired him in to mollify his mother as much as anything.

Well, Mildred's thinking won't clear up till she's out from under Barney's influence. The day she decides to leave him and bring herself and the children back home that's the day she'll see what a nightmare she's been bluffed into.

"If I was a man ..." Ella Purvis thought, feeling her helplessness, feeling her forefinger twitch, almost hearing Bang! and again Bang!

Patrick also lay awake. He was thinking about the truck driver south of Mexico City who had waved them around him and then had speeded up and slowed down to keep them in the wrong lane facing oncoming traffic all the way around a long blind curve on a mountain road. Patrick had finally come to a dead stop, the truck had driven away, the game over. Patrick had driven the van with all his family in it, all their lives and goods in it, to the right side of the road, and continued on.

And this was what it all came to, teaching a child who would never need it to recognize primary colours and to count to ten. He knew he was tired to the point of hopelessness. He knew he was drunk to the point of hopelessness. He knew he would feel better in the daylight, when he was rested. But now, sleepless, he felt it keenly, that his life was a ruin, that he had no prospects.

• • •

Ella Purvis was right, Barney did hope Patrick would satisfy his mother. He also hoped Patrick would satisfy his children. Above all the hoped Patrick satisfied Mildred. That achieved it would be possible for Barney to relax and be satisfied.

Patrick was the latest item in Barney's ongoing attempts to keep the two women he loved appeased enough to pretend they were content. They were merciless. They never let him be easy.

In his domestic economy Barney was more like the Indians than he was like a Patron. The Indians walked the road carrying all their goods on a wooden frame tied to their backs, a frame so large they were sometimes hidden by it. They moved along with only their two legs showing and they only stopped when it became necessary to rebalance the load. Like the Indians Barney moved through his day, a living breathing marketplace, burdened by tallying. Patrick was the latest rebalancing of his load.

When Barney met Mildred she was studying music. The Piano. The Voice. She was lean and fine-boned with an angling lift to her slim neck that made him think of Nefertiti. She walked and turned to look at him in a way that broke his heart.

She was unlike the women he had known, his mother and sisters, who, when they were angered, would go icy and remote. When Mildred was angry she went fiery, raised her voice, prepared to fight. He would smile and tease and watch her anger grow until it seemed she would kill him if she could and he was charmed by it. He had to have her.

He wooed her, appointing himself her future. She agreed that it seemed likely. He won her.

In their early days love made them flexible, created an atmosphere that melded and overrode their differences. They liked thinking they had the best of all of it. Kentucky horses and Yankee know-how, brought to this unlikely place, this throwback to plantations and house-servants and indentured workers. Their personal terrain included Mildred's peacocks and orchids, Barney's expansive generosity.

Domestic geographies have all the problems of adjacent nations. Self interest and expedience conflict with earlier agreements. What had dovetailed bulges, becomes untenable and must be reconsidered.

There came a time when it had all gone slightly wrong. Not wrong enough to end, just wrong enough to have lost the glow of assurance. The couple remembered that they were each a person, noticed that what the other implied was their shared common good was often what suited that person best. In short, romance faded.

Romance, for Mildred, seemed to have included everything kind and gentle. When she looked at Barney now she was bored, and quite casually cruel. Barney continued stubbornly to love her, would not give up the earlier sight he had.

And what did Mildred love?

She loved her orchids that could be brought into the house when the blooms were splendid and put back outside when they faded. She loved her horses that could be brought out and ridden and turned over to the stable hand when she had finished. She thought sometimes of how she had ridden when she was a girl. That youthful exuberance would never risk these horses. These horses were too good to hazard. She had a passion for her horses. When they sweated it only enhanced them. Their sleek coats shone.

As for Barney, she would have liked him more if he had loved her less. She longed to be free of him, to breathe a little, longed to be in the city alone, in the world alone. Horses glowed but a sweaty, over affectionate husband was only a nuisance, wet patches under his armpits, his shirts stained and stuck to his back.

"Go change your shirt!"

"I'm working. I'll change clothes when I'm done."

They both knew she was unreasonable, that she was saying something else. She was saying he spoiled her pleasure. All that she loved in her life, her marbletop table, the shining crystal, was hateful when it must be paid for by Barney's unrelieved presence.

By the time the children's education became an issue all discussions between Mildred and Barney had become specific and unilateral. Mildred wanted a house in Guatemala City. She wanted to stay there during the week and let the children attend the American School. She wanted to come back to the finca only on weekends. "And summers," she told Barney. "We would be here all summer long."

Barney insisted that the children be tutored at home. He hired a young German who was passing through.

Two years of haphazard tutoring had left Virginia unable to read. David's eyes went blank at the smallest bit of daily arithmetic. Now Carolyn was old enough to begin her own sortie into what had been described to her by her older brother and sister as tedious and awful.

Mildred was biding her time.

Barney was on the hot seat.

Patrick was Barney's last hope.

FOUR

"Well, here we are," Patrick said smiling.

The four first-graders, shiny and clean, waited to see what school was.

Carolyn Shaw raised her hand. She had been briefed by her older brother and sister. If she wanted something she must raise her hand.

"Yes, Carolyn?"

"Please, may I go home?" Her lip was quivering.

"We're only going to be here an hour today." Patrick said, "just to let you all see how it is and what we've got, Look." He took packs of coloured paper from a shelf, crayons, scissors—a little bribery. He handed them out to the children.

Carolyn raised her hand.

"Yes, Carolyn?"

"Please, I want to go home now."

"It won't be long, Carolyn. Everybody can go home at eleven."

The child sat looking at her desk. The other three children were colouring a picture of Little Bo Peep with her sheep and her dog. Carolyn sat waiting for the hour to be over, her eyes filled with tears.

Patrick pretended it was eleven at ten forty-five.

Every morning for the first week Carolyn began the class with her hand in the air, a hopeful flag for a hopeful rescue, and asked to go home. Patrick answered, "You can go when the other children go, Carolyn."

The first time she joined in the class was during a blackboard story. A stick-figure girl was moving along the blackboard in a continuing adventure. The children were inventing the story. Patrick was drawing it.

"And when she got there, what happened?"

"She started crying!" John yelled. It was his constant

addition. John saw to it that boys, girls, puppies, kittens, and inanimate objects wept their way through to all the happy endings.

"O.K." Patrick had resigned himself to it, "she started crying." He drew a long line of little circles from the girl's eyes, down her dress, to fall in widening puddles on the ground. Now that was crying! John relaxed back, satisfied.

"Why was she crying?" Patrick asked.

Carolyn spoke up softly, her lip and chin quivering.

"Because she couldn't go home?"

Kerry, put with the first graders, went quickly from the eagerness of a child ready for a party, to the sullenness of a child deprived of one. Patrick gave him paper and crayons and asked him to draw a picture. He drew a few squiggles of colour on the page and brought it to the blackboard to show Patrick who was carefully printing three letter words on the blackboard. Patrick asked him to draw another picture. The third time Kerry brought his pad of paper with him, stood next to Patrick and drew a single line on the page. The next picture was another line on the next page. Patrick was using more time telling him to draw a picture than it took him to draw it.

"Tony's a fool to insist that Kerry's a first grader!" Mildred announced. "He knows better!" and she went to talk it over with Helen. Kerry had spent that morning's session shoving the other children's papers and crayons onto the floor.

Until the school it had been a functional pretence in the Grisanti household to treat John and Kerry like twins. It had worked while John was a toddler and still felt within the span of Kerry's limitations. Now, tensions were growing in the Grisanti household. Antonio saw that the school was letting him down. It was the school that was causing him to feel this way.

"Tony never had to admit that Kerry has a problem before," Helen told Margaret. Then she said, "From the time Kerry was born Don Cesar has never called me by my name. He always calls me Señora, like I'm the housekeeper."

Antonio agreed to let Margaret work with Kerry. Antonio was giving the school another chance.

• • •

The season was on the turn, but slowly. The rain should be stopping but only paused, let brief bits of sun show through, then began again. Days and nights passed with no sight of the sun or the moon.

The house Don Cesar had given over so grudgingly for the tutor sat on the downhill side of Los Cedros. It made a perfect dam for all the water running downhill when it rained.

When the house was being built a metal pipe was laid into the cement floor to let the water drain. It worked according to plan when the pipe was clear but in this intermittent weather a day or two would pass without rain and the cool dark pipe would become irresistible to frogs. They would climb into the pipe and be happy there until it rained again and they were drowned. When enough frogs had died in the pipe to form a solid block the water would begin accumulating on the uphill side of the house. A small lake would begin to pour in a solid sheet, inches deep, over the walkway between the main house and the slat-walled building that held the kitchen and the bathroom.

Margaret hiked her skirt high, shoved it into the waistband to hold it, tied a square of pink plastic around her shoulders and, barefoot, waded into the uphill side of the house to clear the drainpipe.

She stood in knee-deep water and poked at dead frogs with a bamboo pole. She didn't know it was dead frogs she was poking. The obstruction was dense and would not move. She poked harder and the plastic square untied itself and slipped away. Rain and the run-off from the roof soaked her through.

Finally the mass gave way with a great gulping suck. On the downhill side of the house a gelatinous mess of frog bone and skin fell the ten feet from the end of the pipe onto the ground and was pummeled into further disintegration by the falling water. The water level began instantly to drop. Now they would be able to go from the house to the kitchen without taking off their shoes and wading.

Margaret went into the kitchen, en route to the bathroom where she could wash her feet and dry herself with a towel.

"In Los Estados Unidos," Juana, the fourteen year old Indian girl hired to help, said in a tone usually reserved for prayer, "do all of the women have a stove like this one?"

The stove stood high on four legs and fed kerosene to four burners out of a bottle that was filled and inverted into a cradle at one end. Kerosene spilled when the bottle was being filled and again when the bottle was being inverted into its holder, just enough to make a stinking mess. When the wicks weren't trimmed properly they poured a stinking stream of smoke into the air. The oven, a separate "advantage," was a square metal box that sat over a burner, an inset temperature gauge measuring the heat inside, like measuring the heat of a tin can put over fire. The numbers were instantaneous and incorrect.

It was a duplicate of the stoves in all the farmhouses of Margaret's childhood, hated by her mother and her aunts. They had all got rid of it at the first chance. And here Margaret had found it after the intervening years, all its problems intact, waiting for her.

Juana's feet were bare. She had never owned a pair of shoes. This was her first job in a non-Indian household. She had become an instant partisan of all things American.

She courted amazement. She was prepared to hear that all the women in that place had this stove.

The first time the Doughertys went to Guatemala City after Juana started working for them Margaret had thought she would buy shoes for her. She had put paper on the floor for the girl to stand on so she could draw outlines of her feet. Juana wouldn't do it.

"I cannot wear shoes," Juana had said. "I am naturale. Naturales cannot wear shoes."

"But some naturales wear shoes," Margaret said.

"A woman who is naturale, if she marries a Latino she can wear shoes. If I wear shoes the people will laugh. Then, when the shoes are old and no good, when I do not wear shoes people will laugh again."

Juana loved this modern kitchen she had come to. She moved, barefoot, around the rough cement pila with its three spillaway sinks, her hair in glossy braids, her eyes shining. She poured kerosene into the bottle for the stove, cleaned the spill with no dampening of her pleasure.

Margaret continued through the rough kitchen to the bathroom for a towel. She scrubbed her hair and face dry, dressed in dry clothes, rolled her sleeves up and returned to the kitchen, to the day's laundry. To the pila, a monster of poured concrete, a constant spill of water brought from a nearby creek in a four inch pipe poured into a central well four feet deep, three feet square. When the central reservoir was filled the water spilled through grooves into cement sinks along the three sides of the well protruding into the kitchen. A hard-rubber plug let the water collect in a sink then a piece of wood put into the groove stopped more water from running in than was needed. The sink nearest the stove was for daily kitchen use. The other two were reserved for laundry.

Margaret had tried, just once, letting Juana wash the clothes. She watched while Juana, on a flat stone brought from the creek, rubbed a stain away by rubbing a hole where it had been. She resigned herself to it that washing clothes was her own dire destiny. Every day she stood at the pila scrubbing and swishing sheets and shirts and dresses and the endless diapers.

And dreaming her fourteen million dollar daydream.

A letter or a phone call comes to her and there it is, fourteen million dollars. Just enough to let her give a million dollars to each of her relatives who need it, sock back a million for each of the kids, a million for Patrick (community property? ha! forget it, but she won't be stingy). All that money disposed of ritually she can begin to be greedy ... an island of their own, a house with wide verandas painted pale blue.

(What was that on the kitchen table? How did a clutter of mud get on the kitchen table? It was worse than that—it was mud and dead spiders! Margaret thought of spells and black magic, someone had brought a curse of dead spiders to the house! But when she looked at the ceiling over the table she saw the track of a dirt-dauber's tunnel. It had fallen away from the ceiling. She looked at other mud tunnels scattered over the kitchen ceiling, caught onto the rough wood. Dirt-daubers always seek water. But the dead spiders? To feed the dauber's eggs when they hatch? She was looking at a whole describable food chain!)

There'll be nursemaids, speaking assorted languages, for the children—to let them learn properly. And the children will be beautifully clean and cared for.

There'd be no diapers with worms in the baby's stool.

When Margaret went to Barney for medicine he said worms were the single largest killer of babies here. He said worms could so clog a baby up that any food it ate would be vomited up again. When the church bell rang and it was for a baby, Margaret would ask Juana what the baby had died of, and her answer was always that the baby had died of vomiting. Margaret gave Anna the medicine Barney had given her and the baby passed clots of worms, some not quite dead, still wriggling.

Would fourteen million be enough to guarantee no more worms?

With Juana's help Margaret twisted the soapy water out of the heavy sheets. Juana held one end, twisted in one direction and Margaret held the other, twisted in the other direction. The sheets were wrung out, rinsed up and down in the sink refilled with clean water, wrung out again, and hung to drip on rope in the uphill garden. Margaret didn't need Juana's help with the diapers, she could wring them out herself. The problem with diapers was just that there were so many.

The diapers finished, she filled one of the sinks, put the piece of wood into the groove to stop more water coming in, poured American soap powder (bought in Guatemala City for an exorbitant price) into the cold water, swished it around with her hand to dissolve it, filled the sink with the latest diapers. In the other sink she put cotton skirts and blouses and shirts. Tomorrow, when the clothes had soaked as clean as they could get by soaking she would scrub at whatever stains were left.

Some stains wouldn't come out, wouldn't fade with the soaking and wouldn't respond to being scrubbed. In the weeks they had been here some of their clothing had shown an inclination to gather stains. Margaret was resigned to it that they would leave this place in clothes as splotched and patterned as guerilla camouflage.

"They're clean," she told herself.

It was as much as she could do.

Tonight was the night for their last typhoid shot. It was Friday. Patrick would lie in bed, feverish and shaking and bad-tempered and pathetic, all of Saturday. Patrick always reacted strongly to shots.

They had been invited to dinner at the Shaws. That meant an ironed shirt for Patrick, an ironed blouse for herself. And if there weren't enough diapers dry for the night she would iron them dry.

She got on with it.

• • •

"If the eyes aren't right it's all wrong. No matter how good the rest of it is what it all really hangs on is the eyes. Now, those eyes are perfect!"

The eyes that looked out of the painting over Mildred's fireplace had the quality Mildred treasured of seeming to look back at anyone who looked at them. It seemed to Margaret that they were looking at her but she knew they were also looking at Mildred who had painted them.

"She died before I could paint her from life. I painted that from a photograph. She was my favorite. You can imagine how worried I was when it came time to paint the eyes. If the eyes went wrong I'd just have had to throw the whole thing out and start again. There's no point in trying to paint over bad eyes. They just slide around and look oily.

"I have a friend in Kentucky that paints people and she says the same thing is true with people. If the eyes aren't right the whole thing's wrong.

"When it came time to paint the eyes of Freeborn Lady I felt like a diamond cutter. I kept putting it off. But one morning I woke up and I knew that that was the day.

"It was a miracle. It was like the paint brush took over. I was just the medium letting the paint brush do whatever it wanted to do. And the next thing I knew, there the eyes were perfect."

"Did you paint the picture that Tony and Helen have?" Margaret asked.

"Yes, but it's not as good as this one," Mildred said modestly. "The eyes aren't right."

And indeed they weren't. It was a cockeyed horse that graced the Grisanti's fireplace wall. A horse that couldn't look effectively back at anyone no matter where they stood.

This room was testimony to Mildred's assorted refinements. Built-in bookshelves held only hardcover books, a dictionary-stand held a gigantic, permanently open, dictionary. The piano was open, keys at the ready, sheet music above. The feeling was that Mildred went from piano to dictionary at the drop of a hat, smelling the blooming orchids as she passed, looking through the picture window at her peacocks. On the piano a clay bust of her dead cousin, sculpted by her dead uncle, faced into the room.

"Art has always run in my family," Mildred told Margaret when she learned that Margaret, meaning to be a painter, had studied at the Slade in London. Margaret found she had become an acceptable ear for Mildred's heartfelt interests.

It sounded more like Art had a bicycle as Mildred listed uncles and aunts and cousins, all got to by Art. Margaret felt like a fox set loose in the henhouse, holding her sense of humour down in this room where the dead cousin looked across at the dead horse that looked back.

The other guests for dinner were Alberto, thin and dark and very tall, and Hamilton, short, squat, and sandy coloured.

It was generally accepted, even by Barney, with an occasionally obscene, mocking reference, that Hamilton was in love with Mildred. He played the Southern role of a gentleman admirer who would never presume. As a courtier he was sufficient but dull. He didn't drink much. He wasn't vulgar. He had the good manners of a limited imagination.

"Call me Ham," he said to the Doughertys when they were introduced.

After dinner Barney boiled the needle in a pan on the kitchen stove, attached it to the hypodermic, gave Patrick his final injection of the series, disengaged the needle, dropped it back into the boiling water to be sterilized for Margaret.

"You getting these in your stomach?" Hamilton asked Margaret, the bottle of serum in his hand.

"In the arm."

"You're supposed to get them in your stomach."

"I've always had typhoid shots in my arm."

Hamilton, who knew perfectly well they were not getting the shots in their stomachs, smiled and held the bottle toward her.

"This isn't for typhoid. This is for rabies. See here, on the label."

They all looked at the label which said RABIA.

They would have to wait a week and start the typhoid injections again, from the first.

"You can tell the kids," Margaret said to Barney.

The next morning Barney stopped by with a metal dog-tag stamped with yesterday's date and the word RABIES.

"This is for Patrick. He deserves it. He can wear it around his neck."

Patrick only grunted when Margaret gave him his dog-tag on its chain. He would think it was funny later. Much later. Right now he lay shivering and miserable in his bed and would be there all day long.

• • •

Margaret, finished with the day's laundry, began to catch up on her letters.

"Dear X, I spent a part of the morning getting some meat for the week. The way one does it (when it's pork) is one goes to the family that's killing their pig, it's a racket that reaches the ears miles away, and gets some in a basket and brings it home. This morning they were dressing it out over a table in a dark back yard with the women of the family hunching over a tub cleaning entrails, washing out the intestines. Despite the way it sounds it all looked very clean. No blood around and the pig neatly skinned on the table and everyone slightly festive. I bought a hind leg and some skin to render out into cracklings and cooking oil."

It was usually the baker who killed pigs. He had an eye for money, sold bottled beer and boiled sweets. He lived just down the hill so when a pig was hoisted by its hind legs it was easily heard by Margaret who, therefore, had the best access to pork. She was pre-empted from the good cuts of beef which were always reserved for Don Cesar's household and for Doña Mildred and Doña Helen.

The butcher and baker flanked the village. The first building on the road on the downhill side was the baker's, and uphill, past all the cinder-block company houses that had been freshly washed with pink now that the rains had stopped, was the meat shop of Tomas, the butcher.

Once a week Tomas killed cattle and dressed out the carcasses, hanging them upside down on metal hooks. He charged fifty cents a pound for meat of whatever description and put his thumb on the scales besides.

He was substantial. The Indian women who were his customers weighed less than one of his legs. His belly could have feasted the whole Los Cedros population.

Don Tomas, the women called him, ducking their heads in respect while he charged them fifty cents for a saucerful of gristle and fat dyed red by lying with the bloody innards.

He stood among the carcasses, giving special attention to the special customers and keeping a sharp eye on his assistant who served up the weekly saucer of meat to the Indians with no loss of profit.

La Professora Dougherty was written on the front of Margaret's monthly account book. The first month's bill had caused a crisis. Checking through it Margaret found a series of progressively inspired mistakes. Each error was a slightly larger reckoning in Tomas's favour.

Margaret took the book to Tony in the office. "How do I deal with this?" she asked him.

"I'll deal with it."

Half an hour later Tomas, red-faced and furious, was at the door. His fat was in the fire, perspiration running down his face from the downhill walk. And to return he must walk uphill.

He had come to tell her that her book was not yet ready. She had been sent the wrong book. The mistake was his assistant's.

"But my name is on the book."

"This is the book of the Profesora at Santa Maria del Monte. There is no problem. Your book will be ready tomorrow."

Tomas smiled through his rippling anger that could not be controlled. He wiped sweat from his face with a flowered handkerchief.

Not only was the name on the book Margaret's but the weekly lists of purchases were the same as her own list. It was only the addition that had sprung a new growth principle.

Ah, well.

"I will have my book tomorrow?"

"Oh yes. Señora. Tomorrow you will have your book."

Margaret wrote.

"We're the only people in the country who have more than a hundred dollars a year and less than a hundred thousand. The six of us in this house comprise the entire middle-class of Guatemala."

Some middle-class, always up to her elbows in soapsuds.

"The kitchen has walls made of slats spaced apart so that creatures come through at night, Possums (only once, only one) and dogs and cats. At first they only came one at a time ..."

The spaces between the upright slats were so narrow

that only very small dogs, starved thin and desperate, could work their way through, driven to it by the smell from the emptied garbage can.

Anyone who went to the bathroom in the middle of the night could find themselves jerked from yawning half-sleep into the terrified yelping nightmare of some poor creature that, in its panic, could not work back through the narrow slit. The dog would explode, running mindlessly, shrieking with fear, throwing itself against the slatted walls.

It didn't happen every night but the nights it did were memorable.

"... but now they've started to come in families. A brown and white dog I've been chasing away every day and night has begun to bring her two puppies. And one of the cats has laid a family in the roof. One of the kittens got separated from the others and got itself to where the mother couldn't get it. It yowled all afternoon and into the night and finally in the middle of the night Patrick took a table and put a chair on it and climbed onto the roof, removed one of the corrugated tin sheets with a hammer and got it down. The mother, who's wild, won't take it back so now I'm feeding it with a doll bottle and it stays warm at night under a lighted lightbulb. It's very little, has HUGE fleas. I didn't realize until I saw them that somehow I'd expected little cats to have little fleas."

FIVE

On the road between Tapalapa and Los Cedros de San Juan there was a pyramid in a cane field. It was on Don Alessandro's finca, half a mile from the main buildings.

One building in that main lot, as ramshackle as the rest but larger, with a rotting wooden porch, was Doña Inez's home where she had been brought as a bride. It was the house of the Patron who had been, until last year, Don Roberto, Alessandro's father. Now it was the home of Don Alessandro.

Don Roberto was in the pyramid.

When Inez came from Germany she was shocked to realize that she was expected to live in this rickety old house together with two other brothers, one of whom had a wife and children, and with the lustful old man, Don Roberto. Don Roberto's mistress was the "schoolteacher," a fifteen year old latino girl he found clerking in a shop in Tucunan. When the girl had first come to the finca to live she had looked as if she might be a school teacher. She had been awkward, in stiff shoes, skirts with white cotton blouses. Her new position had its effect on her: by the time Inez arrived the schoolteacher was wearing satin blouses and a hat that she decorated with dyed chicken feathers.

The single bathroom in the house, a recent improvement, was got to by passing through the bedroom of Alessandro and his bride. It was a family joke that the newly-weds were walked in on. At night there were the people who passed through the bedroom for the sake of the joke.

In those earlier times Inez had more influence with her husband. Her unhappiness, her weeping and pleading, caused him to take over a small building across the road from the main house, to convert it and improve it for a place for them, away from the family. It could not be more than a separate bedroom, it was so small. It did not qualify as a honeymoon cottage, was made of cinderblock and would have a rough cement floor and a corrugated tin roof when it was finished, but Inez dreamed of it. She laid awake nights thinking of the little house that would give them privacy.

The trenches had been dug for water pipes and the cement floor had been poured when Don Roberto died and Alessandro became the new Patron. Overnight he turned into his father. Plans for the small house were abandoned. There were other things more important to a man with Don Alessandro's new responsibilities.

He became obsessed with the idea of honouring his father: he would build a mausoleum to hold his father's body, to honor his memory.

The old man was sealed into a metal coffin and stored in a back room of the house while Don Alessandro had a large clearing made in the middle of adjacent cane field. This act of filial devotion would be seen from the road. It would be a declaration to every passing driver. Workers were set to cutting stone into square blocks for the foundation, the blocks were brought to the clearing and were laid in a square with sides forty feet long from corner to corner. Cement blocks completed the step pyramid, thirty feet high, with a central black pit of a room where Don Roberto's coffin, lighted by candles, lay in state. A priest had been hired for the event and was worth the money, everything that could be touched was blessed. The candles inside were still flickering, a bit of pathos, when the final cement blocks were laid and Don Roberto was sealed off.

Everyone breathed a sigh of relief.

The day was hot and dry, the ground was rough and soft and filled with cane stubble. But now everyone could adjourn to the refreshments and the sagging shaded porch of the old house.

The schoolteacher had come to pay her final respects in a hat wreathed around with purple chicken feathers. After the service she and the new Patron went off to one side of

the pyramid and talked and laughed. They stood close together. Her high heeled shoes bit into the soft ground. They
stood and laughed in the clear hard sun of the dry season,
forgetful of the old man dead and gone, sealed into the
pyramid where candles were eating away the last breath
of air.

The woman who had been a thorn in the flesh of the family during the old man's lifetime became reserved for Doña
Inez alone.

The schoolteacher stayed on to teach.

When Inez tried to talk about her to Alessandro he
turned fiercely, as his father had turned before him, to say
"The children must have a school!" And to add on his own
account, "No one will say that the school my father began
was closed by me when he died."

For the final blow Alessandro told his wife that the family house had been good enough for his father and it was
good enough for him. They moved into Don Roberto's room.
The schoolteacher who was thus dispossessed moved into
the little house that was to have been theirs.

The old man's death that Inez had hoped for as a blessed
relief became the time when Inez found herself barely toler-
ated. She saw her husband become the rich and handsome
Patron who respected his father, kept a mistress and shot
his leg.

•   •   •

"I couldn't let him take it home, so I couldn't let any of them
take them home." Patrick handed Margaret John Grisanti's
drawing.

The first graders had been told to draw their families. In
John's picture his mother was the largest figure, John was
the next largest, Kerry and the family servants were roughly
the same size. For his father John had drown a round black

dot, biting into the paper with his pencil, given the black dot a tiny pinpoint head and feelers for arms and legs. Antonio was cramped onto the page like a squatting spider.

"I asked them all to do another one and he did the same thing again."

John would probably, given a third chance, have drawn one more squashed father.

Margaret cut shapes out of red and yellow and blue paper. Wadded more red and yellow and blue paper into balls to be thrown into pans and waste baskets tied around with red, yellow, and blue. Collected magazines from the other two households to be looked through for yellow bananas, red apples, blue sky.

Every morning Kerry arrived to toss colours into their matched containers. He would say the colour as he threw. By the end of the first week he could identify all three colours accurately. Half a year's work done.

The second week they began to count to ten. One toy. Two windows. Thee eggs. Seven saucers. By the week's end Kerry could count to ten. He had forgotten red, yellow, and blue.

When Margaret tried teaching the two together the words jumbled in his mind. Red became five. Three blocks would be a colour.

But they liked each other. Kerry was happier.

He showed Margaret a swagger dance he did to delight the Indians. Someone had taught him to pull his penis from his pants and jiggle it while he danced. His father had whipped him for it. His mother had been unhappy. Now he saw Margaret was one more. He would keep his dance for the farm workers. He could find plenty of laughers. A small life of his own. Shoved away by John, who wanted nothing to do with him now, he would go rambling along the road to someone sympathetic. He would go to the baker or the butcher. He would go to the church and wait for the bell to ring.

When the rain stopped sounds from the street could be heard. A coughing like vomiting. Margaret looked out. A small girl was doubled over, her face red with seizure, her mouth running a stream of saliva onto the road, onto her clothes. Her lungs had emptied all the air and fought to pull more in. She shook in a spasm, caught between the cough that would not stop and the battle her lungs were making. Farther along the road the child's mother, impassive, a small baby held in her rebozo, tied onto her back, waited. When the coughing slowed and the child could breathe, when she was normal enough to continue they walked downhill to the baker's.

Margaret went for the mail.

Don Cesar was on the porch of the office. He had no interest in speaking to this woman who began to talk about whooping cough, about the serum provided free by the government to any finca owner who would take the responsibility for doing the immunizing.

"It would take one man," he lifted a forefinger, "one full day to give the children the first injection. He would write their names in a book. For the second shot they must all come again a week later. Some of them would not come back. Others who had not come the first time would come the second time. Then there would be the third time. The same again. Then there would be the next time! And the next! It could go on for months!"

He glared at Margaret. "They are animals. They live and die like animals!"

He had expected trouble from these Americans and here it was. He was enraged by the stupidity of the Indians, the stupidity of the government. The stupidity of this fool of a woman who wasted his time.

That afternoon there was no electricity in the Dougherty

house. Patrick had no light at his desk, couldn't read or write. He went looking for Tony. Tony, puzzled, went to the electric switches. The line was switched off. Don Cesar had given orders that the tutor's house was only to have electricity at night. Tony explained to his father that the tutor needed light for his desk, to get on with his work. The lights were turned on again. The point had been made. Anyone living on Don Cesar's finca was dependent on his good will.

• • •

There was only one person in all the world whom Don Cesar could not dominate, the one person he adored, his daughter Dolores-Rosa.

He watched her be courted by Salvatore with an overwhelming jealousy burning in his stomach and his heart. He had brought Salvatore from Italy, in part, to be Dolores-Rosa's husband, but he had not meant this. He saw that he had made a mistake. Now that he saw Salvatore more particularly he wanted nothing to do with him. He decided to return the young man to Italy, send the package back to the store.

For the first time in her life Dolores-Rosa found that she must fight for her rights as the spoiled baby of the family and its only girl. For the first time Don Cesar found himself being fiercely denied by one of his children.

They were both accustomed to having their own way. They brought their special weapons to the battle. Don Cesar took Salvatore's money as a General cuts off an enemy's supply line.

Dolores-Rosa had energy enough for both of them. She had the energies of a young woman passionately in love and the energies of a child who shrieks in the aisle of a toy shop, "You said I could have it!" and will not be distracted. And she had all her older tricks. She flooded her tiny lace handkerchiefs with tears.

Don Cesar held firm. Explained to the child and to the woman in each her own terms. Told the child that the next one would be better. But the child was overwrought, her face a feverish red. She wanted this one. Her lips quivered. To the young woman in love the father explained she could never be happy with someone so far below her own capacities. She deserved the best. It was her happiness he had in mind.

Dolores-Rosa scorned him. It was her heart he took so lightly. A woman's heart. Her heart was breaking.

In Central and South America the heart is an entity. Has left the body behind and walked out on its own. It adorns shop windows, churches, sitting rooms, bedrooms, doctor's offices. It is pictured in gold paper, in glued-on sparkle, in rich red paint dripping with drops of red-paint-blood.

"She means to have a Hollywood production," the father recognized, furious.

Even now, she told him, she could not eat. She was too unhappy to eat. Everyone else also told him that she was not eating. It shook the grandiose foundations of the household in Guatemala City.

Dolores-Rosa was refusing to eat.

Her self-imposed hunger strike lasted for the better part of two days, impressive for one not experienced in self-denial. She would have fooled them all into thinking it was longer but Don Cesar anticipated her. Planted little traps—threads and light sprinklings of flour in the kitchen and pantry. Ah, this miserable business was taking up all his time.

He was amazed by Dolores-Rosa's pig-headedness.

"I will never give him up!" she insisted, her bosom heaving. She was a proper Italian. She threw herself around in anguish and anger. Collapsed into soft chairs. Flung herself onto couches. All her curves were brought to the fore by the anguished drama.

Don Cesar thought bitterly of his own nuptials straight as a stick, that woman, Dolores-Rosa's mother. "You will never have him!" he roared in answer.

$\bullet \quad \bullet \quad \bullet$

Barney and Patrick drove the necessary distance to pleasure in Barney's jeep, to Tapalapa, to cool their throats in a cantina. Without saying so they meant to make a long afternoon of it.

In Tapalapa the emaciated dogs that habitually slept in the dirt streets had roused themselves and gone looking for shade. As the sun moved along its path the dogs would lift again, thin shanks trembling, to follow their chosen bit of coolness.

Barney braked and parked in a swerve. Barely missed a dog that didn't stir. Dust rolled after the jeep in a cloud and followed the two men as they lifted a piece of printed cloth, entered a room that seemed dark after the brilliant sunlight. The air inside was not cooler.

The owner, nervous, intending to please, disappeared through an interior door to bring the men two cold beers. His wife, very short and fat, came into the room as he left it. She was as slow as he was quick. Moved toward an electric cord dangling near an electric plug in the wall. When these two were joined an overhead fan began to turn. A token of good will. It made no appreciable breeze. Flies resting on the blades flew off to rest elsewhere.

"I know I'm an anachronism." Barney lifted his fourth beer in a toast to the day and Patrick did also. "The day my Indians start hiding in the bush to kill me and my family, we leave. But the others won't. They'll treat it like an epidemic. They'll haul out their grenades and automatic rifles and they'll kill Indians until it's back to normal. They really think they can make this last forever." For Barney, an educated man in a feudal economy, fast in a slow time, to say he was an anachronism synchronized him.

"I'm lucky!" he insisted. "It's just a weird piece of luck. I like being here but I know the difference. I'm not stuck to this place." He waved to the owner for two more beers. "I can take my family and go back to the States." One more of Barney's maneuverings.

When the two men shifted from beer to whisky the owner's daughter, a girl of twelve, came into the room to play a scraping song on a violin while her younger brother danced, an empty case of beer bottles balanced on his head. Barney and Patrick watched.

"Somebody had to think of that and the poor little bastard had to practice that to do that," Patrick shook his head, wise and sad and drunk.

Two swallows may not make a Spring but two drinkers do make a quorum, make the motion and second it. Instantaneous unanimity, old buddies at large. The men shook their head at the pathos of the entertainment. Ordered another drink. It seemed the least they could do.

I've got my guns, too," Barney admitted. "I don't mean to be a fool about this. I've got enough to get us out of here, to get us to the city. But I'm not going to fight a war when the Indians do their turnaround. The money I could put into grenades I put into keeping a stock of medicine and vaccine for my Indians. Hell, I don't even have to pay for the vaccine. The government gives it to me. Not a single kid died on my place when this whooping cough epidemic went through. It's on the long slide," Barney insisted, depths of meaning in the phrase. "It's already on the long slide. Well, let it hap'n, Cap'n."

No lights in the house. The two old buddies, surrounded by provisions, food and bedding, were lying on the floor in the dark living room, talking. Campers on the living room floor.

They had driven home to San Felipe in the dazzling cold light of a full moon.

"Full moom," Barney called it, his head exposed. He was moomstruck, he insisted. He would go home to his wife, to the woman he loved . . . "and we'll go up to the lake, and ride the boat all over the lake, under the full moom!"

A note from Mildred said she was at Margaret's and would be home later. Barney made his preparations. Gathered sleeping bags, bread, eggs, bacon, milk, coffee, whiskey, gin, limes, salt and pepper, heaped it in a pile on the floor of the living room. He and Patrick settled down to wait for Mildred's return. She would, Barney had no doubt of it be happily surprised.

There was only the jeep outside to show that the two men had returned. Mildred and Margaret walked through the dark to the kitchen light switch. The kitchen was immaculate and empty. Mildred walked further, turned the light on in the dining room. Light that spilled into the living room and the two women saw the men lying on the floor among the groceries. Their faces were mocking. The boys in the tree who wait for girls to look up and see them there, knowing they are looked for and will be seen. An old mythic face they wore, the two of them, to be discovered by looking. The two women were large, looking down. Black silhouettes. Their long shadows fell forward, onto the men.

"Surprise!" Barney laughed.

Mildred turned away to Margaret.

"We," and she also laughed, "had better make a pot of black coffee."

"You and me," Barney drawled his alternate proposal "are going to the lake and drive the boat around in the moomlight, moonlight, the full moon light!"

"I don't intend to go up to any lake with you! You're drunk," Mildred answered.

"I do intend," Barney said, sounding not at all drunk, "for us both to go to the lake with each other!"

Their two voices moved into place like experienced duelists. Mildred made a countermove. She sat on the floor next to Barney and stretched out on the floor beside him.

"You don't really want to go all the way to the lake," she almost crooned. "It's so far. All that driving."

She rubbed his cheek with her fingers, a domestic

temptress. It was as much for the other couple, Mildred's drama, as it was for Barney.

Barney, surrounded by the clutter of his plan, watched her all too wisely. In no mood for this coy manipulation.

"We are going to the lake and we are going to ride in the boat." His voice was sharply enunciated as if a different man spoke.

It was ugly to see Mildred, body stiffening as if she had fallen. Her seductive proposal rejected. She sprang to her feet, away from Barney, with all the animal grace she lacked in the lying down. She took her fighting stance, hands on hips, legs spread.

Barney watched her transformation smiling. A hateful smile. This is the battlefield they know well. They were moving to this from the moment Mildred looked down and Barney looked up.

"We better go," Patrick began the slow process of rising to his feet. He had not been dizzy lying down. Now the room was spinning. "A man standing up is drunker than a man lying down," he announced.

"You're not going anywhere!" Barney ordered, poking the air with his finger.

As if the air ricocheted Patrick slid down again, to lie prone. "Well," he agreed, "maybe not."

"You're my friend," Barney announced, hauling paper cups from a brown paper bag, "and we're going to have a drink on that!" He unscrewed the cap from a square bottle. Ignored the paper cups, tilting it to his mouth for a long drink. Passed it carefully across the intervening space to Patrick's waiting hand. Patrick held the bottle, the flunky side-man.

Margaret watched. Wished she and Patrick were elsewhere. Mildred whirled away from the spectacle of her drunken husband, rushed for the kitchen, pulling at Margaret as she passed, to take her along. No room in this drama for innocent bystanders.

In the kitchen, Mildred banged the kettle.

"Whenever we go to the city our friends avoid us!" She filled the kettle with water. "They know he'll end up drunk and spoil the evening!" She crossed the floor, put the kettle on the stove. To boil the water for the coffee they both knew Barney would not drink. "He used to be a lot of fun but now he's not any fun at all!"

No way to change the subject—Barney's history as a drunk. The men's liquid afternoon had become a tempestuous night. Whenever Mildred paused for breath Barney could be heard in the next room dealing Mildred's intimacies out to Patrick. "... her lousy boyfriend! She's not sour when he's around! That's why I let him ... He's like the dumb runt that hangs around the outside of the pack when there's a bitch in heat. He's not going to get any but it's as close as he can get to the action. That's as good as he gets, just hangs around." And Mildred, hearing, was provoked to go further. More intimate detail.

A dangerous situation, Margaret thought. The two were telling more than they would want to be known. They raised their voices, the husband and wife, greedy that the other hear their secrets being told.

"Daddy Frank had to have Barney's mother committed she got so bad! He put up with it until he couldn't stand it any more. He just had the ambulance come for her. It took two attendants and Daddy Frank to get her into a strait jacket. Barney's just like her. He's just a crazy drunk!"

"... drunk as David's sow! And throwing ashtrays and furniture! They had to chase her all over the house, right through the dining room where Daddy Frank and the children were having dinner. She started throwing dishes at them! Wedgewood! That's when Daddy Frank had to step in. He was a big man."

"... sexy dresses I buy to keep her from looking like what she is and make her look like something worth climbing into bed for. She's a bad tempered bitch!" Barney turned his head to yell "BITCH!" toward the kitchen. "Listen," he turned back to Patrick, "don't ever get involved with a frigid woman. Don't …" his voice fell away, trailing in the thought of it.

"… got her cornered and held long enough for them to shoot a needle into her. Knocked her out. And they didn't turn her loose until she was cured! She thanked Daddy Frank for it later! She thanked him. And Barney's as bad as she was."

Mildred went quiet briefly, dreaming of the advantages of strait jackets and hypodermic needles. All of it brought to a flat stop. And to be thanked for it later. Barney thankful.

"… never wanted me. Never once! No, there was once, Tony got a dirty movie and we all watched it. Seeing that piece of trash made a difference to her."

"Foul-mouthed and mean. He gets drunk and paws at me. There's nothing in the world worse than lying in the same bed with a wallowing, stinking drunk and having him think he wants to make love to you. It's like a pig settling into a mud-wallow! That's all he means about going to the lake. I could be anybody! He sure doesn't mean anything romantic by it."

They're going to hate us tomorrow, Margaret thought.

•   •   •

Margaret and Patrick were sitting on their front porch when Don Cesar came driving up the hill. The jeep crested the top with a little bounce and Don Cesar was bounced on the seat. A cluster of four or five barefoot children standing nearby laughed to see Don Cesar made ridiculous. His fierce face dispersed them. He glared across the road at Patrick and Margaret who pretended to be deep in conversation, to have seen nothing.

Don Cesar was not deceived by the Doughertys' pretense. He went to the office and threw their electric switch again, just to keep things straight.

"We haven't got any electricity," Patrick told Antonio.

Antonio went to the switch and turned it back on.

The next day Helen told Margaret that all the workers had been told they must whip their children when they got home that night. Don Cesar had seen to it that the children who laughed at him were punished.

• • •

Dependents like the Doughertys were no problem for Don Cesar. He simply dealt with them. His sons were no problem for him, he simply despised them. But Dolores-Rosa ...

Behind Don Cesar's back his wife, Doña Theresa, helped the young couple at every step along the way. She knew Don Cesar better than anyone. She had lived with him all her adult life.

During the First World War Cesar Grisanti was a soldier in the Italian army. He slogged with all the others through the mud and misery of a foot soldier's life. Every unexpected rest was a miracle, something to be remembered.

There was a week when his company waited for the Isonzo floods to recede, let them through to where no one wanted to be, under enemy fire, lives and legs and arms and eyes in desperate jeopardy.

The young soldier spent that week camped with a family in their small house. Three rooms, overcrowded and wet. He tried to forget his fears. He ate watery stew and rough bread and played with the children. One child, a girl of four or five, was his particular favorite. She had a remarkably beautiful face and talked to him with an unnatural seriousness. Charming.

Twelve years later, having performed the coup that secured his father's holdings to himself, having begun his life, he decided to marry. He had kept up a correspondence with the family. He sent to them for that child.

She came, grateful as her family was grateful. Who

could have foreseen it, that a simple act of kindness would have such a reward?

Don Cesar had seen photographs of Theresa's face. She had fulfilled her earlier promise of great beauty. But her body was a child's. No breasts at all. No hips. Nothing to answer the fantasies he had had, waiting for her.

She had known nothing at all. Her mother had told her nothing at all. She fought him until she understood what was what.

He had got three sons and a daughter off her. She kept a house well, saw to its comforts, never questioned anything he did. And he had never had to fear that passion might drive her into the arms of another man. He had expected a frigid woman, seeing that body, and he got a frigid woman.

Now she lived in the grand house in the city, beloved by her children and her grandchildren. When Don Cesar visited he had his own rooms in the house.

Doña Theresa was not passionless.

All the adoration she had been prepared to give to Don Cesar she had given to her church and to her children. Now she meant to confound her husband's intentions. To secure her daughter's happiness. She had been bought, but her daughter would marry for love.

"Love!" Don Cesar spat, walking his land. "They will talk of love, women. Give them everything, give them Eden, and they will contrive love to spoil it all!" Love was the serpent's apple. He spat with disgust.

He thought of the lively child Dolores-Rosa had been. His bright angel. Now she was demonic, possessed by love. She meant to spoil his final days.

His final days.

He was a man who would die.

He deserved consideration! He deserved Dolores-Rosa's filial respect!

He must, for his own peace of mind and his daughter's

future, choose a husband for her who met his standards.

"How can you want to throw yourself away? How can you want to marry a fop who lies on his bed all day doing nothing for his keep?"

"He was working until you took his duties from him! He is a man! Do you think he will keep asking you to give him something to do when you only insult him?"

The qualities Don Cesar had hoped for in his sons, he found in his daughter. Single-minded. Self-centered. A rock.

"I only want to know you will be happy," he insisted, "then I can die in peace."

"You can die on roller-skates!" his soured angel snapped. She had had enough of him.

"You will have a dying father's curse on your stupid head!"

• • •

The school was a success. Each of the three households had a first-grader, flushed and proud, reading SEE . . . JANE . . . AND . . . SPOT . . . JANE . . . CAN . . . RUN . . . RUN . . . JANE . . . RUN . . .

"See here, she's running! Spot's running, too!"

Eyes would move again to the text, faces freeze into a stilled expression and the story would resume. SEE . . . SPOT . . . AND . . . JANE . . . RUN . . . The eyes would lift, faces shine. The information was joyous. Pictures proved what they had just read. The content was not tedious.

Except to Antonio.

Since all the households were talking about their first graders, hearing them read, he must also listen to John.

"Yes, John. That's good," he would interrupt, bored before he was halfway through the first page. John's pleasure faded at his father's lack of interest. Antonio, ready for anger, would turn to quiz Kerry. According to what was being worked on this week Kerry either knew colours or he knew numbers.

"Some teachers!" Antonio sneered.

The books Virginia could read now were standard texts for American schools. The images began with falling leaves. Autumn, moved into winter snow and ice. Virginia had never seen Winter. The refrigerator became important. Living for months in the refrigerator.

A part of learning is accepting the reality of what you don't know except as you're told it. The world is round. China. Hottentots. Virginia accepted Winter. But when she was told in History about feudal systems, that they no longer existed, she looked out the window.

• • •

boom . . . . boomoom . . . . boom

A crew of men in tin hats began the dry season work on the dirt roads. Drills. Boxes of explosive. They shattered boulders that had floated high in the year's rains, drilled holes in rock, placed charges, stopped traffic at both ends of the danger zone, counted explosions. When the number was what it should be the cars were let go. There would still be a few seconds, bits of rock clattering down. Then the cars drove slowly forward over sharp edged debris hidden by a thick carpet of torn and blasted leaves. The rough road had become a seeming meadow. The smell of chlorophyll was pungent.

Each day the sound was louder as the workers came closer along the road. What had begun as muffled thunder became a giant's footsteps, a heavy thudding approach.

In Mildred's living room the large window was crisscrossed with masking tape, X marks the spot, as was Helen's picture window, to keep the vibration of the explosions from the shattering the glass.

boomboom . . . . . . boom . . . .

Kerry's attention was distracted by the explosions.

"This?" Margaret held up a blue beanbag.

"Red!" Kerry angled his head to look at her to see whether his guess was right.

Margaret shook her head and continued to hold the beanbag before him.

"Look! It's the same colour as your shirt is. What colour is your shirt?"

"Blue!" He was right and knew it. His face broke with his grin of triumph. "Blue! Blue! Blue!" he pointed at the blue crayon, blue paper, blue shirt.

Before Margaret could change the game on him, ring in another colour and another mistake he grabbed up his small straw bag and reached into it.

"Ornch!" he held up his orange. It was his daily joke.

"Right!"

• • •

Tony was not satisfied. He was being fobbed off with second best. He paid a third of the salary plus a house. He insisted on having the real teacher for Kerry.

Patrick moved the first graders an hour earlier in the morning and fitted Kerry in. Kerry continued to learn colours one week and numbers the next.

The Grisanti household eased out. Kerry was in the real school. Tony stopped testing him, no longer made Kerry count objects, name colours as he pointed at them.

Patrick and Kerry would often walk around San Felipe during their lesson. Blue sky. Green trees. Five bushes. And Kerry would tug at Patrick when they passed the church. He was a simple-minded potential murderer within what he thought was the case. He wanted to ring the bell. He thought ringing the bell caused death.

• • •

When Salvatore was certain that negotiations were at a standstill he bought two airline tickets to Italy.

What deceit! Don Cesar was struck to the heart by the couple's blatant disregard. Even Judas had not flaunted his infamy. This man, Salvatore, would have flourished airline tickets in the face of Christ!

And now Don Cesar saw that the couple could really leave. They could go to Italy and be happy there. They could leave him here in this damnable place that ate his life away year by year. He would be left without the consolation of Dolores-Rosa.

Don Cesar changed his tune. "That poor woman has gone through enough hell for you," he told his daughter, meaning her mother. "It is enough. If you must ruin you life I cannot stop you, but I will not let you continue to make her suffer."

To the others, his wife, his sons, he added. "She would have gone to Italy and starved there. Here we can at least see that her fop is kept in work."

It was Don Cesar's equivalent of a blessing.

The plans for the wedding began, a festive blend of armistice and victory.

SIX

In November there was good news for the Doughertys and there was bad news.

The good news was a letter to Patrick from a publisher in New York asking him to write a novel for them.

"We hope you're interested," said the man who signed his name under Sincerely.

The moon poured a greyed brilliant light onto the garden, everything was shades of grey. Margaret's hands shone white as did Patrick's hands and his face when he turned toward her. They were sitting on a low stone wall in the downhill garden. They each had a beer. A quiet celebration made more quiet by Patrick's unhappiness. He was wishing he was somewhere else. New York. Even New Mexico. Somewhere there were friends who would know how much this meant.

Margaret was sympathetic but wondered why she didn't count.

To share this moment that should have been festive for them both meant that she must watch it turn to dust in his mouth. Ah, but it was against her nature. It was her good news, too. She would be a festive friend if he'd let her.

He turned and in the moonlight there were tears in his eyes.

The son of a bitch. My own beloved. She put her arm around his shoulders. She wanted him to be happy. She wanted his heart to have some ease. She held him.

But inside herself there was the sound of music from a far off valley, a small party was going on in a hidden room. The shadows of an improved future were in her head. She celebrated secretly, not to interrupt his sorrow.

They had one beer, and another, and they went to bed.

The bad news came in the scantily furnished two-room office of the doctor in Tapalapa.

"I can't be pregnant," she told him.

He shrugged.

"I don't mean I don't have reason to be pregnant. I mean I can't have another baby. We have as many children as we can provide for. Will you do an abortion?"

"It is illegal."

"Do you know anyone who will do it? I won't have another baby."

The doctor looked at her intently, then he took a piece of paper and wrote a name and address on it.

Alfonse Schmidt/Numero 5/Calle de les Hermanas/ Guatemala City.

"He was a doctor," the doctor said. "Now he does this."

"Should I telephone? Should I send a letter?"

"He has no telephone. What could he write in a letter? You must go there in the daytime to make arrangements. He does not live at this place."

Margaret and Patrick drove through the still unfamiliar city, looking for the street name, the number. The place was vacant. A lost last hope.

"We have to ask. Somebody might know where he went." Desperate, Margaret went to the corner grocery store. She asked the two men there about Dr Schmidt.

The two held a laugh in. They knew what was what. There was a lounging in their bodies. One of the two began to give her directions, she thought it was directions, too fast for her to understand.

Patrick came into the store to stand with her. The two men became more polite. One of them walked out to the street, pointed along it, said a number.

The doctor was in. One of his legs was shorter than the other. He was dirty. Stoned on something—his eyes couldn't be seen into. Morphine? For the leg?

They stood in a grimy tiled foyer. The doctor invited

them in to a room with an examining table with stirrups, a glass case with instruments. Impoverished. Bits of paper were caught to dirt at the floor's edges and in the corners with the same settled solidity of litter in the street.

The doctor was in no fit shape to deal with anything surgical but he wouldn't say so. What he said was that he must sterilize his instruments—they must return at four. Leave half the money.

Patrick looked at Margaret. The look of this place had reminded him of the risks.

"You don't have to do this," he said. "We can work it out."

"I'd be eight months pregnant when we have to drive north. I don't want another baby. Four is enough."

"You want to do this?"

"I can't not do it. It'll be O.K."

She meant to hear nothing, see nothing. It wasn't courage, it was beyond that, it was mindless, she was in trouble, she needed a solution.

Patrick was pale and quiet with it. They nodded and agreed that they would be back at four o'clock.

On the way to the city they had decided on a luxury, they would stay tonight at the Hilton Hotel. The smallest room was still beyond their means, but they would do it.

The doctor over and done with they would have a good bed, twin beds in the circumstance, and room service.

The room cost twelve dollars, paid to a tall, very thin, very black, young man who swirled in a circle away from them, all the way around, picking up the room key as he passed, a dance step. He was the best looking person Margaret had ever seen, their key in his hand.

They bought two slick cover American magazines to be read later. It would be as good as a hospital.

Dr Schmidt wore a white overall. His eyes were normal. Margaret took off her skirt and underpants, climbed onto the table with the stirrups. They were always cold, these tables, even the fancy padded ones covered in phony leather. This one was masonite, a home built job. The ceiling she looked at was a dozen shades of grey. Water stains ran down the walls. Someone had boiled water in this room, over and over, letting it condense on the ceiling and run down the walls, marking them. One simple paint job would make all the difference to this room.

Dr Schmidt had no anesthetic. He loaded a needle for a local injection, he inserted the needle. She felt the shot. They waited for her to be numb enough to let him begin.

The local was ineffective. When Dr Schmidt made his first move Margaret gave a choked scream and told him so, in English, the language didn't matter.

The doctor loaded another needle, gave her another injection. She felt it.

Margaret's fingers were crossed. I hope I come out of this normal. I hope he isn't going to leave me a bleeding corpse. I hope by the time I'm in bed at the Hilton Hotel I'm not there with a fever and an infection. The local doesn't work, you bastard, you're using sugar water and hoping I'm suggestible.

"I cannot give her more. It is dangerous. If I give her too much she can die."

That's a laugh, Margaret thought, that's a laugh.

Patrick was not reassured by the implication that the doctor wanted Margaret to come out of this alive.

"You don't have to do this," he insisted.

"I'm going to do this!" and she looked past him to tell Dr Schmidt. "Do it. Just do it."

Her head was woozy, maybe the stuff was working in her head. It wasn't working in her body where every scrape was a pain. What did she know? Maybe it would have hurt more without his lousy injections. Maybe she was being spared part of it but didn't know it ... She was counting hundreds to help time pass. Eighty-one. Eighty-two.

"Tell me when you're halfway through," sweat running

on her skin ... one hundred ... one ... two ... in this cold room where moisture collected and ran down the walls.

"I will tell you."

... forty-seven ... forty-eight ... The end could happen if the middle could happen ... eighty-four ... eight-five ...

"We are maybe halfway finished now."

Counting on her fingertips with her thumb. Hundreds of hundreds.

... thirty ... thirty-one ...

"How much more?"

"Just a little more."

... seventeen ... eighteen ... nineteen ...

"How much more?"

"We are almost finished."

... one ... two ...

The time did come when he was finished.

He untied the rags he had used to tie her feet to the metal stirrups. He adjusted a pad to catch the bleeding. The two men helped her to climb off the table and to stand. She felt a shake in her legs. She couldn't move her feet. Patrick helped her to walk, his arm around her waist. It was over. Ah, she remembered how to walk. It was over. Another ordeal to count into the count. How I spent the war.

White sheets. High pillows. Two Hershey bars. The good life. Let them eat cake, Vogue, Cosmopolitan. Window shopping, the glossy pages. The American Way of Life. Where all the bills are paid, the rooms are new, the women are slim, the men are attentive. There are no wilted flowers. Babies don't have worms in their diapers. Lemonade springs and the bluebird sings on the Big Rock Candy Mountain. Room service brings bacon and tomato sandwiches with little toothpicks trimmed out like picador lances. In bed. On a tray. A bottle of beer to wash it down. Oh, God, she hurt from her heart to her feet.

Patrick, charged with adrenaline, paced the floor. A shape like a dark cloud. He was filled with a force that would not ease.

"There are slobs all over the world being supported by money they don't have to work for! Writing books like a sweet little hobby! Look at Lowell!" He raged at the room, at the walls, at Margaret. "Look at Lowell with all that money and the prizes! And the job at Harvard!"

Margaret was surprised. "Do you want to teach at Harvard?"

"Me? Of course not! I don't mean I want what he's got! I mean I want what I need!" He paced. "If I ever get into the same room with Lowell I'm going to punch his face in! I'm going to walk over and clip him! Just one good punch! Right in the face!"

. . .

Oscar, Barney's office worker, made a bus trip to the city. Returning home his bus had a flat tire just as it left the city limits. The passengers climbed out to wait while the driver dealt with it. When the tire had been changed they reboarded.

While many of them were still in the aisle a second bus passed, its horn blaring.

Without a thought the driver on the stopped bus raised his foot from the clutch and was in pursuit. The people still in the aisles were thrown to the floor. Bus number two stopped to let off passengers and Oscar's bus passed it, horn blaring.

In the flush of his simply won triumph the driver called an apology back over his shoulder. It was important to the scheduling, he explained, that he be ahead of the other bus.

When he stopped for a passenger the other bus passed him, exultant. The dilemma was clear.

He passed the second bus when it stopped to let

someone off. When a passenger on his bus wanted off he parked in the road, dead centre. The other bus could not pass. The other driver blasted the air with his horn, to no avail, then slung his door open; he was coming out.

Oscar's bus, its passenger disgorged, roared away. And was stopped by a slow truck. Bus number two passed in the oncoming lane.

The passengers and their stops became cursed objects. They came hurtling off with whatever of their luggage they could carry, a salvaging operation. What they could not grab and carry they saw leaving on the departing bus.

Whichever bus was behind must take extraordinary risks in order to pass. Oncoming traffic was driven off the road at the sight of the two buses coming at them, neck and neck. Now whenever the second bus passed its driver would cut in short, to crash the rear back corner of his bus against the front corner of the bus where Oscar's driver sat.

The next thing was that Oscar's driver stopped stopping. The passengers on his bus, and on the other bus when that driver grasped the new strategy, were made prisoners, insignificant cargo.

The driver of bus number two made a decision. He got just far enough ahead to have the time to stop his bus across the road. He opened the door and climbed out. He was a big man, very powerful. Oscar's driver was smaller but game, given the length of chain he took in his hand as he left his own bus. He walked to where the other man stood and proceeded, with his chain, to beat the other man to the ground. When the larger man's assistant tried to join the fight a passenger from Oscar's bus pulled a gun from a hip holster and said, "This will be a fair fight." Apparently the chain served, in his imagination, to equalize the difference in size.

The fight over, Oscar's driver climbed back into his bus with the passengers who decided to try it again, drove around the end of the parked bus, and continued on. To be passed and bumped only minutes later by the other driver, blood pouring down his face.

When Oscar's driver resumed the race the passenger with the gun lurched his way forward along the aisle and insisted, "You will begin to stop!" holding his gun to the driver's head.

The other bus, victorious, disappeared out of their sight down the road. The bus became a bus again. And Oscar arrived home to tell the tale.

In the city, the same week, a drunk was put off a city bus, hauled forcibly by the driver to the door and shoved out. As the bus drove away the drunk pulled a gun from somewhere and began shooting after the bus. The driver stopped, put the bus in reverse gear, came backwards against the man, carrying him up over the curbing to crush him to death against a building.

• • •

And there was a war.

It began on Friday and ended on Monday without any help from the General in charge in troops nearest the front, who could not be found. He had taken himself into his favorite whorehouse for a long weekend beginning Friday morning.

Near where the General sported, an airplane was hauled onto the runway of an airport and blown up. The President, in a military hard-hat and a business suit, was filmed and photographed standing courageously near the wreckage. THE PRESIDENT VISITS THE FRONT! blared the headlines and the television sets, and there he stood, his jaw firm. He had again, just before an election, saved Guatemala from the communists.

A home for old people was burned down, to prove that the enemy would go to any lengths. It was a particularly brutal piece of foolery, eight of the more incapacitated inmates died in the fire. Two ambulances and a fire engine collided at the main intersection nearest the hospital, killing a driver and another patient who had been in one of the ambulances.

The General emerged on Monday night to learn that the war had been fought and won without him.

Hostilities over, the President's wife invited the noncommunist citizens to show generosity and compassion. She asked for donations toward building another, grander, institution where the old one had been. There were few contributions. Too many cynics had seen this all before in various guises. Rumour made it clear why the war had lacked a General and that the burned airplane had been so derelict it had been hauled onto the airfield by a tractor. The general opinion was that the government had burned the building down and the government could rebuild it.

But in the more gullible countryside a man who was said to be a communist was hunted through his own fields and shot by his neighbours. He ran, desperate, through coffee bushes and was caught at a creek, men and dogs in a racket at his back. They shot him on his own land and left his body to rot. His family fled. His holdings were confiscated and sold cheaply to a friend of the President.

SEVEN

The road that passed the Doughertys' house climbed uphill twenty-five miles to San Ysidro, where it leveled off at a volcanic lake. The grades were so steep that without enough weight over the back wheels for traction an automobile could sit and spin dust until the driver admitted defeat and backed slowly down to the flat to get speed up for another try. On the uphill grades traffic was always in low gear, motors grinding. The faces of drivers and passengers registered a deferential anxiety.

Downhill it was a race, boisterous and headlong, a downhill fall. Trucks bounced and clashed. The downhill travelers had no pity for the temperately creeping uphill traffic. They waved their straw hats and hooted, to shame the trucks they passed.

Fortunately, there were not too many trucks. Any truck that could take another road to the uplands did so. Only the trucks that must pass the house passed.

The dust would settle in their wake.

The voices of the children playing in the lower garden could be heard again. All the myriad birdsongs and electronic insect sounds would resume. And the sound of Patrick's typewriter. He had begun his book.

He wrote in the late afternoons before dinner, and in the evenings after dinner. No more cookies and trash paperbacks in bed for Patrick. And he wrote on Saturdays and Sundays.

The book was the story of his earlier life in another Spanish speaking country with a different wife and different children.

It was a piece of luck, he told Margaret, to be writing in circumstances so similar. The similarities jogged his memory. His typewriter spanned that time and this, a reassuring staccato.

Margaret liked hearing it, her hands buried in this week's cut of beef. However much she cut away the gristle there was always more. She was putting chunks of beef through a metal hand grinder clamped to a shelf. At intervals too much gristle would have wound around the turning spiral so that the handle wouldn't turn. She would unclamp the grinder and take the whole thing apart, tear the white gristle away, put the grinder together again, clamp it onto the shelf again, grind more meat, take the grinder apart. In terms of the labour hamburger was a luxury.

"Do you have time to read this?" Patrick asked her, coming into the kitchen with some pages.

Margaret wiped her hand dry.

Wagons are coming down the hill into a village. They are coming down beautifully. And here is the hero. He is a young writer. He is writing while his wife does the laundry and sees to the children.

Margaret looked her over, this woman Patrick was living with in his book, would be living with from now on in the time that had been free for the two of them to be together. She, his other wife, wears her brown hair long in a braid, carries a baby slung over her hip. Patrick could have been describing Margaret.

Patrick returned to his typewriter just as he had done in those pages and Margaret, an interchangeable part, returned to grinding meat.

The book Patrick was working on was their real reason to come to this place, Margaret reminded herself. Patrick was a writer. The publisher asking for a book was a windfall. Made their choice be certified as the right one. And now the time must pass that let the book be written.

Then ... Then ...

Things would be quite different then. Margaret the optimist. Margaret the positive thinker, with the meat ground, putting clothes into the pila.

She thought she might cut her hair short.

For a change.

For the sake of the weather. Now that it was Spring, an unlikely November Spring.

It was going to get hotter. She should cut her hair.

As if the soapy water caused it a telephone rang in her head.

They were calling to say she had been given forty million dollars.

What?

Forty million?

Who said that? She couldn't believe her ears. What had happened to her usual fourteen?

Her daydream had just given her a raise. Not a moment too soon.

· · ·

Barney, half-drunk, returning from the city, hit a bicyclist. The man bounced onto the hood of the car, struck hard against the windshield cracking in clusters of concentric circles, then he rode over the roof and fell back off the car in a heap. Barney, blinded by the suddenly opaque windshield, stopped the car, opened the door to look out, backed to where the man lay.

He knocked the windshield out with a rock, put the man into the back seat as gently as he could manage, drove him to the city, to the hospital.

The bicyclist recovered slowly. Barney paid the bills.

Within a week of hitting the bicyclist Barney, not at all drunk, hit someone else.

He was driving one of the finca trucks to the city to have work done on the brakes. Patrick was with him. Barney was driving slowly, manipulating the hand brake when braking was necessary. They came around a downhill corner and were, without warning, onto a truck stopped beside a stopped bus blocking the highway. Barney swerved to pass on the wrong side, driving off onto the gravel, his horn sounding all the way. He stopped as soon as he could manage it.

"I hit him," he said, his face white.

"You didn't hit anybody," Patrick said.

"I hit him. He stepped out while I was passing. He got clipped by the side mirror."

The two men walked back and Barney was right. An old man lay unconscious on the roadside. His daughter was crying, leaning over him. She said something to Barney.

"He's deaf. He didn't hear the horn," Barney told Patrick. With a rush of three Great Danes, their tongues lolling, a Patron from a nearby finca rode up on his horse to ask Patrick what was happening. Patrick told him.

"Give her five dollars and tell her she can visit him in the hospital," the Patron said from his great height. And rode away, his dogs keeping with him.

Barney looked at their old man and came to tell Patrick that he was dead.

Mildred was righteous and pleased. She had always believed Barney's drinking had this kind of multiple disaster in it. Would it be a message to him? Wasn't his mother in a straitjacket, hospitalized and cured (however briefly) a message to him?

● ● ●

In the Spring, even a November Spring, thoughts turn to love.

Patrick, writing in the electric light, in the dark room, put his earlier wife in a meadow with wildflowers in her hair.

The baker, his desires awakened by Juana made sleek and glossy with the food she was eating at the Doughertys asked her step-father for her.

And Teodoro, publicly the mailman and privately the government's spy, subjected for the past months to the trails of love, was found wanting in a spectacular fashion.

Long before the Doughertys' arrival he had become enamored of Maria Esperanza Cruz, a young woman who sold groceries, general dry goods, and yardage off bolts of cloth in a shop called La Providencia in Tapalapa. Among those mundane goods Maria shone, a miracle among tin cookware and browning cardboard boxes.

Maria's morning walk to the shop and her afternoon walk, returning to her home, was a daily triumph. As she passed the males who lounged along the street to watch her, her own eyes were modestly lowered.

She had delighted Teodoro by treating him as an eligible suitor. He would delay his morning departure, standing on the sidewalk while his assistant loaded the bus with people and goods. He would let his loaded bus stand waiting while he watched for Maria to come walking along the street.

"Good morning, Maria," he would say firmly, his hat on his head.

"Good morning, Teodoro," she would say softly, raising her eyes to his face and lowering them with an impact that caught his breath in his throat. He would watch her continue past, his brain and body in a boil. He had to have her and could think of no reason why she would not have him. He had his position as mailman for the district. He was respected. And he was unmarried. The wife of his earlier years had died bearing their first child. He was, he knew himself to be, a catch.

Then Don Alessando saw her and that was that.

Who would have a mailman in preference to Don Alessandro?

A decent woman would have preferred him, the answer thudded like a falling rock in his mind. A decent woman would prefer marriage to an alliance!

It was a useless answer. It was his answer and not hers. She wore a new scarf over her shoulders, a shining scarf that must have come from Guatemala City. She answered his good mornings without any caressing look, and passed, left him standing.

What galled him was that she did not know he was more. She thought he was only a mailman. Only a mailman. In this economy of Indians and latinos where one man was a world away from another because it was within his social rights to wear shoes, it was extraordinary to be a mailman.

And besides, he was more than a mailman. He was a secret agent. He had hidden power. He had never pointed and accused, had never told the government "kill that one," "arrest that one," but he could. And they would. Wouldn't they? He didn't know.

Surely there was no need to test his effectiveness. The most direct thing to do was tell her his secret. It would be enough to let her know that he and the government were one. A little fear would engender respect, lessen Don Alessandro in her eyes, cause her gaze to linger on his own face. And then ...

But his power depended on concealment. If he told her his secret he was laying himself and his power into her hands. He was not certain enough of her.

She began carrying a blue plastic purse, shinier than the scarf. She wore a blouse he had not seen, the kind of blouse that must be bought in the city. It was all hateful and unfair.

If he told her his secret and it made no difference to her she would tell Don Alessandro and his usefulness would be over. He might even lose his position as mailman.

He could not tell her.

He must use his power as he had never used it—he would destroy Don Alessandro. The thought exhilarated him, shot him through with a certainty, with courage. He felt heroic. He would expose Alessandro as a communist. The whole family, children and all. They would rot in prison. He drove the rough dirt roads of his route hearing Alessandro scream, his bones breaking. And he daydreamed an immense structure of love story wherein Maria adored him. He could see his own face in the newspapers. He would be pointed out when he walked on the street, Maria clinging to his arm. All for love.

He kept an accumulating bulk of notes on Don Alessandro and his family. The notes grew in bulk without becoming incriminating. Don Alessandro could only be proven to be a very usual tyrant and a fascist. In the meantime he continued to look sleek and content, a satisfied lover.

It was all increasingly suspicious. Each time there was nothing it felt to Teodoro like a further proof. But deep inside himself he was crumbling away. He saw an old man in his mirror. Frustrated desire was eating away at his fat, causing his cheeks to sink in as if he had no teeth.

And however badly Maris treated him, however much she made it clear that she wished he would stay away, he could not bear to not see her. He would follow her to the shop, his hat in his hand, to be a customer. He would buy a small item and stand looking at her. She would become busy, dusting shelves in a flurry of dust that fell on his head and shoulders.

Desperation overcame his sense of self-protection. He decided that he must tell her. She would see that he could put his life into her hands.

At that crucial moment Alessandro shot himself in the leg for the second time.

Teodoro felt the hand of God. God had killed the man who should in all decency have been a provable communist. Teodoro's secret was safe and he would have Maria.

Alessandro lived.

But he was in the hospital. He would be there, then at home, recuperating. He would not be in Tapalapa courting Maria. She would be lonely. Teodoro saw things were as they had been: Don Alessandro was gone, Maria was there to be courted, his own secret had not been told.

He missed Maria passing on the street and went to the shop but she was not there. They told him that she had gone to Don Alessandro's finca to be his nurse. When he had convalesced she would become the finca's schoolteacher.

It pleased the shopowner to torture the mailman. She told him how much money Maria was to be paid, and that she would have her own small house, schoolteacher's house, and she would have an Indian girl for the cleaning and the cooking.

Teodoro's despair was complete.

He lived on in a life stripped of colour, joyless.

Until the fatal day when, after dutifully delivering the mail pouch to the finca's office he turned in the wrong direction, coming out, and entered the house.

He went into the room where Don Alessandro lay napping and he shot him in the head, two times. Then he shoved his gun into his belt and, ignoring the blood on his hands and clothing, returned to his bus and the very quiet passengers. He continued his daily route like a blind horse that knows its way home until a car from Tapalapa filled with men and guns and rope and handcuffs caught up with him and he was taken.

The government wanted the murder overlooked. It was not to their credit and they had their other mailmen who were also spies to consider. The government insisted that Teodoro had immunity.

The finca owners, Barney in particular, refused to let it rest. Barney and the others wanted to make it clear that they did not take it casually that they might be murdered by their mailmen.

The finca owners were too powerful for the government to disregard and Teodoro went on trial.

The trial lasted longer than the government had hoped would be the case. The finca owners insisted. It would have been news if the government had not controlled the newspapers.

Maria came to all the court sessions. He could not bear to look at her she hated him so much. At the trial's beginning he had looked toward her, his eyes pleading, hoping for a miracle; now she knew it, that he had been more than he had seemed. She had gestured a harsh curse sign at him. She was there as a malign influence. She was there to see him humiliated, to add to his punishment. He had ruined her life. He had murdered Don Alessandro, depriving her of his affluent protection.

And she had lost the admiration she was accustomed to, it had changed to scorn and laughter. She could have had her job again at La Providencia, she had even agreed, but the first morning, up and dressed, she thought of that walk along the street and the thought had stopped it all. She could not walk through all those eyes for she had lost more—her beauty had been spoiled.

The day of the murder she had been taking a noonday nap in her little house and had been violently wakened, being beaten by the hysterical woman she had thought was the least problem in her life.

Doña Inez had all the combined strength of misery and triumph in her arms and fists now that she was finally freed to destroy this latest woman of Alessandro's. She meant to make Maria pay for all her ruined hopes. Maria's only thought had been to escape from this crazy woman, to get to Alessando.

"Alessandro will send you away!" she had shrieked, trying to avoid the blows. She had been struggling to open the door, not realizing that Inez had locked it when she came in.

"Alessandro is dead!" Inez had screamed at her.

In that moment of shock at what she heard Maria stood still. Inez lifted a wooden chair and broke it against her face. Now and forever a livid scar ran diagonally across Maria's face and across her ruined nose.

She came to the trial for her hatred as Teodoro had come to the shop for his love.

The government assuaged the finca owners by giving Teodoro a sentence of six years.

He sent messages regularly from the prison that he would kill Barney when he was released.

•   •   •

A bull built of straw stood on sawhorse legs, surrounded by admirers. Giggling fear foreshadowed the event to come.

Every year at Christmas the bull was built at San Felipe, straw was shaped and tied to the sawhorse, a stiff neck and head looking to the front. The body was looped around with a long fuse that passed mysterious clumps of coloured papers.

The Indian who was to be the bull's legs stood nearby. His friends egged him on as he drank from the bottle that was his fee for the night's work.

"Liquid courage," Barney said to Patrick, "speaking of which ..." and he pulled a slim silver flask from his hip pocket.

"Con permiso," an old man, barefoot, his straw hat in his hands addressed Elizabeth Shaw, "Patrona, with your permission we will light the fire."

Mildred's lips tightened. She hated it when her mother-in-law was living at the finca.

"Filthy old drunk!" she thought. She smiled at Mrs. Shaw who smiled back at her.

The crowd moved, restless with excitement, widening the circle around the bull. The fuse was touched with the lighted match. People screamed and scurried as the fuse began to snake its hissing way along the straw. A rattle of firecrackers sounded like a machine gun. There was a sudden roiling of smoke. A rocket shot into the crowd and the show was on. Babies on their mother's or their sister's backs began to cry. No one knew what might happen next. Smoke obscured the air and the bull dipped and charged as the man inside did his part.

The bull never ran in the direction of the Patrona and her guests. They were never deliberately threatened.

Finally the bull lost its racket and faltered, came to a standstill in a continuing welter of smoke. The sawhorse was lifted off the man who stood stupefied, wiping smoke tears from his eyes. It was a joke that he was temporarily deafened. He was a great success. The friend who had kept his bottle safe returned it to him. He uncapped it and drank, put his straw hat on his head at an angle and went with his friends toward the music. The marimba had begun to play near the rough wood floor put down for dancing.

"Look at them," Antonio laughed. "Christmas and Easter they get drunk and dance."

Patrick and Barney finished Barney's brandy, watching the dancers. Patrick was surprised and pleased when an old man, also half-drunk, invited him onto the dance floor. It was a great joke. Patrick and the old man joined the other dancers with the crowd around them laughing.

Juana was also dancing. She had bought a new head scarf, a blouse and a skirt. The Doughertys had given her a blouse and a head scarf brought from the city. She planned to dole her new clothes out among her old ones, wearing something new each day of this long week. On the floor she turned and turned, her face shining with pleasure.

In the crowd the baker watched her. She was in jeopardy. The baker had told her step-father to tell Juana she must marry him. Every day the baker sent a fresh loaf of bread to the step-father. The step-father loved his daily bread. With Juana at the bakery he could have it forever.

"Something is the matter with you," he raged at Juana from his bed. If he could stand he would beat her. If he could walk he would drag her through the streets to the baker, throw her at him. Juana stayed beyond his reach.

"An eye has changed you!" he roared.

"He cannot walk," Juana told Margaret scornfully. "He will die soon."

Other eyes than the baker's watched the young girl turning; the eyes of the women who had married, the eyes of the women who had no chance to marry. It was a scandal that Juana would not have the baker. The women watched her.

• • •

Margaret wrote,

"Dear Allen, Xmas is coming, the geese are getting fat how about that? I'm making doll houses ... hand puppets ... and a stick horse with a papier mache head over a broom ... Joys of motherhood ... but the youngest sits alone as of yesterday. (Other children were walking at not much older but we haven't told her.) Comes the season for Xmas cheer! Wish you were here! Love ..."

A pig was screaming. A pig had been tied by its hind legs and hauled high. The shriek of its final fear was everywhere. Everyone in the village of Los Cedros de San Juan knew that the baker was killing a pig. The racket stopped, absolute.

"Juana, I want a back leg," Margaret told Juana.

Juana wouldn't go unless Alix went with her. They took some money and left.

Good, Margaret thought, that solves Christmas dinner.

• • •

A warm, dark night, stars and no moon. Los Cedros waited in the dark. All electricity had been turned off. Along the village's main road pale squares flickered where rooms held candles.

"The signs would be unmistakable. The magi whose function it was to watch for that anticipated signature of God from their Mount of Victory would have no doubts when, after centuries of anticipation, it appeared at last." According to Ephraim of Syria, the mysterious great star would have "at its centre a glowing cross of brighter light and centered on that would be the face of a child."

At the tutor's house kitchen chairs had been brought onto the cement porch and the family waited, looking through the night toward the far side of the valley. The procession would begin there at the finca always called the "sad" finca.

"Ah! There!"

Across the valley a candle was lighted, others were lighted and slowly, then more quickly, the dots of light formed into a line, a thin, shining thread which began to move along the invisible road, wavering, undulating, luminous, afloat.

The procession disappeared at the far left curve where trees rose higher, reappeared in a triumphant burst of light beyond the butcher shop, coming toward them.

At the front, barefoot and solemn, a piper walked playing his homemade flute. Behind him, high over his head, the Virgin Mary floated, carried on a platform by six men. She had been brought from Italy, with her pink and white face, her pale brown hair. One hand slightly raised, she blessed the terrain she passed. She was to be carried through all the dirt streets of Los Cedros de San Juan, blessing the houses and the people however much they had refused her a resting place. No room to lie her head, until she was replaced on her pedestal, on a bed of straw, in the church where the brujo now stood, swinging the censer to keep the church pure for her arrival.

"Look! There's Juana!"

The children waved but were kept from calling out.

Juana was splendid. Tonight she wore only new clothes.

Her blouse was silky lavender with flowers embroidered on it in blue thread. She wore a headscarf of red and blue roses. She had bought one of the longest candles, a sign of affluence.

As she passed the porch she gave them one quick glance. When the procession had passed each figure became a silhouette, lighted by the carried candle.

The church freshly whitewashed, held flowering branches of poinsettia and bougainvillea in glass jars. A luxuriant bower. The processional candles were doused one by one as the procession entered.

Mary stood beside a waist high manger made of rough wood. The young man who was privileged to make the night's miracle happen waited underneath hidden by curtains.

The long processional, candles flickering to light the magic way, had brought feeling to the surface. The church was filled and silent. The Indians sat in an ancient humility, heads bowed in submission. On Aztec nights like this there were times when the Virgin brought forth an obsidian knife to cut hearts out of bodies. There was no such fear here.

Near midnight, above the eye level of the kneeling Indians, the straw in the manger jiggled and moved, shoved by a twisting of plaster curls painted gold, a pearly forehead, round blue eyes. Following the head came the body, arms gracefully curved and one plump leg bent at the knee. The newborn babe was pushed into place by a brown hand that pulled straw over the opening and withdrew.

The church bell rang midnight, bombas exploded in the night sky outside the church, and the Indians stood to file past the manger, to see the miraculous infant on its yearly straw.

"When they arrived at Bethlehem," says Ephraim the Syrian "they had no fear of having come to the wrong place. The occult knowledge which had brought them there must have clothed in glorious light that place of poverty. And beyond terrestrial forms they saw for a moment the Splendors of the Word Incarnate."

The marimba that Don Cesar paid for began to play. The worshippers filed from their miracle, through the door, straight into the fiesta.

For three days and nights the marimba would play and the bombas explode, twenty-four hours a day, fifty feet from the Doughertys' house.

On Christmas day in the morning Margaret and Patrick and the two oldest girls went to the private chapel at San Felipe. Barney in dark shades ("To keep my eyes from bleeding," he told Patrick), read appropriate scriptures to the gathering, the Doughertys, his mother, his wife, his children, and Daddy Frank who was buried under the floor.

This was the year when Kerry and John were given bicycles. John was seven and Kerry eight. The perfect age, Antonio insisted. To make the point clearer he had taken away the boys' tricycles.

This was the year, for Kerry, when even his toys outgrew his abilities. He had loved his tricycle, spent hours riding it on the cement of the laundry yard behind the house. His bicycle, on its kickstand, stood in its place.

His father who would help him learn to ride it waited for him.

Antonio, already angry, anticipating failure, put Kerry onto the seat and wheeled him in circles. Each time Antonio turned the bicycle loose to let Kerry "ride," it would fall sideways and Kerry would crash onto the cement. His knees and elbows were scraped. His head was banged.

Helen watched through the kitchen window, watched Antonio bully Kerry in his insistence that Kerry be normal, name the colours, count to ten, ride a bike.

"That's not too much to ask! I buy him a God-damned bike for Christmas and you keep out of it! You just keep out of it!"

He only wanted it all to be different.

Was that too much to ask?

He only wanted what was wrong to be right.

Helen withdrew, her son screaming, seeing his only hope go. His father began, again, to walk him in circles.

Kerry twisted his head around to watch, to see when Antonio turned the bicycle loose and at the same moment the boy turned loose of the bicycle handles, grabbed for his father's neck. Kerry's lunge toward Antonio made the bicycle fall toward him. He grabbed the boy and the bicycle, swearing. He pulled Kerry from his neck, slammed him into the bicycle seat and again Kerry, his face twisted into a knot as he cried, outguessed his father. Antonio swore as the bicycle pedal raked down his shin, tore his trousers and he fell. Kerry, Antonio and the new bicycle were in a tangle on the concrete.

Helen fed her husband and her son devilled eggs, iced-tea, coconut cake. She did everything she could to alleviate the hurt. She helped whatever she could reach.

In the plaza by the church the marimba played on.

Juana came to Margaret to say, "A head is on the porch."

"What?"

"The head of a man is on the porch."

"Oh. Lord!"

The head was attached to a body. A drunk had sat on the steps to rest and had rested himself into a sprawl over the steps and onto the porch. A tiny woman sat beside him. When Margaret spoke to her she looked up, a flicker of eyes, then looked straight ahead again, a rabbit frozen in place, hoping the danger might go away.

Margaret returned to the kitchen. Later that afternoon she saw that the head had carried itself elsewhere.

EIGHT

It was nearly noon on the last day of the year.

Mildred woke first in the beige and pink hotel room. She slipped from the bed, adept at not waking Barney who snored at the motion, his face ground into the sweaty pillow. She lifted her dressing gown from a nearby chair, her slip from a pile of clothing let fall the night before, and disappeared into the bathroom.

Barney woke, hearing the shower. The daylight hit his eyes like a hammer. He woke to a pounding in his head ... how many Pernods? His tongue had grown moss and dried to the roof of his mouth.

"Damn. Damn."

The small clock on the bedside table showed him that in a little over an hour they would be meeting up with Ham and Alberto again. Brunch, a long afternoon, then dinner. They would see the old year out, the new year in.

He moved a leg to disentangle the covers. He let the cleared leg fall over the edge of the bed. Stood, shaking. Went into the bathroom for the aspirin bottle. Mildred was obscured by the shower curtain.

In the bedroom Barney poured water from a pitcher into a glass, swallowed two aspirin, fell in a heap on the heaped covers and groaned a joyless groan. He lay there waiting to feel better.

Mildred, her shower finished, was being particular about her face. Some coloured stuff smoothed over all, then pink for the cheeks, blended, then something for the eyelids. After each step of the operation she would draw her head back and examine the effect in the mirror, her eyes squinting and critical.

The bathroom door opened. A flood of steam came into the room that had been comfortable. Barney stood naked in the doorway, rubbing himself red with a towel.

Mildred glanced at him once, then returned to her mirror, something for the eyelashes, something for the lips. She was anticipating this day and night. She meant to be beautiful for it. She ignored Barney who would change the subject if he could.

Barney had no tolerance for invisibility. He walked gracelessly to stand behind her in the mirror.

"Who are you dressing up for?" he snapped, knowing it all.

"Myself." She was at work on her eyes again.

She and Ham would never go all the way. She wasn't a tramp and Ham knew she wasn't. Barney's behaviour would have driven any other woman away long ago. He never remembered what he did, what he said. She was the one left with the accumulating knowledge, the memories he wouldn't remember.

Barney was slamming drawers. He sat on the bed to put on his socks.

Mildred took a dark red dress from the closet and slid it over her head. She began to fasten the tiny jet buttons up the front.

Barney was exasperated with himself, setting the day off wrong. He'd make it up.

They came out of the hotel into the street, walked past plateglass windows displaying luxuries. Reflected in the windows Mildred saw herself, tall and slim and desirable.

Hamilton adored Mildred, held her in a tender esteem. When they had the chance the two longed toward each other, star-crossed lovers. When they had the chance they kissed like adolescents, hot and eager. When they had the chance to do more, well, then there was honour.

She was more of a woman than Barney could ever know, pounding himself drunkenly against the lump of her body until he exhausted himself into her. The little death the French called it, that was all Barney would ever have of her, the silly, graceless, little death.

Mildred and Hamilton believed themselves to be subtle,

but they were not subtle. Midnight was an hour away when Barney began to make caustic remarks under his breath, a mumble the other three ignored.

"... and if you could get it up ... and if you could get her into bed ..." he sneered at Mildred, "truth be known, it's one place she don't ..."

Mildred's voice became louder, sharp. She laughed with Ham and Alberto but she kept her husband in the corner of her vision. She thought she could manage him. She was crossing the time until midnight with a progressively assuaging manner, very like she had crossed a field where a bull was kept when she was a girl. She had believed herself to be adept. Go slowly. Don't show fear. Keep your eye on him. The bull had never charged. If he had charged even once all her successful theory might have gone glimmering.

Barney had reserved a bottle of champagne for midnight but the time was deteriorating. Midnight might never come. He reached with the hand nearest to Mildred and, before she realized what he meant to do, he pinched her nearest breast, hard.

"She jumps just like that," he leaned across the table to Ham, "wherever you touch her."

At ten minutes before midnight they were asked to leave by a frightened waiter.

"You understand, Señora, it is the other customers. I myself would never make such a request."

Barney had left his own unsatisfactory table and gone walking around the room, dropping into whatever chairs were empty near anyone who caught his eye.

Ham and Alberto took a firm grip on him, explained that the police would be sent for if he did not leave now, propelled him from the room, but not before one table was overturned and others knocked around in the struggle.

In the street Barney still fought. The two men kept holding him. A policeman became interested. The three promised that Barney was on his way to bed.

"We're going to get a doctor to give him a shot!" Mildred announced.

There was rope in the trunk of the car. Mildred went for it. They would tie Barney up to make him manageable, then they would find a doctor to give him an injection.

For his own good.

"You're just like your mother!" Mildred hissed. "Daddy Frank knew how to handle you. You need a doctor!"

Mildred's righteous reasoning stained the drunk man's thought ... running screaming through the dining room ... struggling with these two men while his wife watched. He fought with a manic power in the grip of all of them.

When Barney's mother had come running past the table, casting wild eyes at them, at bay, the children had sat in shock. When Daddy Frank stood Barney had thought he was going to help. He helped the men who were after his wife. He struck her down viciously with his fist. Then he came back to the table and sat down. The room was quiet. Dessert was chocolate pudding. Barney ate it.

They brought him down at last, tied around with rope. They shoved him into the back seat of the car. They drove all over the city to find a doctor who was working on New Year's Eve.

The man they found was suspicious but believed the identification Mildred had, proving that this maniac was her husband. The doctor charged a triple price and gave Barney an injection with a dull needle as if he stabbed him.

At the hotel the night clerk asked whether they needed help and was told they could manage. The tied man would stagger a few steps, then be carried. They got him into the elevator, out of the elevator into the corridor, along the corridor, into the room.

Ham and Alberto laid the almost unconscious body on the bed and looked to Mildred ... What now?

Mildred was beginning to be frightened to feel, now all was quiet, the enormity of what had happened.

Ham asked whether he should stay. Out of the question. The two men left. Mildred was alone in the chair, watching Barney on the bed.

He was breathing heavily through his mouth. His nose had bled and his face was swollen from Ham hitting him to knock him out. Ham had decided after Barney was tied, yelling, trying to fight, that the best thing would be to make him unconscious. He had hit the tied man over and over again without knocking him out. Barney's eyes had blanked out with it. He believed they were killing him.

Mildred's anger returned. It was Barney's fault he was so hurt. He could have gone along to a doctor without all that fuss. She thought it was unfair that he was going to blame her for this. He always got hurt when he was drunk and she was expected to accept it all. This was just one more time. Well, this time he could be the one accepting it.

She suddenly realized she was going to have to sit in this chair all night. No room on the bed. She should have told them to put him on the floor. He wouldn't have known the difference. This way they'd both be in lousy shape tomorrow.

She could see the raw wounds where he had fought against the rope on his wrists. God, it was going to be painful taking those ropes off. The blood was dried hard. She couldn't untie him until she was sure he understood. If he woke in the middle of the night and she was asleep he might kill her. She left him tied.

At times during the night Barney tried to change his position. He would groan with the effort.

All night long Mildred dozed and woke and dozed. Until the moment when, on the first day of the new year, she looked at him and he was awake. He was looking at her.

• • •

Barney wore his shirts with the left sleeves ripped off. His arm had swollen to such a size that he couldn't put a shirt on. He had taken every shirt he owned, emptied all his drawers onto the floor, and ripped the sleeves out. Half a dozen shirts had been destroyed outright, made into rags by his violence. Mildred thought he had overdone it. She tried to suggest that six shirts would be enough. He had looked at her, pulling on cloth, and she had gone quiet. The shirts that withstood the amputation were the shirts he wore.

"Look at that!" he said to Antonio, "gaudy as a baboon's ass." His swollen arm, alien and public, poked through the ragged edge of cloth. "It wasn't enough to tie me up and knock me around. They had to find a doctor with a lousy dirty needle!"

Knowing Mildred could hear him in the kitchen Barney yelled toward the door. "A little blood poisoning can pass for an accidental death in this damned house!"

There was a slight click, the kitchen door closing, Mildred had gone out. These days she manipulated doors cautiously, trying to escape Barney's notice.

She had so pre-rehearsed the event of that evening that it had seemed simple. Her assumptions had included a sober, grateful Barney. Daddy Frank had said so.

And when it happened it had all gone wrong. There were no white-coated attendants to hide him in an expensive rest home. There was no doctor in charge to tell her she was brave.

The swelling and discolouration in Barney's arm kept being there, went through colour changes like a sunset. Mildred bought new shirts. Mildred? Someone bought new shirts. They appeared in his drawer and lay there, arms intact.

The world had gone greasy. During all Barney's waking time he slipped and slid. He would sometimes lash out, listening to his own voice, when someone, anyone, came into any room he was in. It didn't help. Help what? A reflex. An old habit. He could have told his mother now that screaming didn't help.

When he stopped yelling at the sight of her, Mildred stopped sneaking her way around the house. She dressed and undressed in the bedroom. Pretended that everything was the way it had always been. That nothing had changed.

Barney's head hurt. He wondered whether he might have a concussion. When he drove it hurt his head. When he drove he had to remember to push on the accelerator. More than once he found himself simply stopped in the middle of the road because he hadn't remembered the accelerator.

At times a thick surge of pain would go through him like a sob, reverberating, as a hollow drum must feel when it's struck.

He had been sitting for hours in dark silence when Mildred came into the bedroom not knowing he was there. She turned on the light and saw him, gasped, scuttled from the room. She was not always so sure that nothing had changed.

· · ·

With Christmas past Juana planned toward Easter. She began to keep eggshells from the morning breakfasts. She would put a small hole in each end of the egg and blow the egg out. She rinsed all the shells and saved them. The Doughertys stopped eating boiled eggs she was so disappointed at seeing the shell be made useless.

The month before Easter Juana and the girls cut magazine pages into coloured confetti and filled the eggs. On Easter the eggs could be broken, harmlessly, over heads. Some of the eggs, well marked, were filled with flour. A bit of coloured paper was pasted over the holes with flour and water paste and the egg was stored away.

By the time Easter week arrived Juana and the girls had an arsenal of eggs. All they needed were enough heads.

Holy Week began with Judas Day. Two uprights of rough wood stood flanking the road. Fifteen feet up a crossbar completed the arch. Dead animals hung from the crossbar, rotting.

When cars drove through Los Cedros de San Juan and passed under the Judas arch they became fair game for the children who ran alongside the car screaming "Hoo-dahs! Hoo-dahs!" at them. The children threw stones, made curse signs, made ugly faces, until the car disappeared down the road. The children would wait for the next car.

On this day the world should stop for grief.

No cars should profane the road by driving on it as if business as usual were possible.

Perfidy had struck and the first Christian, some say the last, had been betrayed.

In the afternoon a grander revenge was exacted. Judas himself was seated in a chair and carried through the village. His face and hands were leather, dark and shiny with age. His arms were the stuffed sleeves of a jacket and stuck straight out in front of his body as if he begged forgiveness. The straw stuffed pants that were his lower body were bent at the hips and at the knees to accommodate his being tied into a kitchen chair. Two long bamboo poles were run under the seat, and carried by two men in a parody of respect he traveled the streets of the village as the Blessed Virgin had done. He wore shoes and socks, a straw hat, a tie. He was better dressed than the men who carried him. He was wearing clothing cast off by Don Cesar years earlier. It delighted them to have this much of Don Cesar on their chair. In the plaza the clothing was carefully removed and folded. The face and hands were skinned. Judas, naked straw, was given over to the children to brutalize. They tear him to bits, pulling at legs and arms. They reduce him to a pile of straw and they burn him to ashes. The clothes and the leather pieces are put away for next year.

At midnight on Easter Eve a new fire was built and lighted in front of the dark church. The fire was blessed. A long ta-per was lighted from it and carried into the church to light the candles there. The bombas crashed in the night sky.

Christ had passed from death to life.

He had risen.

The church bell tolled a reversal of its usual message.

Alix and Lucy and Juana ran riot with their confetti eggs. Susie was initiated into the fun, an egg broken, quite gently, on her head. While she was wondering whether to cry they gave her eggs and showed her how to break them on their heads. She was won over.

A screaming racket of voices brought Margaret out of the house and onto the porch. Children armed with sticks and stones were running past, chasing a small black and white dog. Its fur was soaked with blood. One hind leg was broken and dragging while it ran lop-sided on the other three. Doomed and driven it ran without looking back. The pack of children threw their rocks, grabbed others off the ground hardly pausing.

Margaret ran off the porch and after them to stop it. The dog lay quivering and dying. One thin flank twitched.

The children, standing around it, were as close to being contented as Margaret had seen any group of children since she came here. It was a mundane spectacle for them, death, she thought. They saw it so often. But this one was their own. They made this one happen.

"It was a bad dog," Juana said, seeing Margaret's distress. "It had a sickness."

•　•　•

Patrick's other wife was washing clothes in a creek in that other place where he was spending all his spare time. Some tourists walked past her and stopped to say to each other, in English, how charming it was the native still followed the old customs.

Patrick's other wife returned home to tell him about the tourists. They were both delighted.

It was a kind of success particularly appreciated by ex-students of Harvard and Radcliffe that they could achieve being taken for natives.

• • •

The baker was waiting, continued to send Juana's step-father bread. He meant to have his way.

"No," Juana said when Sunday came, "I cannot go to the market." And, "No, I cannot take the list to Tomas." She stayed in the house, in the kitchen. She was afraid. She had seen looks, heard rumours.

Lucy rushed into the kitchen to ask her mother, "Why are all the people coming?"

Margaret went onto the porch and saw women gathering in the night, in the road near the house. They were carrying candles as if it were a feast day. They were not festive.

There were twenty.

Then there were thirty.

"The posada has come to our house!" Lucy said.

An altered posada. They were thick in the road. The grim faces, lighted by the candles, were turned toward the house. The hags had come, even the young women looked terrible.

Now there were forty.

They meant to take Juana from the house and exorcise the evil-eye from her. If the baker wanted her he should have her. In the kitchen Juana had pulled a chair to the farthest corner and sat there in a huddle.

Now there were fifty.

The children were becoming frightened.

"Why are they there?' the children wanted to know. They wanted to know quickly.

"What do they want?"

In the kitchen Juana had slid from her chair to the floor in a soundless trembling.

Patrick was in the city. Margaret did not want to leave to go for help. She was all that kept the women back. She could not send one of the children for Tony, it was too long and dark a walk up the hill. She stood on the lighted front porch and told the women to go away. They would not look at her.

Don Cesar arrived in a cloud of dust, driving fast and braking harshly. He strode from his jeep to the edge of the porch, looking into the faces and naming names. A few of the outermost women tried to slip away.

"No! You will not leave!"

They stayed to hear their names said and saw that Don Cesar's office clerk was in the jeep, writing down names as Don Cesar said them. Now it was they who were fearful. They were being written into a book!

"I have told this woman not to marry," Don Cesar announced. "Mateo must find another wife!" That explained it. Don Cesar wanted her. She was beyond them.

"If there is any more of this stupidness your husbands will be fined!"

Don Cesar left having ignored Margaret as firmly as the women had done. The women left in his wake, hurrying home, candles extinguished.

Patrick returned from the city to say that they were still legal but the van was not. The van must leave the country. How could the van leave the country?

•   •   •

Barney had gone into spasms and rained dark blood from his ruined head over everything in the room. Mildred's piano. Mildred's marble coffee table, Mildred's books.

He had stood before the fireplace. The first blood to fly hit the portrait of Freeborn Lady.

He had moved violently with the force of the bullet and

then he had jerked and jerked. After that first spattering the rest of the room got its bath.

No question now of his small arsenal saving his life. No question of whether Teodoro was bluffing. When Teodoro came out of prison he would find his work had been done for him.

The two women, mother and wife, went for each other in that bloody room. Blame mattered more then grief. They were as pitiless to Barney in his death as they had been in his life.

The old one had the whip hand. Her allowance of a titular ownership did not extend to the daughter-in-law she despised. It was David who would own the finca when his grandmother died. And Mrs. Shaw was a healthy woman.

The children had come running with the others. They saw their father, saw their mother sagging in the doorway as if she could go neither backward nor forward, saw their grandmother arrive.

It was Ricardo, the man-servant, who had the sense to take the children away, speaking to them gently while he led them far from the two women who were raging.

"You filthy old woman! If you ever want to see your grandchildren again you keep a civil tongue in your head when you speak to me!"

Mildred arrived into the kitchen in a rush, having made her telling blow.

It was true Elizabeth Shaw loved the three children. Mildred was still in her life, therefore, could not be dismissed, not ever, she could only be put in abeyance.

That resolving done, the funeral went smoothly. The two women were there to see Barney laid into the ground a few feet away from Daddy Frank. The floorboards of the chapel were heaped along the side wall, would be made back into a floor later.

The children moved through their days in an uncon-

scious lump, were seldom apart. They were deeply frightened. It was not only the gaudy horror that had been their
father's death, it was also the void afterwards. No one could
take their father's place.

When one of the children cried Mildred would take it in
her arms. Say the ritual soothings that let the living get on
with life. But in her heart she had the exaltation of a sur-
vivor who has come through. Alive. She meant to make the
most of it.

The school lost its meaning for Mildred. This would be
the last year of tutors. Mildred would take the children and
go to the United States or to Guatemala City. The children's
education was assured.

Ham and Alberto arrived to help as they could. Mildred kept
them as guests, put them in the pool house between herself
and Elizabeth Shaw to reduce the waves of hatred she felt
emanating from that other house.

Mildred needed to feel beautiful and all the other things
Barney's suicide cast doubts on.

"Damn him! Even the way he died had to be poisonous
to me! He always just thought about himself!"

Ham and Alberto had been there. They knew how they
had all been forced to take the measures they took. Who
could know that damned doctor would use a dirty needle!

Elizabeth Shaw had been sitting on her verandah, crying and drinking. When she saw Mildred and her guests at
the pool in swimsuits with drinks she came stumbling from
her house, screaming at the two men to leave.

Elizabeth Shaw, undercut by drink, tears running,
turned and started to climb the steps. She seemed weak,
taking the steps one at a time, pausing on each.

Ham went to help her, put his arm under her elbow.

She looked at him with all the hatred and hopelessness
of her loss. A shock entered him with that look. It was the
look Barney had given him when he was tied and helpless

and had had the injection. The look stopped Ham now as it hadn't then. He dropped his arm and left Elizabeth Shaw to climb the steps.

Ham and Mildred sat talking in the altered living room. The blood had been wiped off the horse with a little water. Oil had protected the surface. The furniture and rugs that had held stains were gone. The room felt makeshift.

"Thank God, the piano was closed!"

Mildred, languid in black, brushed her hair back and continued, "How ridiculous that such a terrible tragedy should become a cleaning problem."

Ham cleared his throat, "So ... you think you'll come stay in the city for awhile?"

Mildred looked toward the window.

It was too intimate.

But wasn't this what they had wanted, to have the space and time their love needed? Of course she would go to the city. She was not casual about things that mattered. She looked at Ham and nodded, smiled an almost social smile, as if to say, Yes, I'd love to come to dinner ... Yes, I'd love to come to the city and be in an apartment, in a bed for you to climb into when you've finished your day's work. She felt a twist of dislike for him. It was all made so easy for him.

She smiled and he smiled and relaxed back, thinking "That's settled then."

It occurred to her that he fell short in ambition. They had met when Mildred was shopping for orchids. How long had he managed that little shop? Mildred couldn't believe it paid well. She would see to it that he thought on a larger scale.

The thought of Ham as he would be when he had been improved softened her heart and she smiled a real smile at him. He smiled back.

"After a decent period of time ..." he continued.

"That's a year, isn't it?" Mildred asked. "Isn't a decent period of time a year?"

"I think so. We can look it up."

Well, good lord, that would put the cherry on the top, Mildred thought. We can't tie Barney up and give him blood poisoning with a dirty needle and have him shoot himself and just turn around and jump into bed with each other. That's more than a little excessive.

She relaxed. There was time. She'd take as long as she wanted.

She looked speculatively at the glass in Ham's hand. He noticed and blushed, thinking himself thoughtless. He reached casually, put the drink down, stood up, strolled over to the window. She would see that he could walk away from a drink.

A shadow crossed Mildred's face, watching him. She didn't understand his small drama. Was he trying to make her think he didn't drink?

He drank less than Barney, but everybody did.

Barney's complaint that Ham drank the liquor he had paid for came into Mildred's mind. She looked at him looking through the window, a drinker who pretended that he didn't drink and a cheapskate.

But when he turned and smiled she remembered that she loved him. They would have their chance at happiness.

They tucked their differences away, out of sight.

Manners count for something.

The surface of their new possibility was calm. If, somewhere far below, there were mysterious glimmerings of movement they were surely only the decorative fish that belonged in this particular pond.

•　•　•

The birds were going north and so would the Doughertys. This place, in another twenty-four hours, would begin to be a memory.

Margaret was winding up the packing while Patrick taught his last day at school.

The plywood panel was in place, ready for the double bed mattress which had been stripped of sheets. Margaret was filling the space underneath with the same old boxes. What they arrived with and what they are leaving with are the same. But not really. Not really.

There was a growing stack of leavings in the kitchen for Juana to take. Lucas, her brother, arrived to work his way into the pile, carrying armloads home to the one room Juana shared with her mother and the others and coming back for more. A wooden table and two chairs bought in the marketplace for Patrick to work on were the most impressive items. There were also discarded clothing, paper bags, clean jars with lids, old magazines, cans and bottles half-filled with Crisco, flour, salt, sugar, matches. Lucas went back and forth. Each time he returned a few more of the curious were in his wake.

A cornucopia was flowing.

The watchers held their hands out to Margaret.

Margaret left it to Juana to give anyone whatever she didn't want.

Juana had no problem. She wanted all of it.

Margaret came onto the porch to find a crowd grabbing at the things waiting to be packed. She pulled Anna's bottle out of one woman's hands. And Patrick's books! No, they could not take Patrick's books!

They were too many for her. They snatched at whatever was behind her back whichever way she turned.

"Don Cesar!" Margaret screamed at them as if it were a magic spell. And so it was.

"Don Cesar!"

The women left the porch to stand again in the road.

Juana and Lucas returned from their latest trip. Margaret told them that they must help her until Patrick came home. They had to stay on the porch when she was in the house.

She went in and found two women and a man rifling

through drawers, taking the cutlery that belonged with the house. She grabbed Lucy's teddy bear out of a woman's hands and recited "Don Cesar" at the three until they left.

Patrick retuned from his final day of teaching in time to prevent another rush on the porch.

That night they all slept in the van, ready to leave at the first light.

Patrick woke while it was still dark, backed the van out of the driveway, began the drive toward Tapalapa.

By the time the sun rose they were halfway to the border.

PHOTOGRAPHS

Bobbie Louise Hawkins. Texas. Early 1930s.

Bobbie with her mother, Nora Jewell Hall. Nora worked in a fast photography store, hand-coloring photographs.

London, 1949.

Bobbie and her first
husband, Olaf Hoeck.
Exiting the Gripsholm as
they arrived in Denmark.
December 1949.

Bolinas. Early 1970s.

Working as a disc jockey in Albuquerque. 1957.

Robert Creeley, Bobbie, Kirsten Hoeck, Leslie Hoeck, Sarah Creeley
and Katherine Creeley. Guatamala. 1960-'61.

Bobbie and Robert Creeley. Placitas, New Mexico. Early 1960s.

Bolinas. Early 1970s.

Bobbie, Rosalie Sorrels, Terry Garthwaite. Early 1980s.

Bolinas. Early 1970s.

Bobbie performing a
Ruth Draper monologue at
the Boulder Museum of
Contemporary Art, Colorado.
Late 1980s.

Rosalie Sorrels, Bobbie, and
Terry Garthwaite, Vancouver
Annual Folk Festival.
Mid-1970s.

Joanne Kyger, Allen Ginberg, Bobblie Louise Hawkins, Peter Orlovsky,
Michael McClure and Diane Wakowski at a poetry festival.
Bisbee, Arizona. August 1980.
Courtesy of the Allen Ginsberg Collection. Stanford University.

Bobbie and Junior Burke sitting on the stoop of Anne Waldman's house on
MacDougal Street after rehearsal for Bobbie's play "Life As We Know It."
New York City. October 2002.

INTERVIEW

Most of this interview was conducted over the telephone, starting in July 2011, the same week that Bobbie was moving into a new apartment. As our discussion progressed, we talked about many of her books. Following are excerpts from the interview. The complete interview is online at www.belladonnaseries.org/fifteepoems.html

—Barbara Henning

• • •

Barbara: In your book, *One Small Saga*, the narrator, Jessie, seems to be in a fix. She doesn't have enough money to continue art school and then Axel asks her to marry him.

Bobbie: I didn't have the money to go to college, and not having the money was the truth of the time, but that wasn't why I went with him. I went with him because it was an adventure. There I am, living with my parents in a two bedroom little house in Albuquerque, and here is this Danish architect from Africa and England, saying that he'd like to marry me and take me out of the country. With Olaf, I felt that I was in a place I already knew. I felt less exiled in that circumstance than I did living in a bedroom in my mother's house. When I got on the ship with Olaf and we set off to Europe, it was like now I was in my life.

Barbara: When I read the book, I wasn't thinking about it being you. I thought perhaps she was a character in a novel, perhaps autobiographical, but fiction, too.

Bobbie: Robert Duncan once said there is no such thing as fiction. And that makes more sense than almost anything. And when at one point I started looking back through my stories, I thought, I have almost never written a fictional line in my life. Your mind gets on something and you just meander along with it. I don't think that's fiction. It's all autobiography.

Barbara: Wasn't that what Duncan was talking about in his essay, "The Truth and Life of Myth," experience and imagination are one. And once you start telling any story, you jump into some fictional realm.

Bobbie: And you give yourself the allowance to elaborate. . . . And what you do—if you're going to stay with any kind of energy at all or any kind of validity—you go with whatever sparks in that moment. And it might be that that moment's spark is the only time that it ever occurs in your life. Just that quick little uptake and then you go past it.

•   •   •

Barbara: Before you met Olaf, you were an actor, weren't you?

Bobbie: When I was about sixteen I got into a repertory company in Albuquerque that was intending to make radio soap operas. I was on a city bus in Albuquerque going east on Central and I saw this building with "Art Center" written across the front in neon. Because I thought of myself as possibly being some sort of artist, I got off the bus and went across the street to see what was going on. I found myself in this building with sound proofing on the walls, with all kinds of microphones, and two major studios, each studio with an engineering room. It was a professional set up. I was shown around, and I asked if I could audition, they said yes. That was a break. I got a lot of training in that situation, and they liked what I did. I was the youngest member of the group, I was sixteen, and there was a lot there for me to learn. I was skipping a lot of school and anytime I could get away, I would go straight there and work on phonetics, for example, which helped me get rid of a Texas accent. I didn't want a Texas accent. I wanted to be an elegant person living in a book.

•   •   •

Barbara: What books were you reading?

Bobbie: Oh, honey, anything I could put my hands on. It wasn't as if I had anything like an education. We moved every three months, eight months, so I never finished a year in the same school.

Barbara: Did your mother take you to the library?

Bobbie: Oh, no. My mother read magazines. She was enamored of gothic horror so the magazines that were in the house were *Amazing Stories*, *Astounding Stories*, all of these vampire and werewolf stories. When I was six, they brought out a double billing of *Frankenstein* and *Dracula*. My mother who was hardly more than a child herself, longed to go to that. She was worried about taking me with her, that it might be harmful for a six year old to see these two monster movies. But she took me.

Barbara: I remember seeing those type of movies when I was about that age, too.

Bobbie: Well, they still are. Incidentally doesn't that guy Paul Ryan, the politician, look like a central casting figure for a vampire movie? He's got this very white face and very black hair and it comes down in this little pointy widow's peak.

Barbara: Yes, he does. I think they all look and smell like vampires

Bobbie: So what I read was a lot of gothic horror stuff. When I was about ten, there was a great American sci fi renaissance. Suddenly really good writers were writing science fiction, also a lot of bad writers, but these gothic magazines became "Amazing and Science Fiction Stories." They were what was there to read. At different times, I started going to libraries by myself and librarians would become interested in me. So that they would recommend books like all the Oz books. My reading was completely random. I read a lot of comic books. If you read a lot, it almost doesn't matter what you read, your taste is going to improve. The mind rejects boredom. The mind notices when it gets a higher return. When somebody tells beginning writers to just keep on writing, what is hoped for is that by writing an excessive amount they are automatically going to improve.

One year when I was living in England in London, there was a library between where I was living and the underground. Since I had that regular walk, I thought I'm going to be here a long time. I just started with the A's. It didn't matter if I heard of them or not—I'd just pull a book down and take a taste, looking for something that caught me, and I went through a lot of books, most that I don't remember all that well. And yes, almost all my writing is autobiography because it is almost all the outcome of conjecture. I start thinking about something and it gets hooked in my head. Do you want to hear a good line? Ben Jonson, I came across it a couple of days ago. "A horse that can count to ten is an exceptional horse. It is not an exceptional mathematician."

[laughter]

Bobbie: Isn't that great?

Barbara: It's wonderful.

Bobbie: I love lines like that. People come up with great lines. With *One Small Saga*, I'd be thinking about something, write a piece down, maybe a paragraph, maybe a page, maybe two pages, and maybe later, I'll think, oh do that again, do another, and they don't work, but I chuck them in the box, you know.

•　•　•

Bobbie: What I'm really short on, is transitions. Fielding Dawson was a brilliant transitional guy. Did you ever read him?

Barbara: Yes, I teach some of his stories in my classes.

Bobbie: He wrote an extraordinary book, called *Mandalay Dream*. He was capable of creating an incredible ambiance with the transitional shifts he wrote and I always envied him for it. My inclination is to give the gist of something and then fade to black and then come up with the next gist of something.

Barbara: What's really interesting is all that white space and the way you dip into a life, and the emotion is intensified by the emphasis on line and language.

•　•　•

Bobbie: I didn't even think about using poetic breaks and lines and stuff. That wasn't the approach. I wasn't finding a shaping theory. It was more like this line isn't working. What can I do? Virginia Woolf said technique is finding the specific form and tone for the individual piece that lets you say everything.

Barbara: Interesting that you say "line" and not sentence.

Bobbie: I don't think of it as poetry.

Barbara: Well it is definitely poetic. . . . How did it feel to be the subject of love in Robert Creeley's *For Love*? He dedicated that book to you.

Bobbie: Very flattering. Plus there is a weird thing that people, if they admire a poet and that poet has a woman attached, the implication is that she is some kind of priestess of the art. And that's a pain in the neck. So a lot of people when I was with Bob treated me better than they felt I deserved because of my affiliation with him. They wouldn't have treated me nearly as nicely, but when I was with Bob, I suddenly had some status with them. When I met Bob, he was teaching Latin at a boy's school in Albuquerque for $300 a month. I was working as a disc jockey at a radio station doing the midnight to six shift. We weren't exactly exalted there, except he had these friends he had made at Harvard, Buddy Berlin and Buddy's wife, Maryann and Race Newton. Those two guys had been his closest friends at Harvard and they thought of him as a serious writer. From the time he'd been in Harvard, he'd had correspondences going with Williams and Pound. So he was taken seriously in the outside world. I certainly didn't fall in love with him because he was a writer. He just instantly looked like my guy. I thought I was going to be there forever. But toward the end, I had to get out of there just to save my life as I intended it.

• • •

Barbara: Sometimes through reading we absorb voices and movements and language and it comes back in our own writing. When you came to my chat session this summer, you mentioned that you had taped conversations. Could you talk about that?

Bobbie: Taping conversations was a breakthrough for me. I went back to Texas with my mother because my grandmother was pretty much ready to die. I had written a first draft of *Back to Texas*, but it still needed a lot more on my relatives, and I was going to see all of them. We couldn't go into Texas and not visit everybody. I was really concerned to get the tone right in that book, to get that voice in my ear.

It occurred to me that if I slipped a tape recorder in and made tapes of everybody talking then when I got back home I could listen to it before I started to write and I'd be in the right tempo. I also thought that if anybody started telling stories I could "improve" them and put them in the book. That's the first time I registered how good my relatives were as storytellers. All of the stories were unimprovable. They were honed down into something incredible that I just could not improve. You know how that is, when you move away from relatives you make them less in your mind just in order to make yourself the size that lets you move around. But in "Back to Texas," in *Almost Everything*, there's that story when my cousin Preston says that Mexicans can put a dollar bill on a piece of newspaper and cut around it and every one of those pieces of paper will turn into a dollar bill. And then he turns to my aunt, and says, "Old So and so up there, he used to do that. You have to sell yourself to the devil to do it." My Aunt is saying, "So and so sold his soul to the devil?" And I'm sitting there looking at them. But I'm caught into the story, I still don't get that it's a completed item. I didn't get it until I started transcribing the tape.

Barbara: In *Back to Texas*, there's a story, "When you're stoned on grass," and Jesse/you ramble with words—as happens when stoned on grass—and you have this sudden awareness: "Nothing in my life ever happened that was as important to me as learning to read." Then you go on about the fighting between her mother and father, moving frequently and how she did well in school. Then you end: "Right from the first, reading was my darling pleasure." I like the way you often ramble and segue from narrative to idea.

Bobbie: "When you're stoned on grass and drinking wine. . ." I wrote that, and then one afternoon in Bolinas when the sun was shining and I was sitting out in the garden with Joanne Kyger and John Thorpe. I said, "Ok I've got a story I want to read to you." It was the first story I'd written that I felt was a real story.

Barbara: The frame for *Back to Texas* is this car trip to Texas with your mother, Mae, with the conversations and stories that take place in that car. Did you tape your mother also?

Bobbie: Yes.

Barbara: Was she aware of it?

Bobbie: No. When people know you're taping them, they change their diction. They want to sound more particular, and that means they use a different word choice. At the time, I was transcribing what different people said, and thinking, "Wow!" Literally, that story is verbatim. A lot of the stuff in that book, I did not write. I just copied it. And when I started copying out, I started registering a very interesting connection between my hand and my thought and my ear. And thereafter, I had an improved ability to actually hear how people were talking. It was made much more clear to me somehow. In the prose classes, I often have people bring in overheard conversations, written down. We open the class, just going around the room, and there will be this great stuff, like this guy says, "She's the kind of person you think is usual in every way and then she says, *Vahsss.*"

Barbara: Vase.

Bobbie: Everyone broke up instantly and yet that could never have been described as humor. Everyone in the room got that little jostle in their body. When people are really talking they can be brilliant. In intermittent fast flash statements, suddenly there is that lovely little bit of brilliance never to be said again. As conversationalists we take those moments as a beautiful bonus, and then they're gone, but as writers you should rush to another room and put it on paper, save it out of the void. That's exactly when I find I don't have paper. I usually write on the bank deposit slips in the back of my checkbook. I'll always have more of those than I use. Eric Bogosian's career started with him sitting in bars with a tape recorder. Somebody would start talking to him, and he would come away from it having the voice down exactly. When you start doing it this way, you start using actual words instead of your favorite words. It's a natural inclination to pull away from the actual word that got said to the word you would have used if you had said it. One student told me, "You know even when I was following the tape recorder word for word, when I reread it later, I realized I had changed words."

Barbara. Did you have any trouble with your relatives as a result of taping? Did they discover later on that you had taped them?

Bobbie: I didn't tell anybody. But there was a point when my cousin Marilyn came to live briefly in Sausalito with this boyfriend who had sold her a pair of shoes in Lubbock. My mother telephoned and said, "Marilyn is going to find out about you writing that book, and if she finds out about it,

Ollie is going to want a copy, and if you send Ollie a copy, she's going to let Thelma read it and she'll read that part about when Evertt was in the vets hospital, Doris took his money and spent it. So if you send Ollie a copy, will you take that part out?" She didn't ask for a copy. If she got a copy, Marilyn would have sent it to her.

Barbara: That's hilarious.

Bobbie: I mean my relatives were incredible, and it was all because of that habit of sitting around a big kitchen table with a coal oil lamp and telling stories, just passing around the table from one person to the next. That was a major entertainment. Everyone would laugh even if it was the fiftieth time they'd heard this story because it was like a performance. So as a child I had that background.

Barbara: A student at Naropa this summer was talking to me about her family and how angry they were at her for writing about them.

Bobbie: If she's writing about her family, she shouldn't hit them over the head with it. Write about it but keep it to yourself. The likelihood, but we don't want to discourage the young, is that they will never see it because what you are writing probably won't get published.

Barbara: Her poems were already published, and with the internet now everything is available to those who know how to search.

Bobbie: At that point you decide what matters to you. Telling the truth about something is important, and when you start actually saying what you think is the case, you learn that the other person has a completely different memory of it. The real problem, you can't write about someone without cutting them short, you'll always be giving a limited description. You can never write about someone full scale. That's more writing than you are capable of. You are usually extracting the bit that makes the story work. Anyone reading about themselves realizes they've just been cut off at all the edges. It didn't cause me a lot of trouble with my relatives because by that time, I never saw any of them.

$$\bullet \quad \bullet \quad \bullet$$

Barbara: How did "Back to Texas" get started?

Once I was talking to the editor of *Fiction Magazine*, telling him some stories, and he said, if you write some of those out, I'll stick them in the magazine. So I started writing them. Then they were printed in various places, *Big Sky, Fiction, The World*, and something called *Writing*, and something called *ZZZ*. Then *Back to Texas* was published by Bear Hug Books by Chuck Miller, an incredible artist who did the drawings.

Barbara: How did *Almost Everything* come about?

Bobbie: At one point, one of the editors of Coach House Press (Michael Ondaatje, David Young, Sarah Sheard) asked if they could reissue *Back to Texas*. It had gone out of print at that point and they wanted to include *Frenchie and Cuban Pete*. I said, "Well I have nine new stories we could stick in there, too." Michael said, "Great we'll do all of it." Then I said, "That's almost everything." And that became the title.

Barbara: Now it will be a Kindle as well as a book and maybe it will never go out of print.

Bobbie: That would be fun.

· · ·

Barbara: In *One Small Saga* and elsewhere, you have a narrative voice of a woman who is analytic, someone who solves mysteries.

Bobbie: According to my relatives, I started talking almost immediately. I was a real talker right from the first. I think being a talker saved my life, or it gave me one. There is a Russian fairytale about a prince whose mother died and his father married a terrible woman and the terrible woman instantly stuffs him into the cellar, and she becomes pregnant. His only friend is a mouse and the mouse comes to him and tells him that the infant the queen is carrying is a Baba Yaga, and when the Baba Yaga is born, it is going to eat everyone. So for him to escape, he has to start running now, while the baby is in the womb. He has to go to his father's stable and get on his father's fastest horse and ride to the west as hard and fast as he can go. So the kid gets on the horse and starts riding and he passes a giant who is throwing mountains over his shoulder and he's about to run out of mountains, and he passes three witches who only have one eye between them and they pass it around them. He goes past these things. As he goes west, he grows older. By the time he gets to the west, he's a man and meanwhile as he's going, he begins to hear the Baba Yaga coming after him. The Baba Yaga is sitting in a stone bowl beating the ground at the side like a paddle with a stone pestle, going bang bang bang bang, and she's coming after him. He gets to the end of the world, and the daughter of the moon is up there, his horse takes a flying leap, and he escapes the Baba Yaga and gets to the moon. He marries the moon daughter, and after a time, he starts to feel guilty about all his people who have probably been eaten. He wants to save them if he can, so he goes back down to earth. The moon daughter doesn't want him to go, but he must, so she gives him different sorts of things like a comb or this and that.

He goes back down to earth, gets on his horse and starts riding east. As he rides east, he gets younger. When he passes the giant, he gives him his comb. The giant throws it down and instantly has all these new ranges of mountains. And he gives the witches each an eye. So now he's a child again and he's continuing to go east and he comes finally to the castle. All the outside walls of the building are still up, a huge square, like a box, or a playpen. The prince looks through the trees and sitting in the middle of this big blank space is a giant baby girl. As he watches, the girl shrinks down into normal baby size and comes crawling out.

The story continues, but the thing that caught my attention was this sense that in order to escape you can't wait for the danger. In order to escape, you have to start running right now. And I have the feeling that a lot of artists fall out with their families, not because they're that problematic, but because they register that they have to start running fast. It feels to me like my ability to talk was this, except you know in the south, girls aren't encouraged to be smart, but they are often encouraged to be outrageous, so being able to talk would be part of that. In any case, I became articulate pretty quickly. I was reading anything I could get my hands on, as I told you before. When I started reading, I turned into someone else. I had a wider vocabulary. I've been thinking lately that vocabulary is what matters. Enough words and you have somewhere to go.

Barbara: Last night I was near the end of *Back to Texas*, reading "Aunt Ada came...", when you were talking about leaving with Axel [Olaf], and I wrote in the margin, "Get the hell out of there, Bobbie."

Bobbie: I think most artists are born into families where they don't feel like this is where they belong. I mean you can love your parents a lot. The issue of love isn't the point. Do you know the Englishman, Paul Scott who wrote the *Raj Quartet*? It's a fantastic set of books. It came out as a television series called "The Jewel and the Crown." At one point in his autobiography, Paul Scott said that all the time he was a child he knew there was this difference in him and he also knew that even though it was awkward and problematic, it was something to be cherished. I think most artists have that in them as a child. So it sort of stands to reason that artists think of themselves as having unhappy childhoods because many of them, most of the ones I've known, didn't have that experience that gets described as a happy childhood where there is this lovely conflux of the child and its family.

Barbara: That disjunction may very well be what drives artists to create.

Bobbie: Then there are the times when you have to save your life. You just have to save your life. What Olaf gave me was a chance to save my life and I was extraordinarily lucky to have him come along when he did. Imagine that. That such a thing could happen.

Barbara: In one of the stories in *Back to Texas* you talk about when your grandmother gave you that advice about "ignorance and lice". . . "you don't have to be ashamed of having ignorance or lice, you just have to be ashamed of keeping them," I thought that was great advice.

Bobbie: That's a great line, isn't it?

Barbara: Yes, what was your grandmother like?

Bobbie: She was about five feet tall and raised fourteen kids. She was married three times, actually. Her first husband she married when she was about fourteen and he was about seventeen and he died a couple of years later, and then she married Mr. Hall who was my mother's father. He was apparently a really good man and a nice man and gentle, and they were married and had two boys and three girls who lived. She had a lot of children who just died as babies, but she had two sons who grew up and three daughters who grew up. Then that husband died and she married Mr. Ussery and Mr. Ussery was this mean, awful man who would kick the kids if they came within kicking distance. They were all allowed to go to school until they were twelve, and as soon as they were twelve, they were put out in the fields, chopping cotton. It was a poor economy and that was how people on farms lived. He would be mean and her response was to say, "Yes papa." But meanwhile when one of her boys almost cut off one of her girl's fingers, she boiled a needle and thread and sewed it back on. At one time when we were in a conversation about raising children, she said, "I just had 'em and loved 'em." All of her children adored her and were jealous of each other about her. She was a loving woman.

Barbara: I had a grandmother who was like that. She had nine children, and she was also very special to me.

Bobbie: Grandmothers are really good for kids. They're often good for artists.

Barbara: A whole different shebang than mothering.

Bobbie: I was talking once to the wife of the guy who ran Slavic studies at Harvard. She was sort of heavy set and solid, very Russian, and she said, "Grandparents and grandchildren love each other because they share a common enemy."

Barbara: In another story, "About Grandmother's Hair," you mention how the KKK made your grandfather, I guess that's Mr. Ussery, buy shoes for a child who was walking to school in the snow without shoes. He was a terrible man.

Bobbie: Yes, he was awful.

Barbara: I thought it was interesting that the KKK actually did something good.

Bobbie: The KKK people were like the tea party. They thought of themselves as moral arbiters, keeping things straight. What they thought about themselves is very unlike what we think about them. I think of them as rigid-minded fascist, racists. But the KKK thought they were straightening up the country around them, so that if a kid was going to school barefoot, they could take that into their purview as something that needed to be corrected. With all this cross burning, they thought what they were doing was keeping black people in their place, and that keeping black people in their place was a moral necessity.

Barbara: A twisted and self-serving morality.

Bobbie: When they were *feeling* something they thought they were *thinking*. It's a commonplace error. We all do it to some extent, but an education helps, widens the vocabulary, creates a little humility.

• • •

Barbara: Bobbie, when did you start thinking of yourself as a writer?

Bobbie: When I was in high school, I thought of myself as an artist. It was the only hope I had. In the books I loved, the people who mattered to me were the artists. So that was what I wanted to be. I was right, that was where I had some possibility. What I didn't know was what that meant and I never got straight on that. The two serious art forms, I really thought of were the visual and the writing. When I was with Olaf, my first husband, I was being a painter. I was a student at the Slade when we lived in London. And when we were in British Honduras, I was teaching drawing in a couple of missionary schools as a volunteer. I showed pieces in a couple of group shows. I was always writing too because I liked words on paper. But "literature" as a thing to be involved in felt beyond me. Even after I had published books, I never put "writer" down as an occupation. I always put "self-employed." To call myself a writer sounded very impressive and scary, like bragging.

Barbara: Were you painting when you were living with Bob?

Bobbie: Yes, when we came back from Guatemala, I had a one-woman show at the Jonson Gallery in Albuquerque. Later I had two one-woman shows at the Gotham Book Mart Gallery in New York. And I showed with the Quay Gallery in San Francisco. I also had pieces in seven different books published by Black Sparrow.

Barbara: Were you writing then?

Bobbie: When Bob and I were first together, he had three things he would say. One of them was, "I'll never live in a house with a woman who writes." One of them was,

"Everybody's wife wants to be a writer." And one of them was, "If you had been going to be a writer, you would have been one by now."

Barbara: That was encouraging.

Bobbie: That pretty much put the cap on it. I was too married, too old, and too late, but he was wrong. Anne Waldman asked him once, "Why are you against Bobbie writing?" He said there was only room for one writer in a house. After we were no longer together, someone in New York asked me why I insisted on continuing to write when I knew it upset Bob so much. I remember being at a reading Bob was giving and he started reading a story about the Sufis crossing the desert and being eaten by Ogres. It was a story I had read earlier and elucidated on out of a Sufi book. The woman I was sitting with turned to me and said, "That's your story." And I said, "Not now." But I tend to think of Scott Fitzgerald and how he deliberately dynamited anything that could happen for Zelda. She had a lot of different talents none of which were allowed to develop if Fitzgerald had anything to do with it. Meanwhile, he stole all her stories. He was using her as a resource. I'm sure he thought he was taking care of her because I think he was so self serving, he wouldn't have known the difference. He not only stopped her from writing, he saw to it that his friends wouldn't have anything to do with it either. They wanted her to go on stage, and he told them she was too insecure, so they didn't take her. If they supported her, they would lose him as a friend.

With Bob and I, we kept being together because we were really hung on each other. And then that turned into fighting. We were both so volatile that finally, over and over again, there was only one decision for me to make and that was I had to get out of there. It broke my heart. I had thought I'd be there with him forever. Everything being so chaotic wasn't the point. Edith Wharton said, "I don't know if I should care for a man who made life easy. I should want someone who made it interesting." Bob was the most interesting man I ever met.

•   •   •

Bobbie: I kept wanting Bob to write a book about the time we spent in Guatemala in about 1960, and I would say, remember so and so who was the night watchman who made these balls of mud and shot birds with them, and I wanted him to write that book. And he just kept refusing. Finally, he told me he would never write that book because I had so turned him against it by insisting to him that he should write it. Well, that's actually a classic kind of statement at the end of a relationship. It is saying, there is nothing here, anything here is going to block possibility instead of going forward.

Barbara: So later you wrote the story about Guatemala, didn't you?

Bobbie: That's *The Sanguine Breast of Margaret*, a book that has never been published in the United States and should be published somewhere. At some point I thought, he's not going to write this book, so I think I will. When he would go off to do readings and was going to be gone for three or four days or something I'd bring my cardboard box out of the closet and set it up at the table and go to work. If I had things to do and if he was at home and he was teaching, when he would leave where we lived, after half an hour he had gone too far to come back, so I'd wait half an hour and I'd bring it out, and I'd start some work. He'd be gone for the time the class took plus an hour's drive each way. I'd have everything put away by the time he came home. I wrote the first draft of that book, a not so hot hundred page draft. If he suspected that I was writing, he would sit down with a glass of whiskey and start drinking and then we'd have three days and nights of furniture smashing and all the radios in the house turned up full-volume and the kids trying to sleep. It would just be three days of hell. I think a part of what attracted Bob to me was competences I had within myself, but it was as if once I was within his purview, those competences were only to be used for his needs, in the space where we lived, and not as though they were my own.

·   ·   ·

Barbara: You were in Guatemala in 1960, but you didn't publish *The Sanguine Breast of Margaret* until 1998.

Bobbie: I was working on that book a long time, and I kept thinking about it as my first book even after I published other books because it was the first book I started with a book in mind. I didn't actually finish it until I was here in Colorado, sometime in the 80's. When I was living in England I met one of the editors from North and South. He was a close friend of Lee Harwood's. When I mentioned this book, he said he'd publish it. I never gave him American rights because he was a small press and was only publishing about 500 copies.

Barbara: What did you have in mind when you named it *The Sanguine Breast of Margaret*?

Bobbie: I love the notion of sanguine. "Hope springs eternal in the Sanguine Breast." Margaret seemed to be eternally hopeful, with or without justification, and it is a constant.

Barbara: She's the voice of optimism as they drive an old van through Mexico with four children and only $100. It's an incredible story of endurance—the children, the illnesses, thieves, no money, a drunken husband and then arriving at the finca, employed as lowly tutors in a serfdom. If you wrote most of this a long time afterwards, did you have any trouble remembering?

Bobbie: I wrote it in bits and pieces, but when I went to put together the final book, the big problem I had writing it was that I had gotten so far from it, and every time I would start to write about Bob, all of the worst things would come instantly into my imagination, all of the things he'd done that were shitty and petty. Then I thought that wasn't the whole of it, there was more to it than that. There was a way I felt about this person that I was absolutely blocking now and this book was not going to be a book until I could somehow show him as I thought he was then. On about draft 17, Margaret is standing in the garden and as she's pulling up weeds and cutting back a quince bush, I suddenly decide to go to a hypnotist I'd heard of in Santa Rosa. At this point, of course, I was living in Bolinas and Bob and I were not together. So I drove north on the Lucas Valley road. On the seat next to me I had a tape recorder and a list of questions. I wanted to be hypnotized and taken back to being the person I was in Guatemala and then I wanted the hypnotist to ask me the questions, to have those questions answered by the me I was then, and to get it on the tape. One of the questions I had was, "Did you love him?" And I'm thinking, that is going to be confusing for her because she is there then, so I pull over to the side of the road and I change "Did" to, "Do you love him?" I pulled out and started driving, and I thought, "I could spend the rest of my life saving my past from its future." Then I think, "great line," and I pull over to the side and write it down and then continue. But it didn't work.

Barbara: It didn't work?

Bobbie: I couldn't get hypnotized. She said, with some people it takes two or three goes before you get there.

Barbara: It must have opened up some memories for you.

Bobbie: That night when I went to bed I slept fabulously. It was great. I went to her twice. Something must have happened. I remember lying on this sort of naugahyde couch. I've got my eyes closed, and she says, "You're feeling at peace." And I think, yeah. Then she says, "Just start with your feet and feel the peace come up your body. You're feeling very relaxed." And I think, yes, I'm feeling very relaxed. She says, "You're standing on a cliff side looking over a large garden filled with flowers." I'm imagining this garden full of flowers. She says, "You are at peace with yourself." And I think, that's good. Then she says, "You're at peace with the universe," and I just pop straight up and say, "I can't really go with *the universe.*"

Barbara: You weren't a good patient for hypnosis.
Bobbie: I guess not. The arguments still pertained and it was funny. I did that a couple of times and someone suggested their hypnotist and I went to him once and coming away from him, driving over Mount Tamalpais, I found myself thinking, Ok if I can't come to grips with this, it doesn't mean I'm a horrible person for making Bob sound horrible. If he wants to sound good, he can write his own book. At that point I did away with the whole idea of working with hypnotists.

Barbara: Bobbie, how did having children affect your life as a writer?

Bobbie: The question of time, how you find the time for all of it, that was sometimes an issue. But for the most part all the problems I had with getting on with the work were my own problems. The children and my daily life as a mother were my usual day. For myself, particularly around the business of writing secretly, the question of where I would find time to do anything was very sporadic. And I was an only child and so every time I do something I invent it on my own. Motherhood and trying to be a writer were no different.

Barbara: There are several outstanding stories in the *Sanguine Breast*. In one of them you begin, "Who knows how long it would have continued without the newspaper ad." Then you go on with a description of the life of a cattle tick, making an analogy to human beings and alluding to the relationship between Margaret and Patrick. You talk about the cattle tick leaping and then you write—

For human beings only fairy tales try to solve life with one large leap—"happily ever after". In real life we hang and leap, hang and leap, hoping with each leap that it is a forwarding. For each next effort we gather together our latest fund of enough courage, enough hope, and we leap. And being mistaken takes as much effort as being right. (13)

Bobbie: I got really involved for a while in a great book, called *The Parable of the Beast*. Did you ever hear of it? It is a fantastic collection. One of the accounts is that of the cattle tick. The male cattle tick doesn't even have a stomach. He just comes out, screws, then drops off and dies. The female has all these eggs in her then and she goes looking for a mammal to secure herself on. If she can't find one, she goes out on a bush to the end of a twig, and into a kind of stasis and in that stasis she can literally live for up to thirty years.

Barbara: That's amazing and the eggs are still alive?

Bobbie: Yes, and then at some point a mammal walks by and she smells butyric acid, and springs toward that smell. If she lands on something and it tests out at about 98 degrees, she plugs in a proboscis and pulls in some blood and that blood hits her stomach and all those eggs that were there are instantly made fertile and she lays them on this creature. It's an extraordinary story.

· · ·

Bobbie: After the relationship ended, I was sinking into the ancient miasmal mist, and I thought, if I don't get a more interesting life, I'm just going to lie down and die. I asked Rosalie Sorrels and Terry Garthwaite if they were interested in us touring together. Originally it was going to be a foursome because I also asked Diane di Prima. I saw it as two women writers and two women singers, but Diane was just completely wrapped up in what she was doing, and it took us a year just to get Rosalie and Terry and I into the same room to start knocking stuff around toward a show. We finally put on our first show at Bolinas in the community center. We rented the community center for fifty bucks, put out a hundred chairs and put some chairs to be opened in the back of the room so that when we heard chairs being opened out, it meant that we had each made 100 bucks. We did that show to about 350 people and two days later we did Bread and Roses to 3000. Then we started booking ourselves into tours and we toured for eight years. Every October we'd go to the East Coast. We'd start in New York City and go as far as Montreal, then come back down the coast for a second booking.

Barbara: That's the *Live at the Great American Music Hall*, isn't it? I listened to it last week. It's great.

Bobbie: Originally it was produced as a record by Flying Fish but when they went out of business, Rounder

Records picked it up. Isn't that great? Don't you love Rosalie and Terry?

Barbara: I love the whole thing. I get a sense of your younger life. You're tough and tender and you say these sharp and witty things, and I could hear it, too, in your younger voice.

Bobbie: Meanwhile I published the book with Wesley [*Fifteen Poems]* and then I published *Frenchie and Cuban Pete,* and then *Back to Texas,* and in every instance I published books because people asked me for them. I never had this experience of sending out manuscripts, which I think is a real failing if you are a writer with a career, but I have never been able to figure out what a career is. I mean any career I've had has been inadvertent because people invited me.

Barbara: How did you come to Naropa?

Bobbie: There was a point when Bob and I in 75 were going to come to Naropa in the summer, and Anne Waldman had a way of inviting a particular writer, and then if they had a spouse who had something going on, she'd also invite the spouse and provide a plane ticket and find a little workshop for them or something. We were coming on that sort of basis and when we definitely split, I had a call from Anne, and she said, "Does this mean you won't be coming this summer?" I said, "Well I can't really. I mean if you give me a ticket. I can't really afford to come because there isn't any money involved." And she said, "No, if you come separately from Bob, we'll give you a ticket, we'll give you a salary and we'll put you up, and I'll put you on the calendar." That was an extraordinary act of friendship on Anne's part. And it reassured me enormously. So I came and taught a workshop and did a reading and so forth.

Barbara: Maureen mentioned you are now writing something called "Gossip". Can you talk about this project?

Bobbie: At my age there are all of these free floating stories that happened over the past decades and some of them are my stories and a lot of them are other people's stories but those people have died and I only know those stories because I was told them by those people so it seems to me that it is important to get some of them on to paper. Did you see the piece I did, for instance on John Weiners? That's one of my best stories.

Barbara: Steve Katz is also writing pieces like this, he calls them "Memroids."

Bobbie: I think that is really to the point. All of those early beginnings just get eaten by time and disappear. One of the ones I love is about Edward Dahlberg in Majorca talking to Bob's first wife, Ann Mackinnen. They immediately got into a fierce battle and at some point Edward Dahlberg said "Young woman when your bones are moldering in the dust, mine will be carried through the streets by the cheering multitudes." That is one of the great lines of all time and I don't want that to disappear into the void.

Barbara: Bobbie, do you have anything else you want to talk about?

Bobbie: Well this business you mentioned about the avant-garde, I don't have a problem about the avant-garde because the avant-garde is one of those descriptions that comes after the fact. The thing I have a problem with is having university writing departments treating the avant-garde as if it is a genre and then teaching the students avant-garde. It is one thing to do some experimental writing to broaden your scope, but it is another to treat them to the notion of themselves writing some kind of high-degree specialized literature. It is not true. Anything taught as Literature with a capital L deceives the young and sets them apart from it in a way that dreadfully interferes with their own writing because of course they want to be as high class as they can achieve, and they are told literature is it and they get shoved toward the literary, as if it is a unique event. What it really is is an extraordinary thing within the event of what writing is. It is when the writing is really really good. And to have it treated as separated out from the body of writing—you can separate it out because it is so good. Anything that gets titled has been bagged, and anything that's bagged generally accrues an agenda and that agenda is usually destructive to the next generation.

Barbara: Like trying to get to some end product, but what you really need to do is to be in the present with what you are doing, your writing. Thanks Bobbie. It's been very special talking with you.

BOBBIE LOUISE HAWKINS

Bobbie Louise Hawkins has written more than twenty books of fiction, non-fiction, poetry, and performance monologues. She has performed her work at Joseph Papp's Public Theater, Bottom Line and Folk City in New York City; at The Great American Music Hall and Intersection in San Francisco, as well as reading and performing in Canada, England, Germany, Japan, Holland, and more. In England she worked with Apples and Snakes, read at the Canterbury Festival and the Poetry Society. She was commissioned to write a one-hour play for Public Radio's "The Listening Ear," and she has a record, with Rosalie Sorrels and Terry Garthwaite, *Live At The Great American Music Hall*, available from Flying Fish. She was invited by Anne Waldman and Allen Ginsberg to begin a prose concentration in the writing program at Naropa University where she taught for twenty years.

BARBARA HENNING

Barbara Henning is the author of three novels, seven books of poetry, as well as a series of photo-poem pamphlets. Her most recent books are *Cities and Memory* (Chax Press), *Looking Up Harryette Mullen: Interviews on Sleeping with the Dictionary and Other Works* (Belladonna Series), *Thirty Miles to Rosebud* (BlazeVOX) and *My Autobiography* (United Artists). In the nineties, Barbara was the editor of *Long News: In the Short Century*. Barbara was born in Detroit and moved to New York City in the early eighties. Professor Emerita at Long Island University, Brooklyn Campus, she continues to teach courses for Naropa University, as well as LIU.